Christian Martyrs

Edited by Robert Backhouse

Hodder & Stoughton

LONDON SYDNEY AUCKLAND

British Library Cataloguing in Publication Data
A record for this book is available from the British Library

ISBN 0 340 65636 0

Printed and bound in Great Britain by
Cox & Wyman Ltd, Reading, Berkshire

Hodder and Stoughton
A Division of Hodder Headline PLC
338 Euston Road
London NW1 3BH

'The noble army of martyrs: praise Thee.'

Te Deum Laudamus

CONTENTS

Historical Features

INTRODUCTION

'The history of Christian martyrdom is, in fact, the history of Christianity itself; for it is in the arena, at the stake, and in the dungeon that the religion of Christ has won its most glorious triumphs.' So wrote William Bramley-Moore in his conclusion to an introduction to an edition of Foxe's *Book of Martyrs*. Today, however, despite our living in a 'global village', many, many Christian martyrs, including those of the twentieth-century, are largely unsung heros. This popular history of Christian martyrs gathers together the stories of faithful Christians who gladly gave their lives for their Lord and Master – from Stephen, the first Christian martyr, to those martyred in our own day, at the end of the twentieth century.

This book testifies to the Christian faith of the martyrs and provides overwhelming evidence of the fulfilment of Jesus Christ's words, 'I am sending you prophets and wise men and teachers. Some of them you will kill and crucify; others you will flog in your synagogues and pursue from town to town' (Matt. 23:34). Over 500 Christian martyrs are described in detail – drawn from over 30 countries, over 2,000 years. Another 100,000 martyrs are mentioned in passing. Martyrdoms were so often unreasonable and totally unjust. Tertullian certainly felt the force of this when he wrote: 'The term "conspiracy" should not be applied to us but rather to those who plot to foment hatred against decent and worthy people, those who shout for the blood of the innocent and plead forsooth in justification of their hatred the foolish excuse that the Christians are to blame for every public disaster and every misfortune that befalls the people. If the Tiber rises to the walls, if the Nile fails to rise and flood the fields, if the sky withholds its rain, if there is earthquake or famine or plague, straightaway the cry arises: "The Christians to the lions!"' (*Defence of Christianity*, 40:1–2).

However, the exposure of the corrupt nature of secular and religious authorities is not the main purpose of this book. A.J. Mason provides an excellent answer to the question: 'Why a book on Christian martyrs?' in his own introduction to *Historic Martyrs of the Primitive Church*:

> In sending this book to press, it is my hope and prayer that it may not only instruct and interest, but that it may serve to stimulate its readers to a more ardent devotion to the great cause for which the martyrs suffered. They suffered for liberty of conscience, and the service which they thus did for mankind can never be exaggerated. But it was not for liberty of conscience as an abstract principle. They died for their loyalty to one holy God amidst the immoralities of a corrupt polytheism. They died because they would not even pretend to put anything else on the same level with the Son of God who was crucified for them. They died because they would not abandon the gospels which tell of his incarnate life, nor absent themselves from the Eucharist which he instituted to be the bond between himself and us, and between us amongst ourselves. This faith requires to be held today with a force of conviction like theirs; and perhaps there is no better way to brace and strengthen our Christian principles than by dwelling often upon the triumphs which the same faith has won in the past.[1]

The word 'martyr'
The word 'martyr' derives from the Greek word *martus*, 'witness'. The word was originally used in the Acts of the Apostles for people who were witnesses of our Lord's life and resurrection: 'You will be my witnesses in Jerusalem, and in all Judea and Samaria, and to the ends of the earth' (Acts 1:8). One of the essential qualifications for Judas's replacement was that 'one of these must become a witness with us of his [Christ's] resurrection' (Acts 1:22).

In Christian usage the term 'martyr' soon acquired the meaning 'blood-witness' (see Rev. 2:13), the person who was killed because of his testimony to Jesus. With the spread of persecution the word was used of those who had undergone hardships for the faith, and then 'martyr' was restricted in its usage to those who had suffered death on account of their Christian faith. The martyrs were the heroes of the church.

Literature on martyrdoms
A considerable literature on martyrdom was produced in the early church:

1. Acts of the martyrs

These were the accounts of the trials (not transcripts of the court proceedings but often based on them), of which the earliest is the *Acts of Justin and his Companions* (AD 165).

2. Passions

These were freer accounts of the last days and death of the martyr. The earliest of the authentic passions is *The Martyrdom of Polycarp* (not long after his death in AD 156). 'The most poignant of all the martyrs' narratives is called *The Passion of St Perpetua and St Felicity*. It holds a unique place in Christian annals. During the fourth century it was publicly read in the churches of North Africa. It was so popular that St Augustine had to protest that it should not be put on a level with the books of the Bible.'[2]

3. Exhortations

Important early church leaders, such as Tertullian and Origen, wrote treatises about martyrdom, including accounts of specific martyrdoms.

4. Panegyrics

Panegyrics (public speeches in praise of someone) were made on the anniversary of the martyr's death for the edification of the faithful. Many of these are found in the sermons of the church fathers.

5. Legends

Later legends were little more than historical romances, based on a few facts with numerous embellishments. Such legends are excluded from this book.

In most cases the descriptions of martyrdoms in this book come from eye-witness accounts or from compilations of written records concerning the martyr's death. These descriptions are usually by people who wrote with white-hot passion, often from a totally committed viewpoint, and sometimes unable to exclude a tirade of abuse being heaped on those responsible for the martyr's death. These descriptions have not been toned down for the purposes of this book, but have been left as they were written, to ensure that today's reader captures the atmosphere of the particular martyrdom. The centrepiece to each entry in this book is the account of the actual martyrdom. This is drawn from an appropriate historical source. Sometimes this will be

Foxe's *Book of Martyrs*, at other times the Passions, or Eusebius (who wrote *On the Martyrs of Palestine* as well as entries in his *Ecclesiastical History*), or one of the other reliable accounts of Christian martyrdoms found in Christian writings of recognised credibility, such as Prudentius, Chrysostom, Basil, and Augustine. In the case of martyrdom in the nineteenth and twentieth centuries, details have been drawn from the records of international missionary societies, and such reliable sources as the Keston Institute. This is an appropriate place to acknowledge and thank the many libraries, librarians, archivists, missionaries and missionary organisations who have so freely offered advice and material for inclusion in this book: in particular a deep debt of graitutude is due to The Keston Institute, The London Library, Regent's College Library, Dr Williams's Library, the Catholic Central Library, the Unevangelized Fields Mission (UFM), the Overseas Missionary Fellowship (OMF), the Worldwide Evangalisation Crusade (WEC), the Wycliffe Bible Translators and the Africa Evangelical Fellowship.

Foxe's Book of Martyrs

More entries in the present compilation are taken from Foxe's *Book of Martyrs* than from any other source. Many people have wished that Foxe lived today and had brought his book up to date. The Brownists thought this, as is clear from the following dedication, from a volume entitled *A True Confession of the Faith of the Brownists* (1596):

> Our God (wee trust) will one day rayse up an other John Fox, to gather and compile the Actes and Monuments of his later Martyrs, for the vew of posteritie, tho yet they seem to bee buryed in oblivion, and sleep in the dust.[3]

However, Foxe's writings have come under fire from Catholic writers. For example, Edward Norman has written:

> There has been a consistent production of anti-Catholic literature since the Reformation. Some of the works have been classics of English popular culture, like John Foxe's Book of Martyrs (*Acts and Monuments of these latter and perillous dayes*), first published in 1563. It went through five editions in the reign of Elizabeth I, and, with numerous subsequent republications, became the main source for most people of what Catholicism was like. Foxe represented it as inherently corrupt, authoritarian, foreign, and above all, as implacably opposed to personal freedom.[4]

Catholics have felt so strongly about Foxe's accounts that a book was published in 1870 entitled, *Martyrs Omitted by Foxe, being records of Religious Persecutions in the sixteenth and seventeenth centuries, compiled by a member of the English Church* [not identified]. In this volume, the writer states:

> The object of the compiler of these brief records is a twofold one: To hold up a mirror, that we may see ourselves in our hideous deformity, as breakers of the 'law of love,' puffed up, as we undoubtedly are, with the grossest, because the most unjustifiable, spiritual pride.
>
> It is also to edify the reader with records of the power of faith in many a last conflict, and with exemplifications of the working of that 'law of love,' enabling the sufferer to forgive the persecutor, who, like a second Cain, imbrued his hands in his brother's blood.
>
> ... More than heroes, they [Roman Catholic fellow-Christians who were persecuted and killed] were Christian witnesses to the divine character of the church universal. Their names have been cast out as evil; their good deeds disparaged; their intense faith laughed at; their loftiest motives and last hours misrepresented. But they are not less worthy of our admiration. They were Englishmen. They were English Churchmen. They were sufferers for righteousness' sake. Therefore are they surely blessed. May we all be led to see how craftily the enemies of God's eternal and unalterable truth have put darkness for light, and light for darkness; sweet for bitter, and bitter for sweet; and how successfully souls have been ruined and lost in the process.[5]

The present book includes entries from both Foxe's book and from *Martyrs Omitted by Foxe*.

It is not easy to find an unbiased opinion about Foxe. Certainly his strength was his attention to detail, though it is true that his entries were by no means complete: for example it would appear that he did not have access to translations of documents such as *The Passion of Perpetua*. Perhaps Professor Owen Chadwick can give us the best assessment of Foxe's writings:

> Reformed theologians distrusted the old custom of celebrating a calendar of saints, for they believed the reverence paid to saints to derogate from faith in the one Saviour. But at a very early date Protestant writers began to collect historical materials and stories about the deaths at the stake and upon the scaffold. The most famous and influential were the *Book of Martyrs* by Jean Crespin, a French lawyer who fled to Strasbourg and then to Geneva, and who collected the moving and painful agonies of the Huguenot victims; and the book originally of the same title by the Englishman John

Foxe, who fled abroad during the reign of Queen Mary and wrote his *Book of the Martyrs* at Basle between 1556 and 1559. His work, in its later editions known as *Acts and Monuments*, was influenced by that of Crespin, but Foxe's own genius and the different matter make it a great book in its own right. Both Crespin and Foxe were willing to include the death of persons who might doubtfully be claimed for the Reforming cause, and Foxe included at least two persons who had not died at all; but when every allowance is made to modern criticism, they contain much material still indispensable to the historian of the age, and they were sources of power and faith in the Protestant communities to which they were addressed. In England the Convocation of 1571 ordered a copy of Foxe's book to be placed in all cathedrals.[10]

Historical features

Historical features, which are not actual descriptions of martyrdoms, are interspersed throughout this book so that the reader can more fully appreciate the circumstances of particular martyrdoms. For example, while we may know that the early Christians were martyred for not 'sacrificing to the gods' many people today may have little idea about what 'sacrificing to the gods' entailed. Horrific physical and mental tortures were often the prelude and means of Christian martyrtyrdoms. This book does not dwell on these tortures, but neither does it ignore them. For example, we may read that a Christian martyr was 'tortured with a currycomb on the hobby-horse' but without some explanation there can be little understanding today of what actually happened. Eight historical features detail the tortures Christian martyrs were subjected to in the early centuries, which often were used in succeeding centuries as well.

Readers should be prepared for horrific and explicit accounts. The introduction to a book which has graphic illustrations as well as horrific written accounts of the tortures inflicted on Christians states:

> One often hears that certain tortures were inflicted on the first Christians, but, beyond a few vague hints scattered here and there, it is impossible for unlettered folk to imagine the nature of the sufferings they were made to endure. Probably no more awful lesson of man's inhumanity to man, concentrated into so short a space, can be found throughout the annals of literature.
>
> At first sight the descriptions of these tortures may appear to some minds repellent and unreal; but on closer examination we find ourselves wondering – nay, stricken with admiration and astonishment – at the

moral grandeur of the men and women who held with such fierce grip and
tenacity 'the faith once delivered to the saints'.[3]

Additional background information is supplied alongside the
actual martyrdoms to enable the reader to see what specific challenges
faced our Christian brothers and sisters in previous centuries, how
they responded, where exactly they drew their spiritual strength from
to endure the unspeakable tortures they were put through, and how
they remained 'faithful unto death'.

Choice of entries

The choice of entries for a book of Christian martyrs is controversial.
Who should be in and who should be left out? For example, a number
of Protestant ministers refused to attend Bonhoeffer's memorial service
because, far from viewing him as an authentic Christian martyr, they
viewed his acts as misguided and political. Joan of Arc is not officially
regarded as a martyr by the Roman Catholic Church, but is put in the
category of a 'virgin'. Then, Bishop Hannington is included as a 'martyr' in some Anglican lectionaries, although he was actually killed as an
intruder rather than because of his Christian faith. This book is meant
to be broadly based and includes any person who was put to death for
his or her Christian faith. So, for example, all three people just mentioned are included in this compilation. Also included are people who
died in the place of others, but usually excluded are people like Gladys
Aylward who may have given a life of Christian service in dangerous
places, but who died of disease or because of war or accidents. Butler's
Lives, commenting on St Vitalis' martyrdom in 62, reminds us that

> we are not all called to the sacrifice of martyrdom; but all are bound to
> make their whole lives a continued sacrifice of themselves to God, and to
> perform every action in this perfect spirit of sacrifice. An ardent desire of
> devoting ourselves totally to God in life and in death, and a cheerful readi-
> ness to do and to suffer whatever he requires of us, in order constantly to
> accomplish his divine will, is a disposition which ought to accompany and
> to animate all our actions.[4]

Just because a Christian martyr has an entry in a martyrology it
does not mean to say that all he or she did or said was exemplary.
This point has been underlined in a book referring to Christian saints,
which is equally applicable to Christian martyrs:

It is no part of my purpose to present the saints as perfect, although I would not wish to discourage those who have gained strength from that conviction. The ethical perfection of the saints is not, in my understanding, an article of faith in any Church. St Thomas More is almost certainly the most revered of English saints, but his attitude to heretics is repulsive by our modern standards. St Peter fell and fell again. Augustine's sins before he became a Christian add to the drama of his conversion. But the dismissal of his mistress, the mother of his child, seems harsh to us, though not apparently to him. St Francis of Assisi's treatment of his father makes painful reading. And there are numerous other examples.[5]

The entries are, in the main, in chronological order. However, the first entry is Matthew's account of the crucifixion of Jesus Christ. This is placed at the beginning of the book, not because Jesus Christ's death was a martyrdom, but because so many martyrs referred to Christ's death and because so much writing about Christian martyrs makes reference to his crucifixion. For example, Luke records that as Stephen was being martyred he echoed a prayer Jesus himself prayed: 'Then Stephen fell on his knees, and cried out, "Lord, do not hold this sin against them." When he had said this he fell asleep' (Acts 7:60). The accounts of the martyrs begin with those in the Old and New Testaments, moving on to the martyrs of the early Christian church under the various Emperors. Under Nero (AD 54–68), Peter and Paul were martyred along with 'a huge multitude' who were burned and tortured and put to death in other ways. Under Domitian (AD 81–96) a number of Christians were put to death charged with 'atheism' (not publicly recognising the emperor as a god). Under Trajan (AD 97–117), the most famous martyr was Ignatius of Antioch. Under Antoninus Pius (AD 138–161), the chief martyr was Polycarp of Smyrna. Under Marcus Aurelius (AD 161–180) the best known martyrs were Carpus, Papylus, Agathonica, Justin and his companions, the Scillitan martyrs and the martyrs of Lyons. Under Septimus Severus (AD 193–211) a new era began with Christians being sought out by the state, especially the newly converted and their teachers. During this time Saturus and his pupils Perpetua and Felicitas and their companions were martyred. Under Decius (AD 249–251) many of the martyrs were bishops, such as Fabian of Rome. Under Valerian (AD 253–260) bishops were the main target, along with other ministers as well as Christians of noble birth. Martyrs of the time included Cyprian and Fructuosus. Under Diocletian (AD 292–303), Christians experienced the severest persecutions of the early centuries of the church. This was caused by fear of Christian penetration into the Roman army, incuding even officers of the high command, and into the higher echelons of the civil service. Scriptures were burned and churches destroyed. Under Constantine, in March 313 complete freedom was restored to Christians by the Edict of Milan and persecution and martyrdom eventually ceased.

The first three centuries of the Christian era are probably the best-known period of martyrdoms. In addition to these, this book relates many of the less well known Christian martyrdoms through the centuries (such as the martyrs of the Coptic church), as well as the better known martyrs of the middle ages, the Reformation and modern times.

Twentieth-century martyrs

Christian martyrs of the 17th to 20th centuries are under geographical areas, rather than in a chronological list, although most of these are from the 20th century. There are accounts of the martyrdom of numerous pioneer missionaries throughout the world and the martyrdoms of the first indigenous Christians in a number of countries.

> It appears likely that Dr Paul Carlson was correct when he told Congolese believers, before his martyrdom, that more believers have died for Christ in this century than in all the previous centuries combined. Of course, there is no hard evidence to prove this, since the records of most martyrdoms before the twentieth century are lost, and the names of countless martyrs in this century (those who died in the Soviet Union and China, for example) are not available for scrutiny.[6]

Missionary letters and first-hand accounts of the martyrdoms of Christians are here included of the two places where more Christians have been martyred in the twentieth century than anywhere else: China and Russia.

A great cloud of witnesses

Hebrews 11 refers to those who through faith 'shut the mouths of lions, quenched the fury of the flames, and escaped the edge of the sword', as well as those who 'were tortured and refused to be released, so that they might gain a better resurrection. Some faced jeers and flogging, while still others were chained and put in prison. They were stoned; they were sawn in two; they were put to death by the sword. They went about in sheepskins and goatskins, destitute, persecuted and ill-treated – the world was not worthy of them' (Heb. 11:33–38).

Sadly, just as there were many martyrs in Old Testament days and New Testament days, so there have been countless Christians martyrs through the centuries right up to our own day. The writer to the Hebrews calls these martyrs and other faithful Christians 'a cloud of witnesses' by which 'we are surrounded' (Heb. 12:1). Reading the record of this history of Christian martyrs must sober and challenge us, no matter how easy or acutely difficult our personal circumstances may be. This is the way we should act, once we have viewed the roll of honour of the Christian martyrs, according to the writer to the Hebrews: 'Since we are surrounded by such a cloud of witnesss . . . let us fix our eyes on Jesus, the author and perfecter of our faith, who for the joy set before him endured the cross, scorning its shame, and sat down at the right hand of the throne of God. Consider him who endured such opposition from sinful men, so that you will not grow weary and lose heart' (Heb. 12:13).

Robert Backhouse
Norwich 1995

Notes

1. A. J. Mason, *Historic Martyrs of the Primitive Church* (Longmans, 1906), p. x.
2. Frank Longford, *Saints* (Hutchinson, 1970), p. 23.
3. *A True Confession of the Faith of the Brownists* (1596), reprinted in Albert Peel, *The Noble Army of Congregational Martyrs* (Pilgrim Press, 1948), p. 8.
4. Edward Norman, *Roman Catholicism in England* (OUP, 1985), p. 4.
5. *Martyrs Omitted by Foxe, being records of Religious Persecutions in the sixteenth and seventeenth centuries, compiled by a member of the English Church* (John Hodges, 1870), p. xv.
6. Owen Chadwick, *The Reformation* (Penguin, 1972), pp. 174–75.
7. *Tortures and Torments of the Christian Martyrs, from the De SS. Martyrum Curciatibus of the Rev Father Gallonia*, translated by A. R. Allinson (London: printed for subscribers, 1903), p. vii.
8. Alban Butler, *The Lives of the Saints* (Dublin: Richard Coyne, 1833), vol. I, p. 528.
9. Frank Longford, *Saints* (Hutchinson, 1970), pp. 197–98.
10. J. and M. Hefley, *By Their Blood: Christian Martyrs of the Twentieth Century* (Milford: Mott Media, 1979), p. 589.

PART ONE

BIBLE MARTYRS

Christ's crucifixion

While he was still speaking, Judas, one of the Twelve, arrived. With him was a large crowd armed with swords and clubs, sent from the chief priests and the elders of the people. Now the betrayer had arranged a signal with them: 'The one I kiss is the man; arrest him.' Going at once to Jesus, Judas said, 'Greetings, Rabbi!' and kissed him.

Jesus replied, 'Friend, do what you came for.'

Then the men stepped forward, seized Jesus and arrested him. With that, one of Jesus' companions reached for his sword, drew it out and struck the servant of the high priest, cutting off his ear.

'Put your sword back in its place,' Jesus said to him, 'for all who draw the sword will die by the sword. Do you think I cannot call on my Father, and he will at once put at my disposal more than twelve legions of angels? But how then would the Scriptures be fulfilled that say it must happen in this way?'

At that time Jesus said to the crowd, 'Am I leading a rebellion, that you have come out with swords and clubs to capture me? Every day I sat in the temple courts teaching, and you did not arrest me. But this has all taken place that the writings of the prophets might be fulfilled.' Then all the disciples deserted him and fled.

Those who had arrested Jesus took him to Caiaphas, the high priest, where the teachers of the law and the elders had assembled. But Peter followed him at a distance, right up to the courtyard of the high priest. He entered and sat down with the guards to see the outcome.

The chief priests and the whole Sanhedrin were looking for false evidence against Jesus so that they could put him to death. But they did not find any, though many false witnesses came forward.

Finally two came forward and declared, 'This fellow said, "I am able to destroy the temple of God and rebuild it in three days.'

Then the high priest stood up and said to Jesus, "Are you not going to answer? What is this testimony that these men are bringing against you?" But Jesus remained silent.

The high priest said to him, 'I charge you under oath by the living God: Tell us if you are the Christ, the Son of God.'

'Yes, it is as you say,' Jesus replied. 'But I say to all of you: In the future you will see the Son of Man sitting at the right hand of the Mighty One and coming on the clouds of heaven.'

Then the high priest tore his clothes and said, 'He has spoken blasphemy! Why do we need any more witnesses? Look, now you have heard the blasphemy. What do you think?'

'He is guilty of death,' they answered.

Then they spat in his face and struck him with their fists. Others slapped him and said, 'Prophesy to us, Christ. Who hit you?'

Now Peter was sitting out in the courtyard, and a servant girl came to him. 'You also were with Jesus of Galilee,' she said.

But he denied it before them all. 'I don't know what you're talking about,' he said.

Then he went out to the gateway, where another girl saw him and said to the people there, 'This fellow was with Jesus of Nazareth.'

He denied it again, with an oath: 'I don't know the man!'

After a little while, those standing there went up to Peter and said, 'Surely you are one of them, for your accent gives you away.'

Then he began to call down curses on himself and he swore to them, 'I don't know the man!'

Immediately a cock crowed. Then Peter remembered the word Jesus had spoken: 'Before the cock crows, you will disown me three times.' And he went outside and wept bitterly.

Early in the morning, all the chief priests and the elders of the people came to the decision to put Jesus to death. They bound him, led him away and handed him over to Pilate, the governor.

When Judas, who had betrayed him, saw that Jesus was condemned, he was seized with remorse and returned the thirty silver coins to the chief priests and the elders. 'I have sinned,' he said 'for I have betrayed innocent blood.'

'What is that to us?' they replied. 'That's your responsibility.'

So Judas threw the money into the temple and left. Then he went away and hanged himself.

The chief priests picked up the coins and said, 'It is against the law to put this into the treasury, since it is blood money.' So they decided to use the money to buy the potter's field as a burial place for foreigners. That is why it has been called the Field of Blood to this day. Then what was spoken by Jeremiah the prophet was fulfilled: 'They took the thirty silver coins, the price set on him by the people of Israel, and they used them to buy the potter's field, as the Lord commanded me.'

Meanwhile Jesus stood before the governor, and the governor asked him, 'Are you the king of the Jews?'

'Yes, it is as you say,' Jesus replied.

When he was accused by the chief priests and the elders, he gave no answer. Then Pilate asked him, 'Don't you hear the testimony they are bringing against you?' But Jesus made no reply, not even to a single charge – to the great amazement of the governor.

Now it was the governor's custom at the Feast to release a prisoner chosen by the crowd. At that time they had a notorious prisoner, called Barabbas. So when the crowd had gathered, Pilate asked them, 'Which one do you want me to release to you: Barabbas, or Jesus who is called Christ?' For he knew it was out of envy that they had handed Jesus over to him.

While Pilate was sitting on the judge's seat, his wife sent him this message: 'Don't have anything to do with that innocent man, for I have suffered a great deal today in a dream because of him.'

But the chief priests and the elders persuaded the crowd to ask for Barabbas and to have Jesus executed.

'Which of the two do you want me to release to you?' asked the governor.

'Barabbas,' they answered.

'What shall I do, then, with Jesus who is called Christ?' Pilate asked.

They all answered, 'Crucify him!'

'Why? What crime has he committed?' asked Pilate.

But they shouted all the louder, 'Crucify him!'

When Pilate saw that he was getting nowhere, but that instead an uproar was starting, he took water and washed his hands in front of the crowd. 'I am innocent of this man's blood,' he said. 'It is your responsibility!'

All the people answered, 'Let his blood be on us and on our children!'

Then he released Barabbas to them. But he had Jesus flogged, and handed him over to be crucified.

Then the governor's soldiers took Jesus into the Praetorium and gathered the whole company of soldiers round him. They stripped him and put a scarlet robe on him, and then twisted together a crown of thorns and set it on his head. They put a staff in his right hand and knelt in front of him and mocked him. 'Hail, king of the Jews!' they said. They spat on him, and took the staff and struck him on the head again and again. After they had mocked him, they took off the robe and put his own clothes on him. Then they led him away to crucify him.

As they were going out, they met a man from Cyrene, named Simon, and they forced him to carry the cross. They came to a place called Golgotha (which means The Place of the Skull). There they offered Jesus wine to drink, mixed with gall; but after tasting it, he refused to drink it. When they had crucified him, they divided up his clothes by casting lots. And sitting down, they kept watch over him there. Above his head they placed the written charge against him: THIS IS JESUS, THE KING OF THE JEWS. Two robbers were crucified with him, one on his right and one on his left. Those who passed by hurled insults at him, shaking their heads and saying, 'You who are going to destroy the temple and build it in three days, save yourself! Come down from the cross, if you are the Son of God!'

In the same way the chief priests, the teachers of the law and the elders mocked him. 'He saved others,' they said, 'but he can't save himself! He's the King of Israel! Let him come down now from the cross, and we will believe in him. He trusts in God. Let God rescue him now if he wants him, for he said, "I am the Son of God."' In the same way the robbers who were crucified with him also heaped insults on him.

From the sixth hour until the ninth hour darkness came over all the land. About the ninth hour Jesus cried out in a loud voice, '*Eloi, Eloi, lama sabachthani?*' – which means, 'My God, my God, why have you forsaken me?'

When some of those standing there heard this, they said, 'He's calling Elijah.'

Immediately one of them ran and got a sponge. He filled it with wine vinegar, put it on a stick, and offered it to Jesus to drink. The rest said, 'Now leave him alone. Let's see if Elijah comes to save him.'

And when Jesus had cried out again in a loud voice, he gave up his spirit.

At that moment the curtain of the temple was torn in two from top to bottom. The earth shook and the rocks split. The tombs broke upon and the bodies of many holy people who had died were raised to life. They came out of the tombs, and after Jesus' resurrection they went into the holy city and appeared to many people.

When the centurion and those with him who were guarding Jesus saw the earthquake and all that had happened, they were terrified, and exclaimed, 'Surely he was the Son of God!'

Many women were there, watching from a distance. They had followed Jesus from Galilee to care for his needs. Among them were

Mary Magdalene, Mary the mother of James and Joses, and the mother of Zebedee's sons.

As evening approached, there came a rich man from Arimathea, named Joseph, who had himself become a disciple of Jesus. Going to Pilate, he asked for Jesus' body, and Pilate ordered that it be given to him. Joseph took the body, wrapped it in a clean linen cloth, and placed it in his own new tomb that he had cut out of the rock. He rolled a big stone in front of the entrance to the tomb and went away. Mary Magdalene and the other Mary were sitting there opposite the tomb.

The next day, the one after Preparation Day, the chief priests and the Pharisees went to Pilate. 'Sir,' they said, 'we remember that while he was still alive that deceiver said, 'After three days I will rise again.' So give the order for the tomb to be made secure until the third day. Otherwise, his disciples may come and steal the body and tell the people that he has been raised from the dead. This last deception will be worse than the first.'

'Take a guard,' Pilate answered. 'Go, make the tomb as secure as you know how.' So they went and made the tomb secure by putting a seal on the stone and posting the guard.

¶ The Bible: Matt. 26:47–27:66 NIV

OLD TESTAMENT MARTYRS

Zechariah the priest

Jesus Christ's summary of the history of martyrdom in the Old Testament:

This generation will be held responsible for the blood of all the prophets that has been shed since the beginning of the world, from the blood of Abel to the blood of Zechariah, who was killed between the altar and the sanctuary.

¶ The Bible: Luke 1:50–1 NIV

After the death of Jehoiada, the officials of Judah came and paid homage to the king, and he listened to them. They abandoned the temple of the Lord, the God of their fathers, and worshipped Asherah poles and idols. Because of their guilt, God's anger came upon Judah and Jerusalem. Although the Lord sent prophets to the people to bring them back to him, and though they testified against them, they would not listen.

Then the Spirit of God came upon Zechariah son of Jehoiada the priest. He stood before the people and said, 'This is what God says: 'Why do you disobey the Lord's commands? You will not prosper. Because you have forsaken the Lord, he has forsaken you.'

But they plotted against him, and by order of the king they stoned him to death in the courtyard of the Lord's temple. King Joash did not remember the kindness Zechariah's father Jehoiada had shown him but killed his son, who said as he lay dying, 'May the Lord see this and call you to account.'

¶ The Bible: 2 Chron. 24:17–22

Uriah the prophet

Now Uriah son of Shemaiah from Kiriath Jearim was another man who prophesied in the name of the Lord; he prophesied the same things against this city [Jerusalem] and this land as Jeremiah did. When King Jehoiakim and all his officers and officials heard his words, the king sought to put him to death. But Uriah heard of it and fled in fear to Egypt. King Jehoiakim, however, sent Elnathan son of Acbor to Egypt, along with some other men. They brought Uriah out of Egypt and took him to King Jehoiakim, who had him struck down with a sword and his body thrown into the burial place of the common people.

Furthermore, Ahikam son of Shaphan supported Jeremiah, and so he was not handed over to the people to be put to death.

¶ The Bible: Jer. 26:20–24

NEW TESTAMENT MARTYRS

John the Baptist

Among those born of women there has not risen anyone greater than John the Baptist.

¶ The Bible: Matt. 11:11 NIV (Jesus Christ's assessment of John the Baptist)

At that time Herod the tetrarch heard the reports about Jesus, and he said to his attendants, 'This is John the Baptist; he has risen from the dead! That is why miraculous powers are at work in him.'

Now Herod had arrested John and bound him and put him in prison because of Herodias, his brother Philip's wife, for John had been saying to him: 'It is not lawful for you to have her.' Herod wanted to kill John, but he was afraid of the people, because they considered him a prophet.

On Herod's birthday the daughter of Herodias [although her name is not mentioned in the Bible, Josephus, the Jewish historian, tells us her name: Salome] danced for them and pleased Herod so much that he promised with an oath to give her whatever she asked. Prompted by her mother, she said, 'Give me here on a platter the head of John the Baptist.' The king was distressed, but because of his oaths and his dinner guests, he ordered that her request be granted and had John beheaded in the prison. His head was brought in on a platter and given to the girl, who carried it to her mother. John's disciples came and took his body and buried it. Then they went and told Jesus.

¶ The Bible: Matt. 14:1–12

Stephen

THE FIRST CHRISTIAN MARTYR

All who were sitting in the Sanhedrin looked intently at Stephen, and they saw that his face was like the face of an angel.

¶ The Bible: Acts 6:15 NIV

At the end of Dr Luke's account of the martyrdom of Stephen he adds a detail about the people involved in killing Stephen: 'the witnesses laid their clothes at the feet of a young man named Saul' (Acts 7:58). One consequence of Stephen's martyrdom was the impression it left on the man who was destined to become the greatest teacher and missionary of the early church. A second consequence of Stephen's death, a time of persecution for these first Christians resulting in the spread of Christianity from Jerusalem, is recorded in the opening words of Acts chapter 8: 'On that day [Stephen's martyrdom] a great persecution broke out against the church at Jerusalem, and all except the apostles were scattered throughout Judea and Samaria' (Acts 8:1). Like Jesus, Stephen asked God to forgive his murderers.

Now Stephen, a man full of God's grace and power, did great wonders and miraculous signs among the people. Opposition arose, however, from members of the Synagogue of the Freedmen. These men began to argue with Stephen, but they could not stand up against his wisdom or the Spirit by whom he spoke.

Then they secretly persuaded some men to say, 'We have heard Stephen speak words of blasphemy against Moses and against God.'

So they stirred up the people and the elders and the teachers of the law. They seized Stephen and brought him before the Sanhedrin. They produced false witnesses, who testified, 'This fellow never stops speaking against this holy place and against the law. For we have heard him say that this Jesus of Nazareth will destroy this place and change the customs Moses handed down to us.'

All who were sitting in the Sanhedrin looked intently at Stephen, and they saw that his face was like the face of an angel. Then the high priest asked him, 'Are these charges true?'

To this Stephen replied: 'Brothers and fathers, listen to me! The

God of glory appeared to our father Abraham while he was still in Mesopotamia . . . You stiff-necked people, with uncircumcised hearts and ears! You are just like your fathers: You always resist the Holy Spirit! Was there ever a prophet your fathers did not persecute? They even killed those who predicted the coming of the Righteous One. And now you have betrayed and murdered him-you who have received the law that was put into effect through angels but have not obeyed it.'

When they heard this, they were furious and gnashed their teeth at him. But Stephen, full of the Holy Spirit, looked up to heaven and saw the glory of God, and Jesus standing at the right hand of God. 'Look,' he said, 'I see heaven open and the Son of Man standing at the right hand of God.'

At this they covered their ears and yelling at the top of their voices, they all rushed at him, dragged him out of the city and began to stone him. Meanwhile, the witnesses laid their clothes at the feet of a young man named Saul.

While they were stoning him, Stephen prayed, 'Lord Jesus, receive my spirit.' Then he fell on his knees and cried out, 'Lord, do not hold this sin against them.' When he had said this, he fell asleep.

And Saul was there, giving approval to his death.

¶ The Bible: Acts 6:8–15; 7:1–2, 51–60

James
c. AD 30

The son of Zebedee was one of the twelve apostles of Jesus Christ and brother of the apostle John. This account is the only record preserved in the Bible about the death of any of the first of the twelve apostles.

Jesus said to James and John, 'You will drink of the same cup [of suffering] that I drink.'

¶ The Bible: Mark 10:39

About this time King Herod [Herod Agrippa I] began to persecute some members of the church. He had James, the brother of John, put to death by the sword.

¶ The Bible: Acts 12:1–2

The man who informed against James, causing him to be put to death, was so impressed at the way James testified during his court hearing, that he, too, admitted that he was a Christian. So they were both led away to be executed. On the way, the man who had informed on James asked James to forgive him. The apostle did not immediately answer. He considered for a while, and then said to him: 'I wish you peace', and kissed him. They were both beheaded at the same time.

¶ Eusebius, *The History of the Church*, Book I

St Andrew

This apostle and martyr was the brother of St Peter, and preached the gospel to many Asiatic nations. On arriving at Edessa, the governor of the country, named Egeas, threatened him for preaching against the idols they worshipped. St Andrew, persisting in the propagation of his doctrines, was ordered to be crucified, two ends of the cross being fixed transversely in the ground. He boldly told his accusers that he would not have preached the glory of the cross had he feared to die on it. And again, when they came to crucify him, he said that he coveted the cross, and longed to embrace it. He was fastened to the cross, not with nails, but cords, that his death might be more slow. In this situation he continued two days, preaching the greatest part of the time to the people, and expired on 30th November.

¶ John Foxe, *The Book of Martyrs*, revised with notes and an appendix by W. Bramley-Moore (London, 1869), pp. 4–5

'Concordia'

Peter, before his own death, had the pain of witnessing what must have been worse than death to him. The apostle Paul tells us that Peter was accompanied by his wife on his missionary travels. She was probably with him still when Peter went to Rome, and there preceded him to martyrdom. She may have been one of those women of whom Clement speaks as going through a terrible death for the amusement of the Roman crowds. Peter may have seen his wife taken away to be killed, saying, as he looked on, that he was happy in his heart, 'because she had been called and was going home'. 'He lifted up his voice,' so the ancient story runs, 'and addressed her in a very encouraging and comforting manner, speaking to her by name' – the name had been forgotten; some late legends give it as Concordia – 'and saying, "Remember the Lord, Concordia,"' or whatever her name was.

¶ Clement of Alexandria quoted by Eusebius, *The History of the Church*, Book III; in A. J. Mason: *The Historic Martyrs of the Primitive Church* (Longmans, 1905), pp. 9–10

St Peter

The evangelist John records Peter talking with the risen Lord Jesus Christ. After telling Peter to 'feed my sheep', Jesus predicted how Peter would die: 'I tell you the truth, when you were younger you dressed yourself and went where you wanted; but when you are old you will stretch out your hands, and someone else will dress you and lead you where you do not want to go.' Commenting on these words, John writes in his gospel, 'Jesus said this to indicate the kind of death by which Peter would glorify God' (John 21:17–19).

Outside Rome, on the Appian Way stands a little chapel known as 'Domine, quo vadis?' – 'Lord, whither goest thou?' Bishop Lightfoot, among others, is inclined to believe the story that the Christians at Rome came to Peter at the start of the persecution and begged him to flee from the city. Peter gave in to their pleas. When Peter reached the place where the chapel stands, Jesus Christ met him in the middle of a dark night. The apostle asked his Lord, as he had done before, 'What do you want me to do?' The Lord answered him, 'I go to Rome, to be crucified again.' Peter was quick to understand the meaning behind this rebuke. He returned to Rome and told the Christian brethren what he had seen, and then glorified God by his death, as the Lord had foretold that he would, when he said, 'Another shall gird thee and carry thee whither thou wouldest not.'

¶ Ambrose, *Epistle 21*; in A. J. Mason, *The Historic Martyrs of the Primitive Church* (Longmans, 1905), p. 10

When Herod Agrippa caused St James the Great to be put to death, and found that it pleased the Jews, he resolved, in order to ingratiate himself with the people, that Peter should be the next sacrifice. He was accordingly apprehended and thrown into prison; but an angel of the Lord released him, which so enraged Herod, that he ordered the sentinels who guarded the dungeon in which he had been confined to be put to death. St Peter, after various miracles, retired to Rome, where he defeated the artifices and confounded the magic of Simon Magus, a great favourite of the Emperor Nero: he likewise converted to Christianity one of the minions of that monarch, which so exasperated the tyrant, that he ordered both St Peter and St Paul to be apprehended. During the time of their confinement, they converted two of the captains of the guard and forty-seven other people to Christianity. Having been nine months in prison, Peter was brought from thence for execution, when, after being severely scourged, he was crucified with his head downwards; which position, however, was at his own request. His body being taken down, embalmed, and buried in the Vatican, a church was erected on the spot; but this being destroyed by the Emperor Heliogabalus, the body was concealed till the twentieth bishop of Rome, Cornelius, conveyed it again to the Vatican; afterwards Constantine the Great erected one of the most stately churches over the place.

¶ John Foxe, *The Book of Martyrs,* revised with notes and an appendix by W. Bramley-Moore (London, 1869), p. 6

James the Righteous

This James, not to be confused with one of the twelve apostles, referred to as James the brother of John, was known as 'the Lord's Brother', 'the Just' and 'the Righteous'. The risen Jesus appeared to him (see 1 Cor. 15:7) and this presumably helped him to believe in Jesus, for in John's gospel it is recorded that 'For even his own brothers did not believe in him [Jesus]' (John 7:5). James himself wrote:

Brothers, as an example of patience in the face of suffering, take the prophets who spoke in the name of the Lord. As you know, we consider blessed those who have persevered. You have heard of Job's perseverance and have seen what the Lord finally brought about. The Lord is full of compassion and mercy.

¶ The Bible: Jas. 5:11 NIV

After Paul had successfully appealed to Caesar and was sent off to Rome the disappointed Jews turned their attention to James. They hatched this plot against the Lord's brother, whom the apostles had appointed to the episcopal throne at Jerusalem. They hauled James up in front of a great crowd and demanded that he deny Christ. To their surprise James remained calm and showed unexpected tranquillity before this hostile crowd. James openly declared that our Saviour and Lord, Jesus, was indeed the Son of God. They were unable to stomach this testimony as James was universally acclaimed as a most righteous man.

Clement tells us that they seized James, threw him off a parapet and then clubbed him to death. Hegesippus, in his fifth book, provides the most detailed description of James' martyrdom.

The church was in the control of the apostles, along with James, the Lord's brother, who has always been known as the Righteous. Many people were called James, but only this James was holy from the day he was born. He drank no alcohol and was a vegetarian, and following a Nazirite vow never had his hair cut. Only James was allowed to enter into the Holy Place in the Temple as he wore linen, not woollen, clothes. He was often to be found in the Sanctuary alone, praying on his knees for the people's forgiveness. He worshipped God so much in this way that his knees became as hard as the knees of a camel. Because he was so righteous he became known as James the Righteous.

The Scribes and the Pharisees forced James to stand on the Sanctuary parapet and shouted out to him: 'Righteous one, whose testimony we have to accept, you are leading the people astray and encouraging them to follow Jesus, who was crucified. What do you mean by "the door of Jesus"?' [See John 10:9, 'I am the gate; whoever enters through me will be saved.'] James called back, 'Why do you ask me about the Son of Man? He sits in heaven at the right hand of the Great Power, and he will return on heavenly clouds.' [James' reply 'Why do you ask me about the Son of Man?' shows him using his last moments, like Stephen, to call Jesus by a title which is only used elsewhere by our Lord himself when he spoke about himself.]

Many in the crowd were persuaded by James' words, and cried out: 'Hosanna to the Son of David.'

The Scribes and Pharisees realised that they had made a big mistake in allowing James to testify about Jesus. 'Let us throw him over the parapet so that people will become too afraid to follow him,' they plotted. Then they called out: 'The Righteous one has gone astray'.

So they threw the Righteous one over the parapet, and then stoned him as the fall did not kill him. James knelt down and prayed, 'Lord God and Father, I pray thee, forgive them; they do not know what they are doing.' They continued to hurl stones at him until the son of Rachabim shouted: 'Stop throwing your stones! What do you think you are doing? The Righteous one is praying for you. Then, one of the mob, a fuller, grabbed the club he beat his clothes with and cracked it down on top of the Righteous one's head. So the Righteous one was martyred. He was buried where he fell and his headstone remains there. He was a genuine witness to both Jews and Gentiles that Jesus is the Christ.

¶ Eusebius, *The History of the Church*, Book III

St Paul

Paul wrote:

Christ will be exalted in my body, whether by life or by death. For to me, to live is Christ and to die is gain.

¶ The Bible: Phil. 1:20–21 NIV

In the days when Paul was still Saul, he was no stranger to persecution. He instigated imprisonment and executions on numerous early followers of Christ. After Stephen's martyrdom Luke records that 'Saul began to destroy the church. Going from house to house, he dragged off men and women and put them in prison' (Acts 8:3). On the road to Damascus, and on the day of his conversion, Dr Luke paints a picture of Saul the persecutor of Christians in these words: 'Saul was still breathing out murderous threats against the Lord's disciples. He went to the high priest and asked him for letters to the synagogues in Damascus, so that if he found any there who belonged to the Way, whether men or women, he might take them as prisoners to Jerusalem. As he neared Damascus . . .' (Acts 9:1–3). Most interesting, the words of Jesus that then rang in Saul's ears not only focused on his persecution of Jesus' early followers, but also equated it with persecuting Christ himself: 'Saul, Saul, why do you persecute me?' (Acts 9:4).

After Saul became Paul he was on the receiving end of much persecution for the sake of his Lord. Paul writes about some of his hardships in his second letter to the Christians at Corinth and mentions 'troubles, hardships and distresses; beatings, imprisonments and riots, and sleepless nights and hunger' (2 Cor. 6:4–5). Towards the end of this letter Paul gives more details about the persecution he suffered for the sake of Christ: '. . . I have been in prison more frequently, been flogged more severely, and been exposed to death again and again. Five times I received from the Jews the forty lashes minus one. Three times I was beaten with rods, once I was stoned, three times I was shipwrecked, I spent a night and a day in the open sea, I have been constantly on the move . . . I have known hunger and thirst and have often gone without food; I have been cold and naked . . . In Damascus the governor under King Aretas had the city of Damascus guarded in order to arrest me. But I was lowered in a basket from a window in the wall and slipped through his hands' (2 Corinthians 11:23–33).

At Iconium, St Paul and St Barnabas were near being stoned to death by the enraged Jews; on which they fled to Lycaonia. At Lystra, St Paul was stoned, dragged out of the city, and left for dead. He, however, happily revived, and escaped to Derbe. At Philippi, Paul and Silas were imprisoned and whipped; and both were again persecuted at Thessalonica. Being afterwards taken at Jerusalem, he was sent to Caesarea, but appealed to Caesar at Rome. Here he continued a prisoner at large for two years; and at length, being released, he visited the churches of Greece and Rome, and preached in France and Spain. Returning to Rome, he was again apprehended, and, by the order of Nero, martyred, by beheading.

About this same time saints James, Philip, Matthew, Mark, Matthias, Jude, Bartholomew, Thomas, and Luke the evangelist also suffered martyrdom for the cause of Christ.

¶ John Foxe, *The Book of Martyrs*, revised with notes and an appendix by W. Bramley-Moore (London, 1869), pp. 6–7

Clement, the third bishop of Rome, wrote about some of the sufferings the Christians at Rome went through. Writing to the Corinthian church, Clement, talking about Peter and Paul, calls them 'the champions nearest to our own time, noble examples set in our own generation.' Of Paul, he writes:

Through jealousy and strife Paul showed us what is the reward of patient endurance. Seven times he was imprisoned; he was driven into exile; he was stoned; he preached both in the east and in the west, and gained a noble renown for his faith, having taught the whole world righteousness and having come to the very bounds of the west; and when he had borne his witness before the rulers, he was set free from the world and passed into the holy place, the greatest pattern of endurance.

¶ Clement of Rome, 5, 6; quoted by A. J. Mason, *The Historic Martyrs of the Primitive Church* (Longmans, 1905), p. 8

St John

John the evangelist records Jesus Christ's words: 'Greater love has no-one than this, that he lay down his life for his friends' (John 15:13 NIV).

He was distinguished as a prophet, an apostle, a divine, an evangelist, and a martyr. He is called the beloved disciple, and was brother to James the Great. He was previously a disciple of John the Baptist, and afterwards not only one of the twelve apostles, but one of the three to whom Christ communicated the most secret passages of his life. He founded churches at Smyrna, Pergamos, Sardis, Philadelphia, Laodicea, and Thyatira, to which he directs his Book of Revelation. Being at Ephesus, he was ordered by the Emperor Domitian to be sent bound to Rome, where he was condemned to be cast into a cauldron of boiling oil. [This was a punishment which the philosopher Seneca refers to as being suitable for a slave who had been convicted of a very serious crime.] But here a miracle was wrought in his favour; the oil did him no injury, and Domitian, not being able to put him to death, banished him to Patmos, to labour in the mines, in AD 73. He was, however, recalled by Nerva, who succeeded Domitian, but was deemed a martyr on account of his having undergone an execution, though it did not take effect. He wrote his epistles, gospel and Revelation, each in different style, but they are all equally admired. He was the only apostle who escaped a violent death, and lived the longest of any, he being nearly 100 years of age at the time of his death.

¶ John Foxe, *The Book of Martyrs,* revised with notes and an appendix by W. Bramley-Moore (London, 1869), p. 7

PART TWO

MARTYRS UNDER
THE ROMAN EMPIRE

Persecutions under the Roman Empire (I)

EMPEROR	DATES	CONDITIONS	FAMOUS MARTYRS
Nero	54–68	Persecution 64–8	Peter, Paul
Galba, Otho, Vitellius	68–9		
Vespasian	69–79		
Titus	79–81		
Domitian	81–96	Christians charged with atheism	Flavius Clemens, consul and cousin of Emperor, his wife Domitilla, and Acilius Glabrio, ex-consul
Nerva	96–8		
Trajan	98–117	Pliny the Younger, governor of Bithynia (Letters of Pliny and Trajan, x. 96) instructed in 112 **1** Christians were not to be sought out, and anonymous accusations were to be neglected. **2** Those who were regularly accused and who professed to be Christians were to be punished. **3** People who had never been Christians, or who had stopped being Christians, provided they sacrificed, were pardoned. These guidelines were followed for the next hundred years, until Septimius Severus.	Ignatius
Hadrian	117–38	Comparative lack of persecution	
Antoninus Pius	138–61		Polycarp

Persecutions under Emperor Nero

The secular historian, Tacitus, relates that when the city of Rome was destroyed by fire (AD 64) the report was widely circulated and believed that the emperor himself had caused the fire, or had at least prevented it from being put out.

To stifle the report, Nero provided others to bear the accusation, in the shape of people who were commonly called 'Christians', in detestation of their abominable character. These he visited with every refinement of punishment. First some were arrested who confessed [that they were Christians], and then, on received information, an immense number were convicted, not so much on the charge of arson but on the charge of ill-will towards mankind in general. Their deaths were turned into a form of amusement. They were wrapped in the skins of wild beasts to be torn in pieces by dogs, or were fastened to crosses to be set on fire, and, when the daylight came to an end, were burned for an illumination at night. Nero threw open his own gardens for the spectacle, and made it the occasion of a circus exhibition, mingling with the populace in the costume of a driver, or standing in his chariot. Sympathy was eventually felt for the sufferers, although the objects of it were guilty people who deserved the most extreme punishment: people felt that they were being destroyed not for the benefit of the public but to serve the cruel purpose of one man.

¶ Tacitus, *Annals,* xv.44; quoted by A. J. Mason, *The Historic Martyrs of the Primitive Church* (Longmans, 1905), pp. 7–8

Seven sons of Felicitas

A pious widow, Felicitas, who had seven sons, lived in Rome. By the public and edifying example of this lady and her whole family, many idolaters were moved to renounce the worship of their false gods, and to embrace the faith of Christ, which Christians were likewise encouraged by so illustrious a pattern openly to profess. This raised the spleen of the heathenish priests, who complained to the emperor

Antoninus that the boldness with which Felicitas publicly practised the Christian religion, drew many from the worship of the immortal gods who were the guardians and protectors of the empire, and that it was a constant insult on them; who, on that account, were extremely offended and angry with the city and whole state. They added, that in order to appease them, it was necessary to compel this lady and her children to sacrifice to them. Antoninus being himself superstitious was prevailed upon by this remonstrance to send an order to Publius the prefect of Rome, to take care that the priests should be satisfied, and the gods appeased in this matter.

Publius caused the mother and her sons to be apprehended and brought before him. When this was done he took Felicitas aside, and used the strongest inducements to bring her freely to sacrifice to the gods, that he might not be obliged to proceed with severity against her and her sons; but she returned him this answer: 'Do not think to frighten me by threats, or to win me by fair speeches. The spirit of God within me will not suffer me to be overcome by Satan, and will make me victorious over all your assaults.'

Publius said in a great rage: 'Unhappy woman, is it possible you should think death so desirable as not to permit even your children to live, but force me to destroy them by the most cruel torments?'

'My children,' replied Felicitas, 'will live eternally with Christ if they are faithful to him; but must expect eternal death if they sacrifice to idols.'

The next day the prefect, sitting in the square of Mars before his temple, sent for Felicitas and her sons, and said to Felicitas, 'Take pity on your children, Felicitas; they are in the bloom of youth, and may aspire to the greatest honours and preferments.'

The holy mother answered, 'Your pity is really impiety, and the compassion to which you exhort me would make me the most cruel of mothers.'

Then turning to her children, Felicitas said, 'My son, look up to heaven where Jesus Christ expects you. Be faithful in his love, and fight courageously for your souls.'

Publius being exasperated at this behaviour, commanded her to be cruelly buffeted, saying, 'You are insolent indeed, to give them such advice as this in my presence, in contempt of orders of our princes.'

The judge then called the children to him, one after another, and used many artful speeches, mingling promises with threats to induce them to adore the gods.

Januarius, the eldest, experienced his assaults the first, but resolutely answered him, 'You advise me to do a thing that is very foolish, and contrary to all reason; but I confide in my Lord Jesus Christ, that he will preserve me from such an impiety.' Publius ordered him to be stripped and cruelly scourged, after which he sent him back to prison.

Felix, the second brother, was called next, and commanded to sacrifice. But the generous youth replied, 'There is only one God. To him we offer the sacrifice of our hearts. We will never forsake the love which we owe to Jesus Christ. Employ all your artifices; exhaust all inventions of cruelty. You will never be able to overcome our faith.'

The other brothers made their answers separately, that they feared not a passing death, but everlasting torments; and that having before their eyes the immortal recompenses of the just, they despised the threats of men. Martialis, who spoke last, said, 'All who do not confess Christ to be the true God, shall be cast into eternal flames.'

The brothers, after being whipped, were remanded in prison, and the prefect, despairing to be able ever to overcome their resolution, laid the whole process before the emperor. Antoninus having read the interrogatory, gave an order that they should be sent to different judges, and condemned to different deaths. Januarius was scourged to death with whips loaded with plummets of lead. The two next, Felix and Philip, were beaten with clubs till they expired. Sylvanus, the fourth, was thrown headlong down a steep precipice. The three youngest, Alexander, Vitalis, and Martialis, were beheaded, and the same sentence was executed upon the mother four months later.

¶ Alban Butler, *The Lives of the Saints* (Dublin, 1833), vol. II, pp. 43–4

Timothy

The ageing apostle Paul's warning to his young protégé: 'Everyone who wants to live a godly life in Christ Jesus will be persecuted' (2 Tim. 3:12).

Under Emperor Domitian's reign there were various tales published in order to injure the Christians. Among other falsehoods, they were accused of indecent nightly meetings, of a rebellious spirit, of murdering their children, and even of being cannibals; and at this time, such was the infatuation of the pagans, that if famine, pestilence, or earthquakes afflicted any of the Roman provinces, it was charged on the Christians. The various kinds of punishments and inflicted cruelties were, during this persecution, imprisonment, racking, searing, broiling, burning, scourging, stoning, hanging, and worrying. Many were lacerated with red-hot pincers, and others were thrown upon the horns of wild bulls. After having suffered these cruelties, the friends of the deceased Christians were refused the privilege of burying their remains.

Among the most distinguished of the martyrs of this period was Timothy, the celebrated disciple of St Paul, and Bishop of Ephesus.

St Paul sent to Timothy to come to him in his last confinement at Rome; and after that great apostle's martyrdom, he returned to Ephesus, where he governed the church till nearly the close of the century. At this period the pagans were about to celebrate a feast, the principal ceremonies of which were, that the people should carry sticks in their hands, go masked, and bear about the streets the images of their gods. When Timothy met the procession, he severely reproved them of their idolatry, which so exasperated them, that they fell upon him with their clubs, and beat him in so dreadful a manner, that he expired two days later.

¶ John Foxe, *The Book of Martyrs*, revised with notes and an appendix by W. Bramley-Moore (London, 1869), pp. 10–11

Ignatius

'I battle with beasts ... and would to God I were once come to the beasts which are prepared for me' (Ignatius, writing to Polycarp at Smyrna).

The most illustrious victim of the persecution under Emperor Trajan was the great Ignatius, bishop of Antioch, in Syria.

Emperor Trajan commanded the martyrdom of Ignatius, Bishop of Antioch. This holy man, when an infant, Christ took in his arms, and showed to his disciples, as one that would be a pattern of humility and innocence: he received the gospel afterwards from St John the Evangelist, and was exceedingly zealous in his mission and ministry. He boldly vindicated the faith of Christ before the emperor, for which he was cast into prison, and was cruelly tormented; for, after being dreadfully scourged, he was compelled to hold fire in his hands, and at the same time, papers dipped in oil were put to his sides and lighted. His flesh was then torn with hot pincers, and at last he was dispatched by the fury of wild beasts.

Ignatius had either presentiment or information of his fate; for writing to Polycarp, at Smyrna, he thus described his adventures:

> From Syria, even till I came to Rome, had I battle with beasts, as well by sea as land, both day and night, being bound in the midst of a cruel legion of soldiers who, the more benefits they received at my hands, behaved so much the worse unto me. And would to God I were once come to the beasts which are prepared for me; which also I wish with gaping mouths were ready to come upon me, whom also I will provoke that they, without delay, may devour me. And if they will not, unless they be provoked, I will then enforce them against myself. Now begin I to be a scholar; I esteem no visible things, nor yet invisible things, so that I may get or obtain Christ Jesus. Let the fire, the gallows, the wild beasts, the breaking bones, the pulling asunder of members, the bruising of my whole body, and the torments of the devil and hell itself come upon me, so that I may win Christ Jesus.

¶ John Foxe, *The Book of Martyrs,* revised with notes and an appendix by W. Bramley-Moore (London, 1869), pp. 11–13

The stories about Ignatius' trial and martyrdom are unreliable, but there is no doubt that he achieved his aim, and was torn in pieces in the Colosseum on some 'Roman holiday'. Among Ignatius' seven letters, one is written to the bishop of Smyrna, a man about 40 years old; Ignatius longed 'to see his blameless face' and to have Christian fellowship with one who was 'grounded as upon an immovable rock' – the bishop was Polycarp. To bishop Polycarp, Ignatius wrote, 'The times require thee, as pilots require winds, and as one tossed at sea requires a haven. Be vigilant as God's athlete. Stand firm like an anvil under the blows of the hammer. It is the part of a great athlete to receive blows and to conquer. Be yet more diligent than you are, learn to know the times.'

Pliny's writings

A letter from Pliny the younger, while he was governor of Bithynia, to the Emperor Trajan requested instructions about how to deal with Christians who were brought before him.

I have not taken part in the trial of a Christian, and therefore I do not know what it is that they are commonly punished for, and with what degree of allowance, nor what direction the investigation should take. I have been much perplexed to know whether any distinction should be made between one age and another, or whether the weak and tender should be treated in exactly the same way as the strong; whether those who repent should be pardoned, or whether if a person has once been a Christian he should gain nothing by ceasing to be so; whether the very name Christianity is liable to punishment, apart from disgraceful conduct, or the disgraceful conduct which is attached to the name.

Clearly Pliny thought that there might be nothing to punish in Christianity itself.

Meanwhile, this is the method which I have followed with those who were brought before me as Christians. I have asked them directly whether they were Christians. If they confessed, I have asked them a second and a third time, with threats of punishment; if they persisted I have ordered them to be executed. I had no doubt that whatever the thing which they confessed amounted to, their obstinacy at any rate, and their inflexible stubbornness, deserved to be punished.

There then follows the earliest description of Christian ways given by a non-Christian.

Yet they affirmed that their fault or their error came to no more than this – that it was their custom to assemble on a fixed day before daylight, and to repeat alternately among themselves a song to Christ as to a god, and to bind themselves by an oath – not to any crime, but that they would not commit theft or robbery or adultery, that they would not break their word, and that when called upon to produce a thing entrusted to them they would not repudiate the trust. When this was done, they said that it had been their habit to depart and then come together again later to take a meal, but an ordinary harmless meal, and this they had ceased to do after the issue of my edict forbidding the existence of organised associations, as you commanded.

This made me think it more necessary to find out from two female slaves, who were called *ministrae* (deaconesses), how far the account was true. So I tortured them, but discovered nothing beyond a degraded and extravagant superstition. So I adjourned the hearing and had recourse to you. The matter seemed to me worth troubling you with, particularly because so many people were imperilled. Many of every age and every rank, and of both sexes too, are and will be in danger. It is not only the cities, but even the villages and the country, that are penetrated by this catching superstition.

Eustathius

'We say we are Christians, we proclaim it to the whole world, even under the hands of the executioner, and in the midst of all the torments you inflict upon us to compel us to unsay it. Torn and mangled, and weltering in our blood, we cry out as loud a we are able to cry, That we are worshippers of God through Christ' (Tertullian, Apologeticus, c. 21).

General Eustathius, under Emperor Trajan, was returning victorious from a successful campaign against the Barbarians. And it came to pass that as he did this Emperor Trajan died and he was replaced by Adrian (Hadrian), who was an exceedingly irreligious man, and was more wicked than all the other kings who had reigned before him. And when Eustathius was returning from the war the Emperor went out to meet him, according to the custom of the Roman Emperors, and he brought with him all his nobles, because of the long list of all the places which Eustathius had captured. And Eustathius, because of his valour, whereof he was conscious, and because of his meeting with his wife and sons, was filled to the uttermost with his joy. And when he had come into the city the Emperor went and entered into the temple of Apollo, but Eustathius did not go in with him, and remained outside. And the Emperor called him, and asked him why he did not come into the temple of Apollo, saying, 'Thou must pour out a libation to the gods in return for thy victory, and because thou hast returned from the war, and thou must offer up sacrifices of thanksgiving to them.'

Then the Emperor was wroth when he heard these things from Eustathius, and he made him withdraw from him as if he had been a pagan, he and his wife and his sons, and he spake unto them words of terror and threats of destruction. And the saints neither regarded them nor were they frightened at all. And when the Emperor saw their lack of concern and their faith in the Christ, he commanded them to be taken too the stadium, and for a mighty lion to be let loose in the stadium. And when the lion advanced to attack them he stood still before the saints, and bent his legs and worshipped them, and he laid his head also down to the ground. And afterwards he came out of the stadium and departed. And when the Emperor saw this great sight, and that the wild beast would not attack them, he fell into doubt. And he commanded them to make a brazen bull, so that they might cast the saints into it and burn them. And the multitude gathered together to see the strife and the spectacle of the saints. The Emperor's servants seized them with mechanical devices to lift them up in the brazen bull.

Then the blessed Eustathius entreated the honourable people to allow them to pray, and he spread out his hands, he and his wife and his sons, and they prayed, saying: 'O Lord God of the Powers, whom no man hath ever seen, but whom now we see according to his wish, hearken thou now unto us who cry unto thee. Make thou our prayer to be perfect with one thought, namely the confession of thy name and thy holy faith. Make thou us worthy to be counted among the holy martyrs, and let the threat of this fire which is round about us become to us the dew of refreshing, so that our bodies, O Lord, may gain strength thereby.'

Then the saints delivered themselves over to the soldiers, who cast them into the brazen instrument. And having been thrown in the flame of fire it enveloped them, and they ascribed glory to the Holy Trinity, unto whom victory belongeth, and after a short time they delivered up their souls into the hands of God. And the fire did not scorch their bodies in the least degree, nor the hair of their heads.

And after three days the wicked Emperor Hadrian came to the place wherein the saints had finished their fight, an he commanded that the brazen bull should be opened, so that he might be able to see what had happened to the saints. And when it had been opened they found the bodies of the saints in a perfect state of preservation, and there were no marks of destruction whatever in them, and they seemed to be still alive. And when they had brought them out and laid them on the ground, great awe and wonder came upon everyone who stood near them, and the bodies of the saints were brilliantly white like snow. The evil Hadrian looked on them, was filled with wonder and fear, and went away. The multitude who were standing there cried out, "Great art thou, O God of the Christians! Thou art indeed the only Great God, Jesus the Christ, and there is no other god besides thee. for thou didst not permit any harm to reach the bodies of these saints, nay, they have become brilliantly white and shining, and they send forth great light with glory and gladness."

And when the evening had come the Christians came and carried away the bodies of the martyred saints, and they laid them in an honourable place secretly in the city of Rome.

¶ E. A. Wallis Budge (ed.)., *Coptic Martyrdom in the Dialect of Upper Egypt* (British Museum, 1914), pp. 376–80 (extract from BM oriental manuscript 6783)

Symphorosa and her seven sons
c. 120

Symphorosa was well known for relieving Christians who suffered for their faith. The emperor, whose superstition was alarmed at the answer of his gods or their priests, ordered that Symphorosa and her sons should be seized, and brought before him. She came with joy in her countenance, praying all the way for herself and her children, that God would grant them the grace to confess his holy name with constancy. The emperor exhorted them at first in mild terms to sacrifice.

Symphorosa answered: 'My husband Getusius and his brother Amantius, being your tribunes, have suffered various torments for the name of Jesus Christ rather than sacrifice to idols; and they have vanquished your demons by their death, choosing to be beheaded rather than to overcome. The death they suffered drew upon them ignominy among men, but glory among the angels; and they now enjoy eternal life in heaven.'

The emperor, changing his voice, said to her in an angry tone, 'Either sacrifice to the most powerful gods, with thy sons, or thou thyself shalt be offered up as a sacrifice together with them.'

Symphorosa answered: 'Your gods cannot receive me as a sacrifice; but if I am burnt for the name of Jesus Christ my death will increase the torment which your devils endure in their flames. But can I hope for so great a happiness as to be offered with my children a sacrifice to the true and living God?'

Emperor Adrian said, 'Either sacrifice to my gods, or you shall all miserably perish.'

Symphorosa said: 'Do not imagine that fear will make me change; I desire to be at rest with my husband whom you put to death for the name of Jesus Christ.'

The emperor then ordered her to be carried to the temple of Hercules, where she was first buffeted on the cheeks, and afterward hung up by the hair of her head. When no torments were able to shake her invincible soul, the emperor gave orders that she should be thrown into the river with a great stone fastened about her neck.

The next day the emperor sent for her seven sons all together, and exhorted them to sacrifice and not imitate the obstinacy of their mother. He added the severest threats, but finding all to be in vain, he ordered seven stakes with engines and pulleys to be planted round the temple of Hercules, and the pious youths to be bound upon them; their limbs were in this posture tortured and stretched in such a manner that the bones were disjointed in all parts of their bodies. The young noblemen, far from yielding under the violence of their tortures, were encouraged by each other's example, and seemed more eager to suffer than the executioners were to torment.

At length the emperor commanded them to be put to death, in the same place where they were, but in different ways. The eldest, called Crescens, had his throat cut; the second, called Julian, was stabbed in the chest; Nemesius, the third, was pierced with a lance in his heart; Primativus received his wound in the belly, Justin in the back, Stacteus on his sides, and Eugenius, the youngest, died by his body being cleft asunder into two parts across his chest from the head down.

¶ Alban Butler, *The Lives of the Saints* (Dublin, 1833), vol. II, pp. 90–1

Polycarp
c. 70–155/6

*In the book of Revelation, one of the seven letters is addressed to the
church at Smyrna, and includes these words:*

> *'Be faithful, even to the point of death,
> and I will give you the crown of life' (Rev. 2:10).*

*Polycarp was bishop of Smyrna and the leading Christian figure in
Roman Asia in the reign of the emperor Antoninus Pius. According to
Irenaeus, Polycarp 'had fellowship with John [the apostle] and with
the others who had seen the Lord'. Polycarp's long life made him a
very important link between the early church and the apostles.*

The church of God at Smyrna to the church of God at Philomelium
and to all communities of the holy, catholic church everywhere . . .
We are writing to you, brethren, to tell you how many people suffered
martyrdom, especially blessed Polycarp.

Late in the day Polycarp's pursuers came up together and found
him hiding in a cottage, lying in an upper room. It was within
Polycarp's power to flee from there to another place, but he refused to
do so, saying, 'God's will be done.'

So when Polycarp heard them arrive he came down and talked with
them. The soldiers were amazed at his age and his courage and that
so much trouble had been taken to arrest such an elderly man.

The soldiers brought Polycarp back into the city, riding on a donkey.
The head of the police, Herod, met him. Herod's father, Nicetes,
transferred Polycarp into a carriage, sat next to him, and tried to
make him change his mind. Nicetes urged Polycarp, 'Tell me, what
harm is done if one says that Caesar is Lord? Go on, make a sacrifice
to Caesar, and then you will save your skin.'

To start with Polycarp made no reply, but as they pressed him, he
said, 'I do not intend to do what you advise me.'

Once they had failed to persuade Polycarp they dragged him from
the carriage into the stadium where there was such a tremendous
noise that it was impossible for anyone to be heard.

Polycarp was brought before the Proconsul who also tried to

persuade him to change his mind: 'Think of your old age. Just do as everybody else does and swear by the genius of Caesar; repent; say, "Away with the Atheists".' ['Atheists' here does not refer to people who do not believe in God, but to people, like Polycarp, who refused to acknowledge that Caesar was a divine god who should be worshipped and receive sacrifices.]

Polycarp then studied the crowd of lawless heathen in the stadium, waved his hand in their direction, looked up to heaven with a groan, and said, 'Away with the Atheists.'

The Proconsul was insistent and repeated, 'Swear, and we will release you; deny Christ.'

Polycarp replied:

> Eighty and six years have I served him,
> and he has done me no wrong;
> how then can I blaspheme my King who saved me?

Still the Proconsul urged Polycarp: 'Swear by the genius of Caesar.'

'If you really think that I would swear by the genius of Caesar then you forget who I am. Take note, I am a Christian. If you want to learn the Christian faith, appoint a day, and grant me a hearing.'

The Proconsul replied, 'I have wild beasts and if you do not change your mind I will throw you to them.'

Polycarp said, 'Order them to be brought. We are not allowed to change our minds from what is good to what is evil, only to change from what is evil to what is good.'

The Proconsul said, 'As you despise the wild beasts, you will be destroyed by fire, if you do not change your mind.'

So Polycarp said, 'The fire you threaten me with only burns for a short time and then it goes out. You are ignorant of the future fire of judgment which is never put out and which is reserved for the ungodly. So what are you waiting for? Do what you want to do. I have to be burnt alive.'

Saying these things, and other things as well, Polycarp was inspired with courage and joy, and his appearance was filled with grace, so that not only did it not faint at the many things that were said to him, but on the contrary the proconsul was amazed and sent his own herald to proclaim three times in the middle of the stadium, 'Polycarp has confessed himself to be a Christian.' When this was proclaimed by the herald, the whole multitude, both the Gentiles and the Jews who lived in Smyrna, cried out uncontrollable anger in loud shouts, 'This is the teacher of Asia, the father of the Christians, the puller down of our gods, who teaches numbers not to sacrifice nor worship.' After they had said this they called out to Asiarch Philip requesting that a lion be set loose on Polycarp. But he replied that this would be unlawful, as the games had already ended. Then the crowd decided to shout out in unison that Polycarp should be burnt alive. For it was necessary that Polycarp's vision be fulfilled, which he had about his pillow which he saw on fire while he was praying. Polycarp then turned and said prophetically to those who were with him, 'I must be burnt alive.'

This was no sooner said than done. In a moment the mob collected logs and faggots from the workshops and the baths and the Jews proved to be especially zealous about this, as usual. When the pyre had been completed they were about to nail Polycarp to the stake, but he said,

> Let me be as I am:
> He that gave me power to abide the fire
> will grant me too,
> without your making me fast with nails,
> to abide untroubled on the pyre.

So they did not nail him to the stake but just bound him to it. Polycarp put his hands behind him and was bound, like a godly ram out of a great flock for an offering, a whole burnt offering made ready and acceptable to God. Then he looked up to heaven and prayed:

'O Lord God Almighty, you are the Father of your much loved and blessed Son Jesus Christ, through whom we have received our knowledge of you. You are the God of the angels and the powers and the God of the whole creation and of everyone who worships you. I praise you that you have counted me worthy of this day and hour so that I can be counted as one of the martyrs in the suffering of Christ and then to the resurrection to eternal life of both the body and the soul with the Holy Spirit. May I be welcomed with them today into your presence as an acceptable sacrifice. As you planned that this should happen, may it now be fulfilled since you are the faithful and true God. On account of this and for every other reason I praise you, bless you, and glorify you through the everlasting and heavenly high priest Jesus Christ, your much loved Son. It is through him we come to you in the company of the Holy Spirit, to whom we give glory now and for ever. Amen.'

As soon as Polycarp had completed his prayer and offered up his Amen the fire was kindled. A great flame blazed out, and we who saw it, and who have been preserved to tell the story, saw something marvellous. The fire took the shape of an arch, like a ship's sail blown by the wind, and this made a wall around the martyr's body. His body was at the centre of this, not at all like burning flesh, but like baked bread, or like gold and silver in a furnace. We smelled a sweet perfume in the air, like frankincense or some other precious spice.

Eventually when the unholy people saw that Polycarp's body was not being consumed by the fire, they ordered that he should be killed and they stabbed him with as dagger. As they did this a spurt of blood gushed out and put the fire out, to the amazement of all the spectators.

¶ E. C. E. Owen, *Some Authentic Acts of the Early Martyrs* (Oxford, 1927), Church at Smyrna for the Church at Philomelium

Persecutions under the Roman Empire (II)

EMPEROR	DATES	CONDITIONS	FAMOUS MARTYRS
Marcus Aurelius	138–61		Carpus, Papylus, Agathonica Justin & companions Scillitan martyrs Martyrs of Lyons
Commodus	180–92	Very little persecution	
Pertinax, Didius Julianus	193	Very little persecution	
Septimius Severus	193–211	Persecution now regulated by new edicts. Christians were not accused by a private prosecutor, but sought out by the state. Newly converted Christians, not old Christians, persecuted	Saturus Perpetua & Felicitas

Geta & Caracalla	211–17	Same as Septimius Severus	
Macrinus	217–18	No persecution	
Heliogabalus	218–22	No persecution	
Alexander Severus	222–35	No persecution	
Maximus the Thracian	237–8	Persecution mainly against leaders	
Gordian I, II	237–8	No persecution	
Gordian III	238–44	No persecution	
Philip the Arabian	244–9	No persecution	
Decius	249–51	All Christians had to produce certificates of sacrifice according to the edict of 250. Exile, confiscation of goods, torture, imprisonment on a worldwide scale	Many of the martyrs were bishops: Fabian of Rome
Gallus	251–2	New edict issued to compel Christians to sacrifice	
Volusian	252		
Aemilian	253		
Valerian	253–60	Peace until 257 **First edict** imposed death penalty on Christians who went to their own worship services; bishops and priests were ordered to sacrifice to gods. **Second edict**: Bishops, priests and deacons were to be killed at once if they refused to sacrifice.	Cyprian, Fructuosus & his deacons James and Marian Aemilian
Gallienus	260–8	Cemeteries and other places of worship were allowed. Only little persecution	Marinus

Claudius II	270–5		
Tacitus	275–6		
Probus	276–82		
Carus	282–3		
Carinus & Numerian	283–4		
Diocletian alone	284–6		
Diocletian & Maximian	286–92		
Diocletian & Maximian Augusti (Constantius & Galerius Caesars)	292–304	Diocletian's **first edict** (303): scriptures burnt, churches destroyed, Christians stripped of honours. Many killed. **Second edict**: Christian leaders imprisoned. **Third edict**: Imprisoned clergy tortured cruelly if they refused to sacrifice **Fourth edict** (304): War of extermination: all Christians to be killed if they refused to sacrifice.	
Constantius & Gelerius Augusti (Severus & Maximinus Daia Caesars)	305	Persecution in Europe, Asia and Egypt under Galerius and Maximinus	
Galerius, Maximinus Daia, Constantine (already Caesar, 306), Licinius, Maximian, Maxentius	307–13	Toleration granted to Christians	Marcellus, Cassian Christian soldiers Procopius

In 313 Constantine, through the edict of Milan, gave complete freedom to Christians. Persecution soon stopped.

Ptolemy and Lucius

About the same date as Polycarp's martyrdom, a group of mertyr-doms took place in Rome which illustrate how Christians were put to death just for professing to be Christians.

After a woman had been converted to Christ she refused to join her heathen husband in practices which were against her conscience. Eventually she tried to obtain a 'divorce' – a legal release from her husband. The profligate husband denounced her as a Christian. The woman appealed to the emperor to delay her case coming to trial until she had settled her own private affairs, and the request was granted. The divorced husband turned his anger on Ptolemy, the person who had taught his wife the Christian faith. The husband had a friend who was a centurion. He persuaded the centurion to arrest Ptolemy, and throw him into prison, and 'to interrogate him on this one point, whether he were a Christian.'

Ptolemy, a guileless and truthful man, stated that he was a Christian, and he was condemned to death. As he was led away from the tribunal, a Christian called Lucius cried out, 'This man has not been convicted of adultery, or murder, or robbery, or any other crime; you punish him just because he acknowledged Christ's name. Urbicus, that is not a judgment that suits an emperor called Pius, nor Caesar's son, the philosopher, or the Senate – the sacred Senate.'

Urbicus replied, 'I suppose that you are the same as Ptolemy.'

'Certainly,' replied Lucius.

The prefect then ordered Lucius to share the same fate as Ptolemy. Lucius thanked him, and a third Christian who behaved in the same way was included with the former two.

¶ Justin, *Apol* ii.2; quoted by A. J. Mason, *The Historic Martyrs of the Primitive Church* (Longmans, 1905), pp. 30–1.

The Epistle to Diognetus

A beautiful account of the life Christians lived at this time is contained in a little anonymous writing known to us as the *Epistle to Diognetus.* Diognetus appears to have been a high official, and perhaps, like Pliny, was at a loss to know why he was compelled to take action against the Christians. His informant describes him as 'seeking earnestly to know what God they believe in, and what that worship of him is which enables them to despise the world, and to brave death.'

'Christians,' he tells Diognetus, 'are not marked off from other men by country, by language, or by manner of life. They live in Greek or barbarian cities, according to the appointed lot of each, and follow the local customs in dress and diet and so forth, although the nature of their own social ideal is acknowledged to be wonderful and surprising. They live in their own country, but as sojourners in it; they have their part in everything as citizens, and bear everything like strangers; every foreign country is a home to them, and every home a foreign country. They obey the established laws, and surpass the laws by their own lives. They love all men, and are persecuted by all. Men do not understand them, and condemn them; they are put to death, and find life thereby. They are poor, and make many rich; they lack all things, and abound in all. They are dishonoured, and glory in the dishonour; they are slandered, and are found righteous; they are reviled, and they bless; they are shamefully treated, and they pay respect. They do good, and are punished as evil; when they are punished, they rejoice as if life were given to them. The Jews make war against them as aliens, and the Greeks persecute them; and those who hate them cannot give a reason for their enmity.'

¶ Printed in Otto's *Justin,* or in Funk's *Patres Apostolici,* quoted by A. J. Mason, *The Historic Martyrs of the Primitive Church,* Longmans, 1905, pp 31–2

Apollonius

The philosopher Apollonius was beheaded in Rome in 185.

In the persecution Emperor Commodus inflicted on the Christians Perennis was proconsul of Asia. After the apostle Apollonius, who came from Alexandria, was arrested Perennis put him on trial.

PROCONSUL PERENNIS: Are you a Christian, Apollonius?

APOLLONIUS: Yes, I am a Christian. I fear and worship the God who made heaven, earth, the sea and all that is in them.

PROCONSUL: Be advised, Apollonius, and swear by the emperor Commodus, our lord.

APOLLONIUS: Listen to my defence, Perennis. If you disobey God's commandments you become a criminal because you are denying God. God's commands are full of justice and truth. We believe them to be the word of God and they teach us never take oaths.

PROCONSUL: Sacrifice to the gods and to emperor Commodus' statue.

APOLLONIUS: The sacrifice we Christians offer is one of prayer. In fact we daily pray for the emperor Commodus. Be we believe that he rules not by the will of humans, but through God's decree.

PROCONSUL: I will give you one day to think about your fate.

Three days later Apollonius was asked if he had changed his mind. He replied in this way:

APOLLONIUS: I am aware of the Senate's decree, but my God whom I serve is not made with human hands. I can never worship gold, or iron or bronze or silver, or any deaf and dumb idols. You are wrong on many counts to indulge in such worship. First, you are wrong in God's sight because your idols are unable to respond to you. Secondly, you are wrong in God's sight because you worship the fruit of nature, such things as onions and garlic which once they have passed through the stomach go into sewers. Thirdly, you are wrong in God's sight because you worship animals. Fourthly, you are wrong in God's sight because you worship man-made gods such as Dionysus, Heracles and Zeus.'

PROCONSUL: Senate's decree forbids anyone to be a Christian.

APOLLONIUS: Man's decrees have no power over God's decrees. The more you kill these poor, innocent people, the more God will raise up more of them. Everyone is in God's hands, kings and senators, to free men and slaves. After we die we come to the time of judgment. We do not think that it is difficult to die for the God of truth.

PROCONSUL: So does death give you pleasure?

APOLLONIUS: Perennis, I love life, but that does not make me fear death. But the life which I prefer above everything is eternal life. This is the life that is in store for those who live faithfully on this earth. We

Tortures of the first Christian martyrs
1: The cross and stakes

a. Martyrs suspended by one foot.
b. Martyrs suspended by both feet.
c. Martyrs raised on the cross, head uppermost.
d. Martyrs nailed to the cross, head downwards.
e. Martyrs hung up by both arms with heavy weights attached to the feet.
f. Christian women martyrs suspended by their hair.
g. Martyrs hung up by one arm only, with ponderous stones attached to their feet.
h. Martyrs suspended by both feet with a great stone fastened to the neck.
i. Sometimes the blessed martyrs, after being smeared with honey, were bound to stakes fixed to the ground, and so exposed to the rays of the sun, to be tortured by the bites and stings of flies and bees.
j. Martyrs suspended by one foot; one leg is bent at the knee, which is constricted by means of an iron ring, the other being weighed with a heavy mass of iron.
k. Martyrs suspended by their thumbs, with heavy stones attached to their feet.
l. Christians hung up, and a slow fire kindled underneath to suffocate them with the smoke.
m. Martyrs were suspended by their feet and at the same time pounded with hammers.
n. Martyrs were suspended by the hands, which were tied behind their backs, and heavy weights fastened to their feet and round their neck.
o. Martyrs were suspended by the hands, which were tied behind their backs, and had their shoulders weighed down with lumps of salt. Wooden gags were forced into their mouths.

¶ *Tortures and Torments of the Christian Martyrs, from the 'De SS. Martyrum Cruciatibus' of the Rev. Father Gallonio*, translated by A. R. Allinson (London and Paris, printed for the subscribers, 1903), pp. 34–7

believe in the immortal soul, judgment following death, the resurrection of the dead and that God will be our judge. Even if you believe that all this is foolishness we gladly take these illusions with us which have helped us to live.

PROCONSUL: I hoped that you would say goodbye to your beliefs and join us in worshipping the gods.

APOLLONIUS: I hoped that my words would have opened the eyes of your soul so that you would worship the God who created the world.

PROCONSUL: Even though I would like to set you free, Apollonius, emperor Commodus's decree prevents me. However, I will ensure that your death will not be painful.

Perennis then ordered Apollonius to be beheaded. Perennis responded by saying that Perennis' sentence would bring him eternal life.

¶ Summary from *The Book of Christian Martyrs* (SCM, 1990)

The martyrs of Lyons

Under Marcus Aurelius Antoninus Verus many Christians were martyred, especially in parts of Asia and France. At Lyons the martyrs were compelled to sit in hot iron chairs till their flesh was broiled. Some were sewn up in nets, and thrown on the horns of wild bulls.

To start with they endured like heroes whatever the crowds did to them: shouts of abuse, being dragged along the ground, attacked, stoned, imprisoned, and everything else that wild crowds inflict on their enemies. They were herded into the forum and tried by the tribune and city authorities in front of the whole town. As soon as they confessed Christ they were locked up in prison and had to wait for the governor. When they were later brought before him they had to suffer all the cruelties that were reserved for Christians.

Blandina

Blandina was full of such courage that her torturers fell exhausted from their exertions and did not know what else they could do to her. They could not believe that she still breathed, even though she was full of gaping wounds and her body was a mangled mess. They thought that one of their tortures would have been enough to kill her and could not understand how she had survived. Ignoring her great sufferings Blandina still uttered the words, at the end of the day, 'I am a Christian. I have done nothing to be ashamed of.'

Sanctus

Sanctus also endured the ravages of inhuman cruelty with super-human strength. His torturers expected the severity of his tortures to force him to recant. But his resistance was so powerful that when questioned he refused to reveal his name, race, place of birth or nationality. He replied, in Latin, to each question: 'I am a Christian.' The governor and his torturers became so angry with Sanctus that they applied red-hot copper plates to his private parts. Sanctus did not yield as he was strengthened by the divine water of life that flows from the heart of Christ [see John 7:38; 19:34]. However his body bore all the marks of his sufferings and looked like one great wounded mass of flesh, without any human shape left to it. But Christ achieved through this suffering body wonderful things as the opponent of Christianity was completely defeated. Sanctus' suffering also demonstrated to everyone that there is no need to be afraid where the Father's love is present, and that nothing can harm Christ's followers where Christ's glory is present [see 1 John 4:18; 2 Cor. 8:23].

A few days after this wicked people put Sanctus back on the rack thinking that his tortured body would now be unable to resist any further pain, as he experienced excruciating pain at the slightest touch on his body. His torturers also hoped to frighten other Christians by making this example of Sanctus. However, to their amazement, Sanctus' body regained its former shape and he could move his limbs once again. So, through Christ's grace, Sanctus' second time on the rack resulted in his cure and not in further punishment.

Pothinus

Blessed Pothinus, more than ninety years old, and extremely frail, was dragged in front of the tribunal. When he was asked by the governor, 'Who is the Christian's god?' Pothinus replied, 'If you had any understanding you would know.' At that Pothinus was viciously struck to the ground and no allowance was made for his old age. He was then dragged off to prison, barely able to breathe, where he died two days later.

Maturus, Sanctus, Blandina, and Attalus were taken to the amphitheatre so that they could be thrown to the wild beasts.

Blandina, hanging from a post, was given as food to the wild beasts in the arena. She hung there in the shape of a cross and gave great encouragement to other Christians who were martyred. As they looked at her hanging there, they were reminded of the privilege in sharing in Christ's sufferings. None of the wild beasts attacked Blandina that day, so she was cut down and returned to prison.

Attalus

The crowd demanded that Attalus, a man of considerable note, should be brought into the arena. He arrived in the arena, with a clear conscience and fully prepared to face the ordeal, as he had trained so hard in Christ's school. He was paraded around the amphitheatre with a placard on him which read: 'This is Attalus – the Christian', as the crowds hurled all kinds of abuse at him. When the governor realised that he was a Roman he ordered that he should be returned to prison.

Caesar had given orders that they should be put to death by torture, unless they decided to deny Christ, in which case they should be released. The governor ordered them to be put on trial in front of him at the start of a local festival which attracted huge numbers of people. After they were examined again those who were Roman citizens were beheaded and the others put into the arena with the wild beasts. To appease the crowd, the governor put Attalus in with the wild beasts. He was then put in the iron chair and burnt from where he cried out: 'Look what you are doing! You are eating men. But we do not eat people or indulge in any such evil practices.' Just before he died he was asked, 'What name does God have?' Attalus replied: 'God does not have a name like any human person.'

Blandina was brought out, as the crowning glory of these sports. She came with a fifteen-year-old called Ponticus. Blandina and Ponticus had been forced to watch the fate of their fellow Christians and had infuriated the crowd because they had stood firm in their faith. Blandina encouraged her younger Christian brother through all his tortures until he eventually gave up his spirit to God. Blandina then had to endure all the sufferings she had witnessed. She was whipped, thrown to the wild beasts and roasted on the griddle. Last of all she was put in a basket which was tossed by a bull. Blandina's martyrdom resulted in the onlookers admitting that they had never seen a woman suffer such tortures so well for such a long time.

¶ Eusebius, *The History of the Church*, Book V

Epipodius and Alexander

*The persecution at Lyons continued for some years, and Epipodius
and Alexander were martyred the year after Blandina.*

Epipodius and Alexander, friends from their school days, were unable
to escape from Lyons and so lived in hiding in an area in the city
known as Pierre Encise. Thorough search for any remaining Christians was made in Lyons. They were discovered and taken off quickly,
so quickly that Epipodius only had time to put on one shoe, leaving
the other one to be treasured as a relic by the widow who had cared
for them. After three days in prison they were examined and they
confessed that they were Christians. To deprive them of their mutual
support they were tried separately.

   Epipodius bore his tortures bravely. When the crowds shouted for
worse tortures the magistrate, in order to maintain the dignity of his
office, ordered Epipodius to be executed with the sword at once. Two
days later Alexander was brought to the bar. On refusing to offer
incense, he was beaten by three executioners in succession. After they
had finished he still confessed, 'The gods of the heathen are devils. I
commit my will to God Almighty.' The magistrate said that as the
Christians liked to prolong their torments and boast about them, he
would not allow them to do this. He ordered that Alexander should
be crucified without delay. He died quickly as his body was exhausted
through the scourging which it had received. With his last breath he
called on Christ.

¶ Ruinart's *Acta Primorum Martyrum Sincera*; quoted by A. J. Mason, *The
Historic Martyrs of the Primitive Church* (Longmans, 1905), pp. 57–8

Symphorian

*'Martyrdom is fullness, not because it finishes a human life but
because it brings love to the fullest point' (Clement of Alexandria).*

At about the same time as the martyrs of Lyons suffered, Symphorian lived in Autun, a town renowned for being the centre for orgies linked to the Phrygian worship of Cymbele, or Berecynthia. During a great celebration of the festival of this goddess, Symphorian was seen not to give the customary marks of reverence to Berecynthia. Since Christians were being rounded up Symphorian was brought before the governor, Heraclius.

Symphorian said, 'I am a Christian, my name is Symphorian.'

'Are you a Christian?' answered the governor in surprise. 'You must have escaped our attention. There are few of you in these parts. Why do you despise the figure of the mother of the gods, and refuse to worship it?'

'I worship the true God, who reigns in heaven,' replied Symphorian. 'I do not worship the image of a devil. If you would allow me to I would break it up with a hammer.'

The magistrate declared that he was not only guilty of sacrilege, but of treason. After a few days Symphorian was again asked if he would worship the gods, but he refused. 'I fear the Almighty God who made me,' he replied, 'and I serve him only. You have my body in your power for a while, but not my soul.'

The judge condemned him to be beheaded. As he was led out of the gate of the city, his mother called out to him from the city wall, 'My son! Symphorian, my son! Think of the living God. Be steadfast. It is no loss of life for you today, but a change for the better.'

¶ A. J. Mason, *The Historic Martyrs of the Primitive Church* (Longmans, 1905), pp. 58–9

Carpus, Papylus and Agathonica
(161–9)

Carpus, Papylus and Agathonica were martyred at Pergamos at about the same time as the churches at Lyons and Vienne were being persecuted.

While the proconsul was in residence at Pergamus blessed Carpus and Papylus, Christ's martyrs, were brought before him. Having taken his seat on the tribunal the proconsul asked, 'What is your name?'

The blessed one replied, 'My first name and chosen name is Christian, but, if you want to know my earthly name, it is Carpus.'

The proconsul said: 'You are aware of Augusti's commands, that you must both worship the gods who govern the world, so I now order you both to come forward and sacrifice.'

Carpus replied, 'I am a Christian, I worship Christ, the son of God, who came in the latter times for our salvation and delivered us from the deceit of the devil, and to such idols I do not sacrifice. No matter what you may do to me, it is impossible for me to sacrifice to fake representations of demons. People who sacrifice to them are similar to them. For just as "true worshippers" – those who, according to the divine teaching of our Lord, "worship God in spirit and in truth" – are made like God's glory and are immortal with him, taking part in eternal life through the Word, so also those who worship these idols are like the demons and will perish with them in hell. So, be assured, Proconsul, I will not sacrifice to these.'

The proconsul angrily replied, 'Sacrifice, both of you, and don't behave like fools.'

Carpus replied, smiling, 'Perish the gods that have not made the heaven and earth!'

The proconsul said: 'You must sacrifice: for so the Emperor commanded.'

Carpus answered: 'The living do not sacrifice to the dead.'

The proconsul said: 'Do the gods seem to you to be dead?'

Carpus said: 'Would you hear the answer? These were never even men, nor ever lived, that they should die. Do you wish to learn that this is true? Take away from them your homage which you suppose they receive at your hands, and you shall know they are nothing, things of the earth earthy and destroyed by time. For our God who is timeless and made the ages himself remains indestructible and everlasting, being ever the same and admitting neither of increase nor of decrease, but these are made by men and destroyed, as I said, by time. And do not marvel that they give oracles and deceive. For the Devil, having fallen in the beginning from his place of glory, would fain by his own villainy make of none effect the fatherly love of God for man, and being hard pressed by the saints contends with them and prepares wars beforehand and forecast announces them to his own. Likewise also from the things that happen to us daily he, being more ancient than the years, by his experience foretells the future evil which he himself intends to do. For by the decree of God knowledge as well as wickedness are his, and by God's permission he tempts man, seeking to turn him from holiness. Be convinced therefore, O consul, that you are living in no small folly.'

The proconsul said: 'By enduring much idle talk from you I have led you to blaspheme the gods and the Augusti. So that it goes no further with you, will you sacrifice? Or what have you to say?'

Carpus answered: 'It is impossible for me to sacrifice, for I have never sacrificed to idols.'

So the proconsul ordered him to be hung up and scraped. Carpus cried out: 'I am a Christian.' And after this torture had continued for a long time, he was exhausted and unable to speak.

So the proconsul left Carpus, and turned to Papylus, and said to him, 'Are you a councillor?''

And he answered: 'I am a citizen.'

The proconsul said: 'A citizen of which city?'

Papylus answered, 'Of Thyatira.'

The proconsul said: 'Have you any children?'

Papylus answered, 'Yes, and many of them, thanks be to God!'

Then someone in the crowd shouted out, 'He means that some of the Christians are his children in the faith.'

The proconsul said: 'Why do you lie, saying that you have children?'

Papylus answered: 'Would you learn that I do not lie, but speak the truth? In every district and city I have children in God.'

The proconsul said: 'Will you sacrifice? Or what will you say?'

Papylus answered: 'I have served God since I was a youth, and I have never sacrificed to idols, since I am a Christian, and you cannot learn anything more than this from me; for there is nothing greater or nobler than this for me to say.'

So he was also hung up and scraped three times with two instruments of torture at the same time, but he uttered no sound, but as a noble athlete withstood the wrath of the Enemy.

When the proconsul saw their great endurance he gave orders that they should be burnt alive. They were both taken at once to the amphitheatre, so that they might leave this world quickly. Papylus was nailed to the stake, lifted up, and as the fire approached him, he prayed and gave up his soul peacefully. Carpus was then nailed and he smiled on them, so that the spectators asked, 'What are you laughing about?' The blessed Carpus said, 'I saw the glory of the Lord, and

I was glad, and at the same time I was leaving you and have no part in your evil actions.' When the soldier piled up the wood and lit it the saintly Carpus said, as he hung, 'We too were born of the same mother Eve and have the same flesh as you, but looking to the judgment seat of truth let us endure everything.' After he said this, as the fire approached him, he said, 'Blessed art thou, Lord Jesus Christ, Son of God, because thou didst count me also the sinner worthy of this part in thee!' Then Carpus gave up his soul.

A certain Agathonica standing and beholding the glory of the Lord, which Carpus said that he had seen, and perceiving the invitation to be from heaven, immediately raised her voice, 'This dinner has been prepared for me; of this glorious dinner therefore I must take part and eat.'

But the people cried out, saying, 'Take pity on your son.'

The blessed Agathonica said, 'He has God who can have pity on him, for he is the Protector of everyone; but I must leave.' Then she took off her outer clothes and threw herself on the stake, rejoicing. But the spectators lamented and said, 'Terrible sentence, unjust orders!' When Agathonica was lifted up on the stake and felt the burning flames, she cried out three times, 'Lord, Lord, Lord help me, for I flee to Thee.'

And so she gave up her spirit, and was perfected with the saints, whose remains the Christians secretly took up and carefully guarded to the glory of Christ and the praise of his martyrs, because to him belong glory and power, to the Father and to the Son and to the Holy Spirit, now and always and for ever and ever. Amen.

¶ E. C. E. Owen (trans.), *Some Authentic Acts of the Early Martyrs* (Oxford, 1927), pp. 42–6

Justin

(also Chariton, Charito, Euelpistus, Hierax, Paeon, Liberianus)

c. 165

'You can kill, but you cannot harm us' (Justin, Apology).

The Christian church fared worse under the emperor Marcus Aurelius than it had done under any emperor since the times of Nero and Domitian. The most famous martyr under Marcus Aurelius was the philosopher Justin.

Justin, the celebrated philosopher, fell martyr under Emperor Marcus Aurelius Antoninus Verus' persecution. He was born in Neapolis, in Samaria, in 103. About 133, when he was thirty years old, he became a convert to Christianity. Justine wrote an elegant letter to the Gentiles, to convert them to the faith he had newly acquired. As the pagans began to treat the Christians with great severity, Justin wrote his first apology in their favour, and addressed it to the Emperor Antoninus, and to the senate and to the people of Rome in general. This piece, which occasioned the emperor to publish an edict in favour of the Christians, displays great learning and genius.

A short time later, he entered into debates with Crescens, a celebrated cynic philosopher; and his arguments appeared so powerful, yet disgusting, to the cynic, that he resolved on his destruction. Justin's second apology upon fresh severities gave Crescens an opportunity of prejudicing the emperor against the writer of it; upon which Justin and six of his companions were apprehended.

¶ John Foxe, *The Book of Martyrs*, revised with notes and an appendix by W. Bramley-Moore (London, 1869), pp. 14–15

Examination of Justin by the prefect

When they were brought before the judgment seat, Rusticus the prefect said to Justin: 'First of all obey the gods, and make submission to the princes.'

Justin said, 'To obey the commands of our Saviour Jesus Christ is not worthy of blame or condemnation.'

The prefect Rusticus said, 'What doctrines do you hold?'

Justin said, 'I have endeavoured to make myself acquainted with all doctrines, but I have given my assent to the true doctrines of the Christians, whether they please the holders of false beliefs or not.'

The prefect Rusticus said, 'Do those doctrines please you, miserable man?'

Justin said, 'Yes, for the belief in accordance with which I follow them is right.'

The prefect Rusticus said, 'What belief do you mean?'

Justin said, 'That which we religiously profess concerning the God of the Christians, in whom we believe, one God, existing from the beginning, Maker and Artificer of the whole creation, seen and unseen; and concerning our Lord Jesus Christ, the Son of God, who hath also been proclaimed aforetime by the prophets as about to come to the race of men for herald of salvation and for master of true disciples. And I, being but a man, regard what I say to be of little worth in comparison with his infinite Godhead, but there is a power in prophecy, and that I acknowledge; therein has proclamation been made beforehand about him of whom I just spoke as the Son of God. For I know that from the beginning the prophets foretold his coming among men.'

The prefect Rusticus said, 'Where do you meet together?'

Justin said, 'Where each wills and can. Do you really think that we all meet in the same place? Not so: for the God of the Christians is not confined by place, but being unseen fills heaven and earth, and is worshipped and glorified by the faithful everywhere.'

The prefect Rusticus said, 'Tell me, where do you meet, or in what place do you gather your disciples?'

Justin said, 'I lodge above the house of Martin, near the baths of Timothy, and during all this time (this is my second visit to Rome) I have known no other place of meeting but his house. And if any wished to come to me, I imparted to him the word of truth.'

Rusticus said, 'To come to the point then, are you a Christian?'

Justin said, 'Yes, I am a Christian.'

Examination of Chariton and others

The prefect Rusticus said to Chariton, 'What do you say, Chariton?'

Chariton said, 'I am a Christian by God's gift.'

Charito said, 'I am a Christian by the grace of God.'

Euelpistus, a slave of Caesar, answered, 'I also am a Christian, freed by Christ, and share by the grace of Christ n the same hope.'

Hierax said, 'Yes, I am a Christian, for I worship and adore the same God.'

Paeon said: 'I received from my parents this good confession.'

Euelpistus said, 'I listened indeed gladly to the words of Justin, but I too received Christianity from my parents.'

The prefect Rusticus said to Liberian, 'And what do you say? Are you a Christian? Are you an unbeliever like the rest?'

Liberian said: 'I also am a Christian; for I am a believer and adore the only true God.'

Rusticus threatens the Christians with death

The prefect Rusticus said to Justin, 'Listen, you that are said to be a learned man, and think that you are acquainted with true doctrine, if you shall be scourged and beheaded, are you persuaded that you will ascend to heaven?'

Justin said, 'I hope if I endure these things to have his gifts. For I know that for all who so live there abides until the consummation of the whole world the free gift of God.'

The prefect Rusticus said, 'Do you then think that you will ascend to heaven, to receive certain rewards?'

Justin said, 'I do not think, I know and am fully persuaded.'

The prefect Rusticus said, 'Let us now come to the pressing matter in hand. Agree together and sacrifice with one accord to the gods.'

Justin said, 'No one who is rightly minded turns from true belief to false.'

The prefect Rusticus said, 'If you do not obey, you will be punished without mercy.'

Justin said, 'If we are punished for the sake of our Lord Jesus Christ we hope to be saved, for this shall be our salvation and confidence before the more terrible judgment seat of our Lord and Saviour who shall judge the whole world.'

So also said the other martyrs, 'Do what you will. For we are Christians and offer no sacrifice to idols.'

¶ Eusebius, *The History of the Church*, Book VI

The Scillitan saints

Records about martyrdoms inflicted by the sword in Scillium, part of the African diocese of Carthage, are contained in Acts of Martyrdom. *These are the oldest Acts in existence in Africa, and are excellent examples of Acts as they are based on official reports, and have very little added by any editors. Seven men and five women, who became known as the Scillium martyrs, appeared before Saturninus at Carthage.*

In the consulship of Praesens, then consul for the second time, and Claudian, on 17th July, Speratus, Nartzalus and Cittinus, Donata, Secunda, Vestia were brought to trial at Carthage in the council chamber. The proconsul Saturninus said to them, 'You may merit the indulgence of our Lord and Emperor, if you return to a right mind.'

Speratus said, 'We have never done harm to any, we have never lent ourselves to wickedness; we have never spoken ill of anyone, but have given thanks when ill-treated, because we hold our own Emperor in honour.'

The proconsul Saturninus said, 'We also are religious people, and our religion is simple, and we swear by the genius of our Lord the Emperor, and pray for his safety, as you also ought to do.'

Speratus said, 'If you will give me a quiet hearing, I will tell you the mystery of simplicity.'

Saturninus said, 'If you begin to speak evil of our sacred rites, I will give you no hearing; but swear rather by the genius of our Lord the Emperor.'

Speratus said, 'I do not recognise the empire of this world; but rather I serve that God, whom no man has seen nor can see. I have not stolen, but if I buy anything, I pay the tax, because I recognise my Lord, the King of kings and Emperor of all peoples.'

The proconsul Saturninus said to the rest, 'Cease to be of this persuasion.'

Speratus said, 'The persuasion that we should do murder, or bear false witness, that is evil.'

The proconsul Saturninus said, 'Have no part in this madness.'

Cittinus said, 'We have nobody else to fear except the Lord our God who is in heaven.'

Donata said, 'Give honour to Caesar as Caesar, but fear to God.'

Vestia said, 'I am a Christian.'

Secunda said, 'I wish to be none other than what I am.'

The proconsul Saturninus said to Speratus, 'Do you persist in being a Christian?'

Speratus said, 'I am a Christian.' And all agreed with this statement.

The proconsul Saturninus said, 'Do you want any time to consider your position?'

Speratus said, 'When the right is so clear, there is nothing to consider.'

The proconsul Saturninus said, 'What have you in your case?'

Speratus said, 'The books, and letters of a just man, one Paul.'

The proconsul Saturninus said, 'Take a reprieve of thirty days and think it over.'

Speratus repeated, 'I am a Christian.' And all were of the same mind.

The proconsul Saturninus read out the sentence from his note book: 'Whereas Speratus, Nartzalus, Cittinus, Donata, Vestia, Secunda, and the rest have confessed that they live in accordance with the religious rites of the Christians, and, when an opportunity was given them to return to the ways of the Romans, they persisted in their obstinacy, it is our pleasure that they should suffer by the sword.'

Speratus said, 'Thanks be to God!'

Nartzalus said, 'Today we are martyrs in heaven, thanks be to God!'

The proconsul Saturninus commanded that proclamation be made by the herald, 'I have commanded Speratus, Nartzalus, Cittinus, Donata, Vestia, Secunda, Veturius, Felix, Aquilinus, Laetantius, Januaria, Generosa, to be led out for execution.

They all said, 'Thanks be to God!

And so all were crowned with martyrdom together, and reign with the Father and Son and Holy Spirit for ever and ever. Amen.

¶ Eusebius, *The History of the Church,* Book VI

Perpetua and Felicitas

Perpetua was martyred 7th March 203 in the amphitheatre at Carthage. She was about twenty-two years of age.

The persecutions about this time extended to Africa, and many were

martyred in that part of the globe; the principal of whom was
Perpetua, a married lady with an infant child at her breast.

Pages from Perpetua's diary, written from prison

When I was still with my companions, and my father in his affection for
me was endeavouring to upset me by arguments and overthrow my
resolution, I said, 'Father, do you see this waterpot lying here?'
'I see it,' he said. And I said to him, 'Can it be called by any other name
than what it is?' And he answered, 'No.'
'So also I cannot call myself anything else than what I am, a Christian.'
Then my father, furious at the word 'Christian', threw himself upon me
as though to pluck out my eyes; but he was satisfied with annoying me; he
was in fact vanquished, he and his devil's arguments. Then I thanked the
Lord for being parted for a few days from my father, and was refreshed by
his absence. During those few days we were baptised, and the Holy Spirit
bade me make no other petition after the holy water save for bodily endurance. A few days later we were put in prison; and I was in great fear,
because I had never known such darkness. What a day of horror! Terrible
heat, thanks to the crowds! Rough handling by the soldiers! To crown all
I was tormented there by anxiety for my baby. Then my baby was brought
to me and I suckled him, for he was already faint for lack of food. I
obtained leave for my baby to remain in prison with me and my prison
suddenly became a palace to me, and I would rather have been there than
anywhere else.
The procurator Hilarian said to me: 'Spare your father's white hairs;
spare the tender years of your child. Offer a sacrifice for the safety of the
Emperors.' And I answered, 'No.'
'Are you a Christian?' said Hilarian. And I answered: 'I am.'
Then he passed sentence on all of us, and condemned us to the beasts.
I sent at once the deacon Pomponius to my father to ask for my baby. But
my father refused to give him. And as God willed, neither had he any
further wish for my breasts, nor did they become inflamed; that I might
not be tortured by anxiety for the baby and pain in my breasts.

As for Felicitas, she was also visited by God's grace. Being eight
months pregnant, and as the day for the spectacle grew near she was
in great sorrow in case her pregnancy prevented or delayed her
martyrdom, since it is against the law for pregnant women to be
exposed for punishment. Her fellow martyrs were also deeply grieved
at the thought of leaving so good a comrade and fellow-traveller
behind alone on the way to the same hope. So in one flood of common

lamentation they poured their prayers to the Lord two days before the
games. Immediately after the prayer her pains came upon her. And
since from the natural difficulty of an eight-months' labour she suffered much in childbirth, one of the warders said to her: 'You who so
suffer now, what will you do when you are flung to the beasts which,
when you refused to sacrifice, you despised?' And she answered:
'Now I suffer what I suffer: but Another will be in me who will suffer
for me, because I too am to suffer for him.' So she gave birth to a girl,
whom one of the sisters brought up as her own daughter.

The day of their victory dawned, and they proceeded from the
prison to the amphitheatre, as if they were on their way to heaven,
with happy and gracious looks; trembling, if at all, not with fear but
joy. Perpetua followed with shining steps, as the true wife of Christ,
as the darling of God, abashing with the high spirit in her eyes the
gaze of all, Felicitas also rejoicing that she had safely given birth so
that she might fight the beasts, from blood to blood, from midwife to
gladiator, to find in her second baptism her childbirth washing.

For the young women the Devil made ready a mad heifer, an
unusual animal selected for this reason, that he wished to match their
sex with that of the beast. And so after being stripped and enclosed in
nets they were brought into the arena. The people were horrified,
beholding in the one a tender girl, in the other a woman fresh from
childbirth, with milk dripping from her breasts.

They were brought into the open, that, when the sword pierced their
bodies, these might lend their eyes for partners in the murder. When
Perpetua's turn came to receive the sword, she was struck on the bone
and cried out, and herself guided to her throat the wavering hand of the
young untried gladiator. Perhaps so great a woman, who was feared by
the unclean spirit, could not otherwise be slain except she willed.

O valiant and blessed martyrs! O truly called and chosen to the
glory of Jesus Christ our Lord! He who magnifies, honours, and
adores that glory should recite to the edification of the church these
examples also, not less precious at least than those of old; that some
new instances of virtue may testify that one and the self-same Spirit is
working to this day with the Father, God Almighty, and with his Son
Jesus Christ our Lord, to whom belong splendour and power
immeasurable for ever and ever. Amen.

¶ E. C. E. Owen (trans.), *Some Authentic Acts of the Early Martyrs*
(Oxford, 1927), pp. 78–92

Tortures of the first Christian martyrs
2: Wheels, pulleys and presses

a. Martyrs had their limbs interwoven in the spokes of a wheel, on which they were left exposed for days until they died.

b. Martyrs were bound on a narrow wheel, which was revolved, so that their bodies were horribly mangled on iron spikes fixed underneath.

c. Martyrs were bound to the circumference of a wheel which was then revolved over a fire kindled underneath.

d. Martyrs were crushed in the press, just as grapes and olives are pressed in making wine and oil.

e. Martyrs were bound, sometimes by their hands, and sometimes by their feet, to the ropes of the pulleys one way and to the stakes the other; then the ropes were pulled tight, according to the judges' instructions, and their bodies were miserably stretched and racked.

f. Martyrs, with hands bound behind their backs, were hoisted in the air by a rope and pulley above spikes or sharp flints below them, on to which they were let fall.

¶ *Tortures and Torments of the Christian Martyrs, from the 'De SS. Martyrum Cruciatibus' of the Rev. Father Gallonio, translated by A. R. Allinson (London and Paris, printed for the subscribers, 1903), pp. 58–61*

Nichomachus, Dionysia, Andrew, Paul

At Troas, three more Christians were presented to proconsul Optimus, Nichomachus, Andrew and Paul.

Nichomachus said 'I am a Christian,' when asked about his religion. The other two said the same.

The magistrate said, 'Sacrifice to the gods, as you are commanded.'

Nichomachus answered, 'As you are aware, a Christian may not sacrifice to devils.'

He was hung up and tortured for a long time. He bore the torture until he was completely exhausted and could hardly breathe. The unhappy man cried out, 'It is a mistake. I never was a Christian; I sacrifice to the gods.' He was instantly taken down. The sacrificial flesh was put to his dying hands and lips as he last spasm seized him. He fell forwards, and, gnawing his tongue, died an apostate.

There was a young girl, sixteen years old, called Dionysia, among the spectators. She was a Christian. This sight so horrified her, that she could not help crying out, 'Poor, miserable wretch! For the sake of one short moment you have indescribable pains that will last for ever.'

Dionysia was dragged forward.

Optimus asked, 'Are you a Christian?'

'Yes,' she replied, 'I am a Christian. That is why I am sorry for that poor man, because he could not endure a little to find eternal rest.'

'He is at rest,' replied the proconsul, 'the great Diana and Venus have taken him. Now follow his example and sacrifice, or you will be roughly handled and then burned alive.'

The girl replied, 'My God is greater than you, so I am not afraid of your threats. He will enable me to endure whatever you inflict on me.'

The next day, Andrew and Paul, Nichomachus' two companions were brought before the judge again. The priests of Diana were set on them being punished. The two men refused to sacrifice to Diana or to any other god. They said that they could not recognise any of the devils whom the heathen worshipped, and that they had never worshipped any other than the only true God. The crowd were incensed and the proconsul thought it best to hand them over to them to be stoned to death, rather than the more usual form of execution. Their feet were lashed together, and they were dragged outside the town to die.

Meanwhile, the young Dionysia had spent a night in dreadful pain at the hands of ruffians. In the morning, as she was being led to be sentenced, she met the crowd who were dragging Andrew and Paul to their death. With a quick movement, she managed to free herself from her guard, and flung herself on the other Christians, crying, 'Let me die with you on earth, that I may live with you in heaven.' But the proconsul would not allow her to share their kind of martyrdom. He gave orders to Dionysia to be separated from them and to be beheaded.

¶ A. J. Mason, *The Historic Martyrs of the Primitive Church* (Longmans, 1905), pp. 137–9

Tortures of the first Christian martyrs
3: The wooden horse and other instruments

a. **The wooden horse, or hobby horse**
   - The horse was an engine of wood fashioned to resemble a real horse, and having two small, channelled wheels, or pulleys, in the two ends, which were hollowed out to receive them. Over these axles ropes were led and the wheels revolved, by which means the person tied to them was racked and stretched in different directions.
   - The tormentors took ropes and tied one to the martyr's feet and one to the martyr's hands, which had been twisted behind him.
   - The other ends of these ropes were attached to a winch or windlass which was fixed to the horse's legs. As the windlass was turned, so the body of the martyr was stretched, until every limb was strained and every joint dislocated.

b. **Stocks:** wooden contrivances, where prisoner's legs were constrained, constricted and confined. Blessed martyrs had their legs stretched and forcibly drawn apart even to the fourth and fifth hole of the instrument.

c. **Shackles:** wooden instruments with round holes, into which feet and necks of prisoners were inserted, and fixed there in such a way that they could not withdraw them again.

d. **Thongs:** a kind of bond used for securing the feet or neck. Martyrs, firmly bound with thongs around their feet and hands, were violently tugged by four men in all directions until limb was torn from limb.

e. **Fetters:** snares or nooses in which feet were secured.

f. **Manacles** – 'The English heretics at this present moment [1591] are busied unceasingly in malignantly and cruelly afflicting them of the orthodox faith by means of iron manacles, or handcuffs as they call them. These are a sort of instrument whereby a man is hung up and tortured, his two hands being put through an iron ring toothed inside, and violently squeezed. Indeed, so fierce and intense is the pain that unless the back is allowed to lean somewhat against the wall and the tips of the toes to touch the floor, the man will fall incontinently into a dead faint.'

g. **Neck collar:** a sort of necklace or neckband for condemned criminals, made of wood or iron, which imprisoned their necks firmly.

h. **Chains:** iron bonds in which slaves or prisoners are made fast to hinder their escaping.

> ¶ *Tortures and Torments of the Christian Martyrs, from the 'De SS. Martyrum Cruciatibus' of the Rev. Father Gallonio*, translated by A. R. Allinson (London and Paris, printed for the subscribers, 1903), pp. 68–70

Cassian

Cassian was a Christian schoolmaster, and taught children to read and write at Imola, a city twenty-seven miles from Ravenna in Italy. A violent persecution was raised against the church, probably that of Decius or Valerian, and Cassian was taken up, and interrogated by the governor of the province. As he constantly refused to sacrifice to the gods, the barbarous judge having informed himself of what profession he was, commanded that his own scholars should stab him to death with their iron writing pencils, called styles; for at that time it was the custom for scholars to write upon wax laid on a board of boxed wood, in which they formed the letters with an iron style or pencil, sharp at one end, but blunt and smooth at the other, to erase what was to be effaced or corrected.

Cassian was exposed naked in the middle of two hundred boys; among whom some threw their tablets, pencils, and penknives at his face and head, and often broke them upon his body; others cut his flesh, or stabbed him with their penknives, and others pierced him with their pencils, sometimes only tearing the skin and flesh, and sometimes raking in his very bowels. Some made it their barbarous sport to cut part of their writing-task in his tender skin. Thus, covered with his own blood, and wounded in every part of his body, he cheerfully bade his little executioners not to be afraid; and to strike him with greater force; not meaning to encourage them in this sin, but to express the ardent desire he had to die for Christ.

¶ Alban Butler, *The Lives of the Saints,* Dublin, 1833, vol. II, pp. 230–1

Trypho and Respicius

Trypho and Respicius were Christians from Apamea, in Bithynia. The head of police had arrested the Christians in response to Decius' edict and had brought them to Nicaea for trial. They were told they must choose between sacrificing to the gods and being burned alive. They said that to be burned alive for Christ would be a great privilege, and encouraged the magistrate to carry out the edict's instructions.

'Sacrifice,' said the magistrate. 'I see that you are mature, intelligent people.'

'Ah,' cried Trypho, 'in our Lord Jesus Christ we have indeed a good understanding.'

As the command was given that they should be tortured they threw off their clothes and freely offered themselves to their executors. This went on for three hours. The judge, who did not want them to be killed if it could be helped, sent them back to prison. It was a common practice for Roman governors, when they wanted prisoners to comply with their demands, to take them with them from place to place, loaded down with chains and fetters. The governor of Bithynia was going on a hunting expedition, and he forced Trypho and Respicius to go with him. It was bitter winter weather, and the ground was frozen hard, so Trypho's and Respicius' feet were covered with chilblains.

When the expedition was over, they were examined. 'Will you be corrected in the future?' the magistrate asked.

'We correct ourselves every day, before the Lord,' Trypho answered, 'whom we serve without ceasing.' They were returned to prison and when they were next brought out before the magistrate, he said to them, 'Have compassion on yourselves, and sacrifice to the gods. I think that you are beginning to become wise.' But these kind words could not make them change their minds.

'The best compassion we can show ourselves is to unwaveringly confess our Lord Jesus Christ, the true Judge, who shall come to judge everyone's deeds.'

The magistrate ordered nails to be hammered through their feet and then for them to walk through the wintry streets of the town. The men said that the nails had only pierced their shoes, and not their flesh. The magistrate, astonished at their perseverance, had their hands tied behind their backs and had them thrashed until their persecutors were exhausted. The claw and the torches followed, but without effect. At last the judge said, 'Stop being stupid. Think how men of your age should act.'

Respicius answered that they would never bow down to stocks and stones, because they served the true God, and him only, 'As we have such a Lord,' he said, 'no pains can ever separate us from his love.'

The following day the judge ordered them to be beaten with loaded thongs. Then he read out this judgment: 'These Phrygian youths, who are Christians, and refuse to obey the imperial commands, are sentenced to be beheaded.' The martyrs were led out to be executed.

They lifted up their hands, crying to the Lord Jesus Christ to receive their souls, and so submitted to the penalty that had been pronounced on them.

¶ A. J. Mason, *The Historic Martyrs of the Primitive Church* (Longmans, 1905), pp. 140–1

Martyrs at Alexandria in Decius' reign
249–51

First an old man called Metras was arrested and commanded to blaspheme. When he refused the local people of Alexandria beat him with clubs, pierced his face and eyes with pointed reeds and then stoned him to death outside the city.

Then they picked on a woman convert called Quinta. They took her to the temple, full of idols, and demanded that she should worship the idols. When she turned away in disgust they tied her feet together and dragged her through the city over the rough roads, and large stones, beating her as she went. They took her to the same place where they had stoned Metras, where they also stoned her.

They then turned their attention to a wonderful, elderly lady called Apollonia. They beat in her head until all her teeth fell out. They then erected a pyre in the front of the city and told her that she would be placed on this and burnt alive if she did not repeat the heathen incantations after them. Apollonia asked for a moment to decide. They released her from their grip but she then jumped immediately onto the pyre where she was burnt to ashes.

They arrested Serapion in his own house. They broke all his limbs and threw him, head first, from the first floor of his house.

No road, no highway, no pathway, was left open to us, either by day or by night. Anybody who did not join in their blasphemous chanting was seized and burnt to death.

¶ Letter from Dionysius to Bishop Fabius of Antioch, quoted by Eusebius, *The History of the Church*, Book VI

Tortures of the first Christian martyrs
4: Scourging

The heathen, after they had bound Christians to the horse, frequently beat them pitifully with rods, cudgels, and whips.

a. **Lashes:** thongs made of leather, employed usually for the correction of slaves.

b. **Cudgels:**
  - Martyrs were tied to a post set upright in the ground, or to a stake or pillar, and persistently beaten with cudgels, strong wooden staffs, until they died.
  - Martyrs were also bound to four stakes, by their wrists and ankles and beaten with cudgels.
  - Martyrs were laid naked on iron spikes and violently beaten with a cudgel.
  - Martyrs were bound hand and foot, laid on the ground, and beaten with a cudgel.

c. **Rods:**
  - Rods for beating offenders were generally made of thin twigs of trees, but sometimes they were made from iron or lead.
  - The custom of the ancients was, when prisoners were scourged, first to strip the same, and then to whip them over the back, or belly, or other portion of the body, with rods or other instruments of flagellation.

d. **Scorpions** were knotty or prickly rods.

e. **Loaded scourges** were a sort of whipping instrument made of cords or thongs, with little lead balls attached to the ends, which were inflicted on the loins, back and neck of a condemned person.

f. Martyrs were buffeted, kicked and pounded with fists.

g. Martyrs were stoned to death.

h. Martyrs had their faces bruised and jaws broken with stones.

i. Martyrs were crushed under huge stones – in the *Acts of the Blessed Martyr St Theopompus* it is written: 'Hereon the holy man was led forth from his prison and stretched face upward on the ground and bound fast to stakes. Then, a huge boulder, which eight men could hardly lift, was laid on his belly.'

¶ *Tortures and Torments of the Christian Martyrs, from the 'De SS. Martyrum Cruciatibus' of the Rev. Father Gallonio,* translated by A. R. Allinson (London and Paris: printed for the subscribers, 1903), pp. 91–4

Laurence

Laurence, the principal of the deacons, was taught and preached under Sextus, Bishop of Rome, and followed him to the place of execution, when Sextus predicted that he should met him in heaven three days after. Laurence considering this as a certain indication of his own approaching martyrdom, on his return collected all the Christian poor, and distributed among them the treasures of the church which had been committed to his care, thinking the money could not be better disposed of, or less liable to fall into the hands of pagans. His conduct alarmed the persecutors, who seized him, and commanded him to give an immediate account to the emperor of the church treasures.

Laurence promised to satisfy them, but begged a short respite to put things in proper order: three days being granted him, he was suffered to depart. Then with great diligence he collected together a great number of aged, and helpless poor, and went to the magistrate, presenting them to him, saying: 'These are the true treasures of the church.'

Provoked at this disappointment, and thinking that he was being ridiculed, the governor ordered Laurence to be immediately scourged. He was beaten with iron rods, set upon a wooden horse, and had his limbs dislocated. He endured these tortures with such fortitude and perseverance, that he was ordered to be fastened to a large gridiron, with a slow fire under it, that his death might be more tedious. But his astonishing constancy during these trials, and his serenity of countenance under such excruciating torments, gave the spectators so exalted an idea of the dignity and truth of the Christian religion, that many immediately became converts.

Having lain for some time upon the gridiron, the martyr called out to the emperor, who was present, in a kind of jocose Latin couplet, which may be thus translated:

> This side is broil'd sufficient to be food
> For all who wish it to be done and good.

On this the executioner turned him, and after having lain a considerable time longer, he had still strength and spirit enough to triumph over the tyrant, by telling him, with great serenity, that he was roasted enough, and only wanted serving up. He then cheerfully lifted up his eyes to heaven, and with calmness yielded his spirit to the Almighty. This happened on 10th August 258.

¶ John Foxe, *The Book of Martyrs,* revised with notes and an appendix by W. Bramley-Moore (London, 1869), pp. 23–4

Cyprian
258

On 30th August at Carthage in his private room Paternus the proconsul said to Cyprian the bishop, 'The most sacred Emperors Valerian and Gallienus have thought fit to send me a letter, in which they have commanded that those who do not observe the Roman religion must recognise the Roman rites. I have therefore made inquiries concerning yourself. What answer have you to give me?'

Cyprian the bishop said, 'I am a Christian and a bishop. I know no other God but the One True God, who "made heaven and earth, the sea, and all that in them is". This God we Christians serve, and him we pray day and night for ourselves, and for all men, and for the safety of the Emperors themselves.'

The proconsul Paternus said, 'Is your will constant in this?'

Cyprian the bishop answered, 'A good will, which knows God, cannot be altered.'

The proconsul Paternus said, 'Can you then in accordance with the order of Valerius and Gallienus go into exile to the city of Curubis?'

Cyprian the bishop said, 'I will go.'

Then the proconsul Paternus ordered the blessed Cyprian to be banished. And as he stayed a long time in exile, the proconsul Aspasius Paternus was succeeded as proconsul by Galerius Maximus, who ordered the holy bishop Cyprian to be recalled from his banishment and brought before him.

Galerius Maximus asked Cyprian, 'Are you Thascius Cyprianus?'

Cyprian the bishop answered, 'I am.'

Galerius Maximus the proconsul said, 'Have you taken on yourself to be Pope of people holding sacrilegious opinions?'

Cyprian the bishop answered, 'Yes.'

Galerius Maximus the proconsul said, 'The most sacred Emperors have commanded you to perform the rite.'

Cyprian the bishop answered, 'I refuse.'

Galerius Maximus the proconsul said, 'Consider your own interest.'

Cyprian the bishop answered, 'Do as you are ordered. In so clear a case there is no need for debate.'

Galerius Maximus having conferred with the council gave sentence reluctantly: 'You have lived for a long time holding sacrilegious opinions, and have formed an abominable conspiracy, and have set yourself up as an enemy of the gods of Rome and religious ordinances, nor have the pious and most sacred Emperors Valerian and Gallienus, the Augusti, and Valerian, the most noble Caesar, been able to recall you to the observance of their rites. So you will be an example to all those who have joined you. Discipline will be vindicated in your blood.

With these words he read from his tablets the sentence: 'It is our pleasure that Thascius Cyprianus should be executed by the sword!'

Cyprian the bishop said, 'Thanks be to God!'

After this sentence the crowd of brethren cried: 'Let us also be beheaded with him.' So there arose an uproar among the brethren, and a great crowd accompanied him.

¶ Eusebius, *The History of the Church,* Book VI

300 martyrs

Perhaps one of the most dreadful events in the history of martyrdom was that which took place at Utica, where 300 Christians were, by the orders of the pro-consul, placed around a burning lime-kiln. A pan of coals and incense being prepared, they were commanded either to sacrifice to Jupiter or to be thrown into the kiln. Unanimously refusing, they bravely jumped into the pit, and were suffocated immediately.

¶ John Foxe, *The Book of Martyrs,* revised with notes and an appendix by W. Bramley-Moore (London, 1869), p. 26

Tortures of the first Christian martyrs
5: Iron claws, hooks and currycombs

a. **Iron claws:** two longish pieces of iron were fastened together, just in the same way as those forming a smith's iron pincers are used to be joined and paired together. Their ends were rounded and towards the ends slightly hollowed, so that little spears or spikes could be fixed there, for the greater convenience of the tormentors mangling those set on the wooden horse or tied to stakes or hung up aloft, whether ordinary criminals or the blessed martyrs. Iron pincers were also used to torture the martyrs.

b. **Iron hooks:** longish sticks, or miniature spears, which had an iron at one end, curved and bent back on itself. These hooks were used to tear the skin off martyrs.

c. **Iron currycombs** for tearing the flesh from faithful Christians: these combs resembled those used to comb wool.

d. **Shards:** sometimes the sides, bellies, thighs and legs of Christians were lacerated in a very cruel way with fragments of pottery. Eusebius, in his *History*, wrote: 'In the Thebaid all hitherto described cruelties were exceeded. For here the tormentors would take shards of pottery instead of claws and tear and lacerate the whole body till they did scrape the skin from off the flesh.'

¶ *Tortures and Torments of the Christian Martyrs, from the 'De SS. Martyrum Cruciatibus' of the Rev. Father Gallonio,* translated by A. R. Allinson (London and Paris: printed for the subscribers, 1903), pp. 106–8

Cyril

At Caesarea in Cappadocia, a young martyr, named Cyril, won great renown. The boy Cyril was wholly unconcerned that the police brought him before the magistrate for openly professing to be a follower of Christ.

MAGISTRATE: I forgive you, boy, and so does your father. He will take you home again. You can have all your comforts of home back if you will be a good boy and think about what you are doing.

CYRIL: I do not mind being punished for what I have done. I am very happy with God, in spite of being turned out. I shall have a better home later on. I am glad to become poor, that I may be rich. I am not afraid of a good death. I see a better life before me.

The magistrate did not want the boy to be put to death. He thought that the sight of an execution would bring him to his senses. He ordered Cyril's hands to be tied, and led to the fire. The officials reported that the boy was unmoved and showed no sign of fear.

MAGISTRATE: You have seen the fire, boy, and the sword. Be good, and you shall enjoy yourself at home again with your father.
CYRIL: It was a great shame that you brought me back from the fire and the sword, which I was prepared to endure.

Some of the bystanders were moved to tears. But Cyril told them that they would have rejoiced if they had known where he was going. He asked for no better way of spending his life. And so he went to his death.

¶ A. J. Mason, *The Historic Martyrs of the Primitive Church* (Longmans, 1905), pp. 199–200

Leo

Leo, an aged ascetic, lived about this time, at Patara, on the southern coast of Asia Minor.

A friend of Leo's, Paregorius, had been martyred under Decius, and Leo felt deeply grieved that his life had been spared. The proconsul Lollianus visited Patara while the festival to the god Serapis was being held, and the officials used this opportunity to enforce the edict which compelled all the inhabitants to join in the sacrificial acts. Leo saw the people streaming to the festival, and withdrew to pray where Paregorius' relics had been buried, as he often did. He returned home with his mind full of the thoughts of his martyred friend. That night he dreamed that he and Paregorius stood in the middle of a river in full flood. In spite of the current Leo saw that he could easily reach the point Paregorius had reached in front of him.

The next day he set out for his friend's grave, travelling on a road that went past the temple of Fortune. Leo cast caution aside. He went into the temple and broke the lamps and tapers, shouting aloud, 'If you think that the gods have any power, let them defend themselves.'

Leo was arrested and brought before the governor. He defended his actions by saying that lights and tapers were vain and senseless things, and that what the true God cared about was a contrite heart and humble soul. He exhorted the magistrate to honour God and his only Son, the Saviour of the world and creator of souls.

The magistrate replied that this was irrelevant to the charge. He was told that he would be set free, so long as he obeyed the edict, but Leo refused to worship gods that were no gods. Leo was lashed, but Leo's heart was caught up with the Lord, and he seemed to feel nothing. The patient magistrate was willing to forgo an act of sacrifice if Leo would only repeat after him the formula, Great are the gods.

'Great they are,' answered the martyr, 'to destroy the souls that believe in them.' At last the patience of the official ran out. Giving in to the demands of the crowd he ordered the old man to be dragged away by the feet and thrown into the fast flowing stream that passed through the town. Leo burst out with thanksgiving to God who allowed him so soon to be reunited to his friend Paregorius, and prayed for the conversion of his killers. He was dead before they reached the rock from which they hurled him.

¶ A. J. Mason, *The Historic Martyrs of the Primitive Church* (Longmans, 1905), pp. 200–1

Fructuosus and his deacons

Fructuosus was bishop of Tarragona in Spain, martyred on 21st January 259, during the reign of Emperors Gallienus and Valerian.

During the reigns of Valerian and Gallienus, in the consulship of Aemilian and Bassus, on Sunday 16th January, Fructuosus the bishop and the deacons Augurius and Eulogius were arrested. In prison Fructuosus was resolute, rejoicing in the Lord's crown, to which he had been called, never stopped praying. With him were the brethren, cheering him and asking him to keep them in mind.

The next day, still in prison, he baptised our brother, Rogatian.

On Friday 21st January Aemilian the governor ordered, 'Admit Fructuosus the bishop, and Augurius and Eulogius.'

The officials replied, 'They are in court.'

Aemilian the governor said to Fructuosus the bishop: 'Have you heard what the Emperors have ordered?'

Fructuosus the bishop answered, 'I do not know what they have ordered. I am, however, a Christian.'

Aemilian the governor said, 'They have ordered that the gods are to be worshipped.'

Fructuosus the bishop said, 'I worship one God, who "made heaven and earth, the sea and all that in them is".'

Aemilian said, 'Do you know that there are gods?'

Fructuosus the bishop answered, 'I know no such thing.'

Aemilian said: 'You shall know later.'

Fructuosus the bishop looked to the Lord and began to pray silently.

Aemilian the governor said, 'Who is to be obeyed, who is to be feared, who is to be adored if the gods are not worshipped and the images of the Emperor are not adored?'

Aemilian the governor said to Augurius the deacon: 'Pay no heed to the words of Fructuosus.'

Augurius the deacon answered: 'I worship God the Almighty.'

Aemilian the governor said to Eulogius the deacon, 'Do you worship Fructuosus also?'

Eulogius the deacon answered, 'I do not worship Fructuosus, but I worship him whom Fructuosus also worships.'

Aemilian the governor said to Fructuosus the bishop, 'Are you a bishop?'

Fructuosus the bishop answered, 'I am.'

Aemilian said, 'You were.' And he gave sentence that they should be burnt alive.

When Fructuosus the bishop was being led out with his deacons to the amphitheatre, the people began to express their grief, as he was greatly loved, not only by the brethren, but by the pagans as well. For he was just as a bishop should be, as the blessed apostle Paul had said through Holy Spirit, a teacher of the Gentiles. So the brethren who knew that he was on his way to so great a glory, rejoiced rather than grieved.

Fructuosus was heard to say, under the guidance, and indeed, in the words of the Holy Spirit: 'You will not lack a shepherd for long, nor will the love or the promise of the Lord fail you either here or hereafter. For what you see in front of you seems the illness of but one hour.' They were like Ananias, Azarias, and Misael, for with them the Divine Trinity was visible. For each of them at his place in the fire the Father was present, the Son gave help, and the Holy Spirit walked in the middle of the fire. When their ropes which bound them were burned they knelt down, rejoicing and assured of resurrection, and, holding out their arms as a symbol of the Lord's victory, prayed to the Lord until they gave up their souls.

¶ E. C. E. Owen, *Some Authentic Acts of the Early Martyrs* (Oxford, 1927), pp. 100–3

Victor the General

Emperor Diocletian went throughout the city, saying, 'When ye shall have finished offering up your sacrifices ye shall eat and ye shall drink at the door of the temple of Apollo and Artemis, and ye shall glorify them, for it is they who have made the heavens, and the earth, and the sea, and mankind.'

And it came to pass that when all the people had offered up sacrifice, it came to the turn of his son to offer up sacrifice. Now he was a young man of nineteen years of age, and he worshipped God, and held his commandments in fear. Romanus the general said to Apa Victor, his son, 'O my son Victor, it is now thy turn to worship the gods of the Emperor, in whose honour the whole city is keeping this feast day, especially Apollo, the greatest of the gods.'

And Apa Victor looked into his father's face, saying, 'O my father, hath this foolishness obtained such a hold upon thee this day as too make thee forsake the God of heaven for the sake of the glory that is vanity? Remember, therefore that which our Lord Jesus saith in the Gospel, "Whosoever denieth me before men, him will I myself deny before my Father, who is in the heavens, and before his holy angels" [Matt. 10:33].'

While Apa Victor was saying these words all the soldiers of the army were looking at him and at his father. Then Romanus said, 'O my son Victor, listen to me, and offer up sacrifice, and let us bring to an end our trouble in this place.'

Apa Victor replied, 'Get thee away from this sin which leads to death.'

And his father was filled with indignation, and he swore an oath, saying, 'By Apollo, the greatest of the gods, I will deliver thee over to the Emperor so that he may destroy thee.'

Apa Victor said to his father, 'Yesterday thou didst worship God and I was thy son; but today I am not thy son, because thou hast made thyself disobedient to God, and thou dost worship idols.'

The Devil filled the heart of the father of Apa Victor, and he made him to deliver Apa Victor over into the hands of Diocletian the Emperor. And Emperor Diocletian made the soldiers fasten Apa Victor's hands behind him, and he tied him to the tail of a horse, and shaved the crown of his head, and suspended a bell from his neck, and four soldiers with palm branches in their hands, beat him, and they dragged him naked round about through all the city, and a herald went before him crying out, 'These things are done unto this man because he will not offer up sacrifice to the gods of the Emperor'; and they went through every part of the city with him.

Apa Victor was then exiled and tortured by Duke Sebastianus. Then the Duke made his servants strip Apa Victor naked, and cut his sinews, and fastened his hands behind him, and drove skewers through him. Then the Duke said to him, 'Offer up sacrifice.'

And Apa Victor said to him, 'I will not offer up sacrifice.'

Later, the Duke ordered his servants to break the joints in his legs and arms until his bones stuck out through his skin. And Apa Victor said to him, "I give thanks unto Thee, O my Lord Jesus the Christ, because all the joy of the Christ has drawn high unto me.'

Then the Duke passed the sentence of death on Apa Victor and ordered his soldiers to cut off his head.

¶ E. A. Wallis Budge (ed.), *Coptic Martyrdom etc. in the Dialect of Upper Egypt* (British Museum, 1914), pp. 256–98
[The above extracts are taken from a translation of British Museum Manuscript Oriental, No 7022. This manuscript comes from a group of Coptic texts of an important series of ten martyrdoms, lives of great ascetics, discourses on asceticism and the history of the angel of death. All of them are dated and written in the dialect of Upper Egypt and were only first published by the British Museum in 1914.]

Sacrificing to the gods

The Emperor Diocletian took counsel and decided to do the things that were unseemly before God, Jesus the Christ; and this is what he did. He made seventy images of gold, and gave unto them the name of 'gods', which they certainly were not. To thirty-five of these he gave names of gods, and to thirty-five the name of goddesses; now the number of his other gods and goddesses amount to one hundred and forty.

And the Emperor Diocletian affixed a decree on the outside of the door of the Palace, wherein it was written thus: 'I, the Emperor Diocletian command that from Romania, in the north, to Pelak, in the south, every man, whether he be eparch, or general, or count, or bishop, or elder, or deacon, or reader, or servant, of free man, or soldier, or countryman, shall worship my gods. And any one among these who shall say, "I am a Christian," shall be remembered, and he shall died by the sword. And as for you, O all ye noblemen of high senatorial rank, and officers at court, ye shall give effect to this decree in such a way that every man shall worship my gods; for these are the gods who give us victory in battle, and it is they who are the protectors of you yourselves, and they give strength unto you and unto the whole army. Therefore, he that doth not rise up early in the morning, and come at dawn to me so that we may go into the temple together and offer up sacrifices to the gods, he, I say, that doth not come here shall be cast into the sea, so that all men may know that I am king, and that there is no other king besides me.'

And it came to pass at dawn, on the first day of the month Parmoute, that the Emperor Diocletian, and all his army, and the eparchs, and the generals went into the temple. And the Emperor took his seat upon the throne, and he caused the herald to make a proclamation, saying, 'O all ye Roman people, come ye and offer up sacrifice.' And the Emperor made an altar of silver and a vessel wherein to burn incense of gold; and he made a great pedestal of gold, and he placed it before the altar so that the statue of Apollo might be set upon it. And the Emperor commanded them to bring frankincense, and the finest flour of wheat, and the purest oil, and rare old wine, and pour them out upon the altar whereon was blazing fire. And afterwards they lighted two hundred candles on golden candlesticks, and four hundred candles on silver candlesticks, and two hundred white horses drew his gods into the temple.

And when they had brought his gods into the temple the Emperor Diocletian stood up on his throne, and he lifted his crown off his head, and set it upon the head of the statue of Apollo, and he bowed down and worshipped it three times, saying, 'Thou art the god who livest, O Apollo,

the greatest of the gods, who dost give unto us victory in war.' And after
the Emperor had worshipped Apollo, his three fellow Caesars Romanus,
Basileides, and Euaios, came and worshipped Apollo also.

¶ E. A. Wallis Budge (ed.), *Coptic Martyrdom etc. in the Dialect of Upper Egypt*
(British Museum, 1914), pp 121–3

James and Marian
6th May 259

*'Do not desire death on a sick-bed, in childbirth, or by a mild fever,
but by martyrdom to the honour of him who suffered for you'* (Tertullian, Fuga, 9; De Anima, 55).

James and Marian were arrested because they persisted in confessing
the Name. They were tortured severely by the police, who also had a
centurion and the magistrates of Cirta, the Devil's priests, to assist
them, as if faith, which sets no store about the body, could be broken
through the mangling of limbs.

Marian was hung up to be torn by his thumbs, and not by his
hands, in order to inflict greater pain. In addition to this different
weights were fixed to his feet so that his whole body would be torn in
two. You were unsuccessful, you wicked pagans, against God's
temple and against the joint heir with Christ. Even though you hung
up his limbs, racked his sides, tore his bowels, my Marian, trusting in
God, grew in spirit as much as he grew in body. Eventually the cruelty
of his torturers was defeated, and he was locked up in prison to the
sound of great rejoicing. There, with James and the other brethren, he
celebrated the joy of the Lord's victory in repeated prayer.

James and Marian were later brought out to be executed by being
beheaded. After Marian as blindfolded, filled with the spirit of
prophecy she spoke about the avenging of the blood of the righteous,
and as if from the height of heaven threatened various earthly
plagues, famines, and earthquakes. Through this prophetic utterance
the faith of the martyr not only triumphed over the heathen but
sounded a triumphant note in the ears of God's saints.

When everything was over Marian's mother, with a joy like that of the mother in the days of the Maccabees, certain that her son's passion had ended, began to congratulate not only him, but herself as well, who had borne such a son.

¶ E. C. E. Owen (trans.), *Some Authentic Acts of the Early Martyrs* (Oxford, 1927), pp. 13–17

Marinus and Asterius

Marinus was noted for his wealth and family at Caesarea in Palestine, and around 272 was about to be appointed a centurion, as he was due promotion to this vacant position. But another soldier complained that Marinus should not be appointed centurion as he was a Christian, and that he should be appointed in Marinus' place. Achaeus, the governor of Palestine, asked Marinus if was a Christian. When Marinus affirmed this the governor gave him three hours to change his mind.

The bishop of Caesarea, Theotecnus, was told about the matter. He went to Marinus and took him away from the tribunal and led him by the hand to the church. There, pointing to the sword which Marinus wore, and then to a book of the gospels, the bishop asked the soldier which he was going to choose. Marinus, without hesitation, stretched out his right hand and took hold of the sacred book.

'Adhere steadfastly then to God,' said the bishop, 'and he will strengthen you, and you shall obtain what you have chosen. Depart in peace.'

Being summoned again before the judge, Marinus professed his faith with greater resolution and alacrity than before, and was immediately led away just as he was, and beheaded.

Asterius, a Roman senator, in great favour with the emperors, and well known to all on account of his birth and great estate, was present at Marinus' martyrdom. Even though he was richly dressed, he took away the dead body on his shoulders, and having sumptuously adorned it, gave it a decent burial. Rufinus adds that Asterius was beheaded for this action.

¶ John Foxe, *The Book of Martyrs,* revised with notes and an appendix by W. Bramley-Moore (London, 1869), pp. 292–3

Victorinus and his six companions
284

These seven martyrs were citizens of Corinth, and confessed their faith before Tertius the proconsul, in their own country, in 249, in the beginning of Decius' reign. After their torments they went to Egypt, either voluntarily or by compulsion, where at Diospolis, the capital of Thebais, they completed their martyrdom, in 284, in the reign of Numerian, under the governor of Sabinus.

After the governor had tried the constancy of the martyrs by racks, scourges, and various inventions of cruelty, he had Victorinus thrown into a great mortar. The executioners began to pound his feet and legs, saying to him at every stroke, 'Spare yourself, wretch. It depends on you to escape this death, if you will only renounce your new God.'

The prefect became furious at his constancy, so commanded that his head should be beaten to pieces. The sight of this mortar, far from intimidating Victorinus' companions, seemed to inspire them with greater ardour to be treated in the same way. So when the tyrant threatened Victor with the same death, he said to the executioner, 'In that is salvation and true felicity prepared for me!' He was immediately cast into it and beaten to death.

Nicephorus, the third martyr, was impatient of delay, and leaped of his own accord into the bloody mortar. The judge was enraged at his boldness, and commanded not one, but many executioners at once to pound him in the same way.

The judge caused Claudian, the fourth martyr, to be chopped in pieces, and his bleeding joints to be thrown at the feet of those who still lived. He expired, after his feet, hands, arms, legs, and thighs were cut off.

The tyrant, pointing to his mangled limbs and scattered bones, said to the remaining three companions, 'You can avoid this punishment. I do not compel you to suffer.'

The martyrs answered with one voice: 'On the contrary, we rather pray that if you have any other more exquisite torment you would inflict it on us. We are determined never to violate the fidelity which we owe to God, or to deny Jesus Christ our Saviour, for he is our God, from whom we have our being, and to whom alone we aspire.'

The tyrant became almost distracted with fury, and commanded Diodorus to be burnt alive, Serapion to be beheaded, and Papias to be drowned.

¶ Alban Butler, *The Lives of the Saints* (Dublin, 1833), vol. I, p. 272

Barlaam

An obscure country life, which this saint had led from his childhood, in a village near Antioch, in manual labour, which he sanctified by a heroic spirit and practice of Christian piety, prepared him for the crown of martyrdom. He was imprisoned for his zealous confession of the name of Christ and when he was called to the bar, the judge laughed at his rustic speech. In spite of his anger the judge could not but admire exceedingly Barlaam's greatness of soul, his virtue, and his meek constancy, which even gathered strength by his long imprisonment. He was cruelly scourged; but no sigh, no word of complaint was extorted from him. He was then hoisted on the rack, and his bones in many parts dislocated.

Amidst these torments, such was the joy which was painted by his countenance, that one would have judged he had been seated at some delicious banquet, or on a throne. The prefect threatened him with death, and caused swords and axes fresh stained with the blood of martyrs to be displayed before him. But Barlaam viewed them without being daunted, and, without words, his meek and composed countenance spoke a language which confounded and disconcerted the persecutors.

He was therefore remanded in prison, and the judge, who was ashamed to see himself vanquished by an illiterate peasant, studied to invent some new artifice or torment, resolving to revenge his gods, whom he thought injured by the saint's constancy. At length he flattered himself that he had found out a method by which the martyr should be compelled, in spite of all his resolution, to offer sacrifice. Barlaam was brought out of prison, and an altar with burning coals upon it being made ready for sacrifice, the martyr's hand was forcibly held over the flames, and the incense with live coals was laid upon it, that, if he shook the coals off his hand, he might be said to offer sacrifice by throwing the incense into the fire upon the altar. The saint, fearing the scandal and very shadow of the crime, though by throwing off the fire to save his hand, he could not be reasonably esteemed to have meant to sacrifice, kept his hand steady whilst the coals burnt quite through it, and so, with the incense, dropped upon the altar. At such an instance of fortitude the taunts and scoffs of the heathens were converted into admiration. God, soon after this victory, called his soldier to himself, to crown him with glory.

¶ Alban Butler, *The Lives of the Saints* (Dublin, 1833), vol. II, pp. 903–4

The Theban Legion
22nd September 286

Diocletian became emperor in 284. His persecution was so terrible that all former persecutions seemed to the Christians as nothing in comparison with it. They called the date of Doicletian's accession 'the Era of Martyrs'.

A remarkable affair occurred in 286. A legion of soldiers, consisting of 6,666 men, contained none but Christians. This was called the Theban Legion, because the men had been raised in Thebais. They were quartered in the East till the Emperor Maximian ordered them to march to Gaul, to assist him against the rebels of Burgundy. About this time Maximian ordered a general sacrifice, at which the whole army were to assist; and he commanded that they should take oaths of allegiance, and swear, at the same time, to assist him in the extermination of Christianity from Gaul. Terrified at these orders, each individual of the Theban Legion absolutely refused either to sacrifice or to take the oaths prescribed. This so enraged Maximian that he ordered the legion to be decimated – that is, every tenth man to be selected from the rest, and put to the sword. This cruel order having been put into execution, those who remained alive were still inflexible, when a second decimation took place, and every tenth man of those living were again put to the sword.

The second severity made no more impression than the first; the soldiers preserved their fortitude and their principles; but, on the advice of their officers, drew up a remonstrance to the emperor, in which they told him that they were his subjects and his soldiers, but could not, at the same time, forget the Almighty; that they received their pay from him, and their existence from God.

'While your commands,' they said, 'are not contradictory to those of our common Master, we shall always be ready to obey, as we have been hitherto; but when the orders of our prince and those of the Almighty differ, we must always obey the latter. Our arms are devoted to the emperor's use, and shall be directed against his enemies; but we cannot submit to stain our hands with Christian blood; and how, indeed, could you, O Emperor, be sure of our allegiance and fidelity, should we violate our obligation to our God, in whose service we were solemnly engaged before we entered the army? You command us to search out and to destroy the Christians: it is not necessary to look any farther for people of that denomination; we ourselves are such, and we glory in the name. We saw our companions fall without the least opposition or murmuring, and thought them happy in dying for the sake of Christ. Nothing shall make us lift up our hands against our sovereign; we had rather die wrongfully, and by that means preserve our innocence, than live under a load of guilt: whatever you command we are ready to suffer; we confess ourselves to be Christians, and therefore cannot persecute Christians, nor sacrifice to idols.'

Such a declaration, it might be presumed, would have prevailed with the emperor, but it had the opposite effect; for, enraged at their perseverance and unanimity, he commanded that the whole legion should be put to death, which was then executed by the other troops, who cut them to pieces with their swords. This barbarous transaction occurred on 22nd September 286.

¶ John Foxe, *The Book of Martyrs*, revised with notes and an appendix by W. Bramley-Moore (London, 1869), pp. 27–8

Tortures of the first Christian martyrs
6: Burning

For all the heathen bade Christians of either sex, to the scorn of Christ, to be racked on the horse and mangled with scourges, and iron claws, and to be stretched in the stocks to the fourth and fifth hole, yet was not their savage rage thereby exhausted. So they would often pour quicklime or molten lead or boiling oil over their fresh wounds, or else order the same to be torn open with shards of pottery or violently rubbed and scrubbed with hair cloths, and lastly, command the unhappy beings in this evil case to be horribly burned with red-hot plates, torches, and blazing brands.

a. **Plates of iron** were heated in the fire and applied to the bare flesh of the blessed martyrs and held there until it had miserably burned the same.
b. **Torches** were made from pinewood or twisted and waxed or pitched rope. Martyrs were torched as they hung from the horse or suspended by their feet by a pulley.
c. **The brazen bull** was the most exceedingly cruel sort of punishment in use among the ancients, into which anyone who was to be tortured was thrown through an opening or door in its side. Then the door was shut, and a fire was lighted about the bull causing the imprisoned person to suffer unexampled agonies, and by their lamentations and cries to imitate the bellowing of a bull. And this brazen contrivance was so cunningly wrought to the likeness of a real bull that movement and voice alone were lacking to persuade folk that it was a living animal.
d. **The brazen pot** was a very capacious vessel made of brass, into which condemned people were stripped and thrown, to be boiled or seethed.
e. **Very large cauldrons,** made of bronze, were filled with boiling oil or pitch, molten lead or wax and the victims thrown in, sometimes head first.
f. Martyrs were forced to walk over burning coals and have boiling pitch poured over their head. Also martyrs were roasted on burning coals as they were made to lie down on the burning coals with their hands and feet bound.
g. Martyrs were sent to sea in a ship filled with combustibles and set on fire.
h. **The frying pan** was a wide open dish or plate, made of metal, which was filled with oil, pitch, resin or sulphur and then placed over a fire. When it began to bubble and boil, then were Christians of either sex thrown into it. Such as had persisted steadfastly and boldly in their profession of Christ's faith, to the end they might be roasted and fried like fishes cast into boiling oil.
i. **The gridiron,** or iron bed, was framed of three iron bars set lengthwise

and a span distant one from the other, one finger thick, two broad, and
of a length suitable for its purpose, with seven or more shorter pieces of
iron placed crosswise, and likewise separated a span from each other.
There were fixed at each corner and in the middle supports, also of iron,
raising the framework a little off the ground and serving as legs. The
victim was laid on the gridiron, with his legs and arms bound to the four
corners, that his tender limbs might be stretched and racked. This done,
fire was set underneath.

j. Martyrs were tied hand and foot to iron chairs which were then placed
over a burning fire. Sometimes a red-hot helmet, or morion, was also
placed on the martyr's head.

k. Martyrs were dressed in heated iron tunics and forced to put on red-hot
shoes, which consumed the flesh from their bones.

l. Martyrs had their eyes burned out with a lighted brand.

m. Martyrs had their hands filled with incense mingled with live coals, which
became so painful to hold that they let them go, and so were said to have
made sacrifice to an idol.

n. Sometimes a red-hot helmet, or morion, was also placed on the martyr's
head. This is illustrated by the history of the martyrdom of St Clement of
Ancyra and that of St Justus, a soldier, where it is written:

> The day of trial of the holy martyr St Justus, who was of the city of
> Rome, a soldier under the Tribune Claudius. Returning once from a
> victory over the Barbarians, he saw a cross appearing before him like
> a crystal, and heard a voice coming from it. Instructed by it in the
> mystery of godly piety, he distributed on his arrival in Rome all his
> goods to the poor, exulting in the faith of Christ.
>
> But when this came to the ears of the Tribune, and Christ's martyr
> would in no way deny the profession he had made, he sent him to the
> Governor Magnentius. Questioned by him and found constant in his
> steadfastness to the Christian faith, he was ordered to be scourged
> with whips of rawhide, and afterwards to have his head capped with
> a fiery helmet, and iron balls heated red-hot to be put under his
> armpits. All these torments the blessed martyr bore unflinchingly,
> blessing God all the time, until he was finally thrown into a furnace,
> where he gave up the ghost.'

¶ *Tortures and Torments of the Christian Martyrs, from the 'De SS. Martyrum
Cruciatibus' of the Rev. Father Gallonio,* translated by A. R. Allinson (London
and Paris: printed for the subscribers, 1903), pp. 115–17

Maximilian

In 295, while Dion, the proconsul of Africa, was engaged in levying new troops, a young man, Maximilian, was brought before him to be measured, as he sat in the forum at Theveste. The proconsul asked him his name, but he answered, 'Why should you want to know my name? I cannot serve in the army, I am a Christian.

There were many Christians in the army and Dion would not listen to the excuse. 'Measure him,' he said.

While they were doing this, Maximilian repeated, 'I cannot serve. I cannot do what is wrong.'

'Measure his height,' said the proconsul. He was five feet ten. 'Let him be marked,' said the proconsul.

Maximilian resisted. 'I cannot do it,' he said. 'I cannot serve.'

'You had better serve,' said Dion, 'or it will be the worse for you.'

'I cannot,' repeated the young man; 'cut off my head if you like, but I cannot be a soldier of the world; I am a soldier of my God.'

Maximilian's father was standing by. It was his business to collect the money paid by conscripts who wished to commute their service for a fine. The proconsul suspected that there was some collusion between the father and the son.

'Who has induced you to behave like this?' he asked the young man.

'My own mind,' replied Maximilian, 'and He who called me.'

Dion turned to Victor, the father. 'Give your son good advice,' he said.

'He knows his own business,' replied Victor. 'He has his own ideas of what is good for him.'

'Serve,' repeated Dion to Maximilian, 'and take the badge.' Dion ordered the officials to hang the lead badge round his neck. But Maximilian resisted having the distasteful emblem put on him.

'I will not take the badge of worldly warfare,' he cried, 'if you put it on me, I shall tear it off. It is of no use. I am a Christian. It is unlawful for me to wear this bit of lead round my neck after receiving the sign of my Lord Jesus Christ, the Son of the living God, whom you do not know, but who suffered for our salvation, whom God delivered up for our sins. All we Christians are his servants. We follow him as the Prince of life and the Author of salvation.'

'Take the badge, I say, and serve,' persisted Dion, 'or you will come to a bad end.'

'I shall not come to an end,' replied the enthusiastic man. 'My service is for my own Lord. I cannot engage in worldly warfare. I have already told you that I am a Christian.'

Dion the proconsul answered, 'There are Christian soldiers in the sacred bodyguard of our lords Diocletian and Maximian, Constantius and Maximus: they serve.'

But no argument would convince Maximilian. 'I suppose,' he said, 'that they know what is good for them; but I am a Christian, and cannot do what is wrong.'

'What wrong do men do who serve in the army?' the proconsul asked.

'I need not tell you,' said Maximilian, 'you know well enough what they do.'

Once more the proconsul urged him to comply: 'Come,' he said, 'serve, or else if you flout service, you are on the way to perish.'

'I shall not perish,' answered Maximilian, 'and if I pass out of the world, my soul lives with Christ my Lord.'

The proconsul's patience was exhausted, and he had the following sentence read out, from his tablet: 'Maximilian has disloyally refused the oath of service, and is therefore adjudged to be beheaded.'

The young man, twenty-one years old, answered, 'Thanks be to God.'

As they led him to the place of execution, he said to the Christians near him, 'Beloved brethren, hasten with all your might and with eager desire that you may be permitted to see the Lord, and that he may bestow on you a crown like mine.' His death was instantaneous.

Maximilian's mother, Pompeiana, received the body from the magistrate, and laid it in her own bedroom. Then she carried it to Carthage and buried it close to the grave of the martyr Cyprian. A fortnight later, the mother herself died, and was buried in the same spot. 'His father, Victor,' adds the simple and touching record, 're-turned to his home with great joy, giving thanks to God that he had sent such a gift before him to the Lord, and determined to follow after.'

¶ A. J. Mason, *The Historic Martyrs of the Primitive Church* (Longmans, 1905), pp. 207–9

Eusebius

'about the end of the third century'

In the reign of Diocletian and Maximian, before they had published any new edicts against the Christians, Eusebius, a holy priest, a man eminently endowed with the spirit of prayer, and all apostolical virtues, suffered death for the faith, probably in Palestine. The emperor Maximian happening to be in that country, an information was lodged with Maxentius, president of the province, against Eusebius, that he distinguished himself by his zeal in invoking and preaching Christ, and the holy man was apprehended, and brought before him. The people stirred up Maxentius, by their furious clamours against the servant of Christ.

MAXENTIUS: Sacrifice to the gods freely, or you shall be made to do it against your will.

EUSEBIUS: There is a greater law which says, 'Thou shalt adore the Lord thy God, and him alone shalt thou serve.'

MAXENTIUS: Choose either to offer sacrifice, or to suffer the most rigorous torments.

EUSEBIUS: It is not consistent with reason for a person to adore stones, than which nothing is viler or more brittle.

MAXENTIUS: These Christians are a hardened race of men, to whom it seems desirable rather to die than to live.

EUSEBIUS: It is impious to despise the light for the sake of darkness.

MAXENTIUS: You grow more obstinate by lenity and entreaties. I therefore lay them aside, and frankly tell you, that, unless you sacrifice, you shall be burnt alive.

EUSEBIUS: As to that, I am in no pain. The more severe or cruel the torments are, the greater will the crown be.

Upon this, Maxentius ordered that he should be stretched on the rack, and his sides rent with iron hooks. Eusebius repeated, whilst he was tormenting, 'Lord Jesus preserve me. Whether we live or die, we are yours.'

The president was amazed at his constancy and fortitude, and after some time, commanded that he should be taken off the rack. Then he said to him, 'Do you know the decree of the senate, which commands all to sacrifice to the gods?'

Eusebius answered, 'The command of God is to take place before that of man.'

Maxentius ordered Eusebius' guards to confine him until the next day. Maxentius went to the prince, and said, 'Great emperor, I have found a seditious man who is disobedient to the laws, and even denies to my face that the gods have any power, and refuses to sacrifice, or to adore your name.'

The emperor answered, 'Let him be brought before me.'

A person present, who had seen Eusebius at the prefect's tribunal, said, 'If you see him, you will be moved by his speech.'

The emperor replied, 'Is he such a man that he can even change me?'

The prefect then spoke, 'He will change not only you, but the minds of all the people. If you once behold his looks, you will feel yourself strangely moved to follow his inclinations.'

The emperor, however, ordered him to be brought in. As Eusebius entered, everyone was struck in beholding the dazzling brightness which appeared in his countenance, the joy and the affecting composure, sweetness, and undaunted courage which shone in his looks and eye, and the gracefulness of his air, and whole mien, which in his venerable old age seemed to breathe an air of virtue above what is human. The emperor fixed his eyes steadfastly upon him, as if he beheld in him something divine, and spoke thus, 'Old man, why are you come before me? Speak, and do not be afraid.' Seeing him silent, he said, 'Speak freely; answer my questions. I desire that you be saved.'

Eusebius answered, 'If I hope to be saved by man, I can no longer expect salvation from God. If you excel in dignity and power, we are, nevertheless, all mortal alike. Neither will I be afraid to repeat before you what I have already declared. I am a Christian: nor can I adore wood and stones; but I most readily obey the true God whom I know, and whose goodness I have experienced.'

The emperor said to the president, 'What harm is it if this man adores the God of whom he speaks, as above all others?'

Maximian replied, 'Be not deceived, most invincible emperor; he does not call what you imagine God, but I know not what Jesus, whom our nation or ancestors never knew.'

The emperor said, 'Go you forth, and judge him according to justice and the laws. I will not be judge in such an affair.'

Maxentius went out and ascended his tribunal, saying to Eusebius, 'Sacrifice, or torments and flames must be your portion.'

Eusebius replied, 'My soul, which is God's, cannot be hurt by your torments. I persevere firm in the holy law to which I have adhered from my cradle.'

The president then condemned him to be beheaded.

¶ Alban Butler, *The Lives of the Saints* (Dublin, 1833), vol. II, pp. 234–5

Egyptian martyrs

Egyptian martyrs at Tyre

We know about the Egyptian martyrs (martyred from 305 onwards), who became shining lights in Palestine and at Tyre in Phoenicia. Nobody could have been but amazed at the harsh floggings, the man-eating beasts which followed when they were attacked by panthers, various bears, bulls enraged by red-hot irons, and wild boars. I saw the courage of these martyrs myself and the divine power of the presence of the One to whom they testified, our Saviour Jesus Christ himself, who was clearly seen in these martyrs. For a long time the man-eating beasts would not go near the bodies of God's beloved people, but rather attacked their handlers. The holy champions stood naked, waving their arms to attack the attention of the wild beasts which left them unmolested. To the astonishment of the spectators this went of for a long time, until a second and then a third group of wild beasts were introduced which then all ravaged the same martyr.

Nothing can outstrip the amazing, fearless courage of these saints and the endurance of their young bodies. A man, not yet twenty years old, would stand up without chains, spread out his arms in the shape of a cross, and concentrate his mind totally on unhurried prayers to the Almighty. A supernatural power stopped the mouths of these wild beasts. Then a wild bull was introduced. The bull attacked and mangled everyone in sight with his horns, except for the group of five holy martyrs, whom he refused to even approach. Even when the bull was provoked with red-hot irons he did not attack the martyrs. Different wild beasts were then sent in but even these did not attack their intended victims. In the end the martyrs were each butchered with a sword. They were not buried in the ground but thrown into the waves of the sea.

Egyptian martyrs in Egypt

Great numbers of men and women and children, who despised this passing life, faced death in a variety of ways for the sake of our Saviour's teaching. Some were flogged without mercy, some put on the rack, some scraped, and some endured countless other tortures. Some were burnt alive, others drowned in the sea, while others gladly bared their necks to the executioner's axe. Some died as they were being tortured, some starved to death, some were crucified like common criminals but some were nailed in an upside down position, head down, to inflict even more pain, and others were starved to death as they slowly died on the cross.

Egyptian martyrs at Thebais

These martyrs were torn to shreds from head to toe with claw-like potsherds until they expired. Women, stripped naked without a stitch of clothing, were lifted up a single foot by rope and so exposed in this shameful way to the crowds. Some were tied to tree stumps and then killed in terrible agony as follows. With the help of machinery the strongest branches of these trees were drawn close to each other and one leg of the martyr was then tied to each of the tree branches. Then the branches were allowed to be released and they flew back to their normal positions and the martyr's limbs were torn apart in a second. They did this, not just for a few days or a few weeks, but year after year. Sometimes ten people were killed in this way and on other days thirty or sixty people were killed. On some days over one hundred people were killed by a succession of different punishments.

As I was in these places, I witnessed these executions personally. Some martyrs were beheaded, others were burnt alive. On some days, so many were killed that the axehead became blunt. I saw a great enthusiasm on the part of those who placed their trust in God's Christ. As soon as one group had been sentenced to death, another group would jump up on the platform and tell the judge that they were Christians.

¶ Eusebius, *The History of the Church*, Book VIII

Tortures of the first Christian martyrs
7: Other instruments of torture

Eusebius says in his *Ecclesiastical History*: 'The hands of the executioners failed, and albeit succeeding one another in relays, the men were wearied out, and the edge of the sword blunted. Myself saw the tormentors sit back exhausted, recover strength, regain breath, take fresh swords – and yet the day not be long long enough for all the torments to be inflicted! Nevertheless, not one of all the band, not so much as one child of tender years, could be frightened back from affronting death; the one and only thing each dreaded was, that when the hurrying sun ended the short day, he should be left behind, divided from the society of his martyred comrades. Thus did they, one and all, steadfastly and boldly trusting to the faith, welcome with joy and exultation a present death as the beginning of eternal life. In a word, while the first batches were being slaughtered, the rest would stand singing psalms and hymns to God, each waiting his own turn of martyrdom, that so they might breathe forth their last breath in praises to the Almighty.'

Mighty the failure of these servants of Satan, and great their foolishness! Verily did they tumble into the pit they had digged for the saints to fall into. Again and again did they condemn – but all in vain – their Christian adversaries to be:

a. stabbed to death with countless blows of iron writing styles [schoolboys' pens];
b. struck over with nails, either their whole body or some special part of it;
c. cut in half with saws;
d. transfixed with spears;
e. pierced with swords;
f. shot with arrows;
g. their bellies to be gashed open and the inwards torn out;
h. their throats to be cut;
i. to be beheaded
j. to be disfigured with brands and markings;
k. their heads to be pounded with axes or clubs, and dashed to pieces;
l. women's bosoms to be amputated;
m. women's tongues, hands and feet, as well as men's, to be cut away;
n. their legs to be broken;
o. stripped naked and led through the public streets
p. buried alive in the earth, either up to their necks, or half buried with arms tied behind them, and left to perish;

q. shut up in a leaden box and drowned in a river.

r. sewn up in a bag, together with a cock, a viper, an ape, or a dog, and thrown into the nearest stream or river.

s. Where two trees could be found growing near together, a branch of each being bent down so as to meet, to either of these one of the martyr's feet was tied in such a way that the boughs which had been forcibly drawn together, when let go, returned with a bound to their natural position and, tearing the man's body in two which was fastened to them, rent his limbs asunder and bare them back with them.

¶ *Tortures and Torments of the Christian Martyrs, from the 'De SS. Martyrum Cruciatibus' of the Rev. Father Gallonio,* translated by A. R. Allinson (London and Paris, 1903, printed for the subscribers), pp. 139–41

Genesius, a comedian

Christ who, to show the power of his grace, and the extent of his mercy, called a publican to the apostleship, honoured with the glory of martyrdom this saint, drawn from the stage. The emperor Diocletian, coming to Rome, was entertained by people on the stage. In a comedy which was acted in his presence, one of the players took it into his head to represent, in a ludicrous manner, the ceremonies of the Christian baptism, which could not fail to divert the assembly, who held this religion, and its mysteries, in the utmost contempt and derision.

This player, Genesius, who had learned some things concerning the Christian rites from friends who zealously professed that religion, laid himself down on the stage, pretending to be sick, and said, 'Ah! My friends, I find a great weight upon me; and would gladly be eased.'

The others answered, 'What shall we do to give thee ease?'

'You senseless creatures,' said Genesius, 'I am resolved to die a Christian, that God may receive me on this day of my death, as one who seeks his salvation by fleeing from idolatry and superstition.'

Then a priest and exorcist were called, that is to say, two actors. They sat next to his bed-side, and said, 'Well, my child, why did you send for us?'

Here Genesius, being suddenly converted by a divine inspiration, replied, not in jest, but seriously, 'Because I desire to receive the grace of Jesus Christ and to be born again, that I may be delivered from my sins.'

The other actors mimicked the whole ceremony of baptism with him, but Genesius in earnest answered the usual interrogations, and on being baptised was clothed with a white garment. After this, other actors, dressed like soldiers, to carry on the jest, seized Genesius, and presented him to the emperor, to be examined, as the martyrs were wont to be. Then Genesius declared himself openly, and said aloud, standing on the stage, 'Hear, O emperor, and all you that are here present, officers of the army, philosophers, senators, and people, what I am going to say. I never yet so much as heard the name of a Christian but I was struck with horror, and detested my very relations because they professed that religion. I informed myself concerning its rites and mysteries only that I might the more heartily despise it, and inspire you with the utmost contempt for the same; but whilst I was washed with the water, and examined, I had no sooner answered sincerely that I believed, than I saw a company of bright angels over my head, who recited out of a book all the sins I had committed from my childhood; and having afterward plunged the book into the water which had been poured upon me in your presence, they showed me the book whiter than snow. Wherefore, I advise you, O great and mighty emperor, and all ye people here present, who have ridiculed these mysteries, to believe, with me, that Jesus Christ is the true Lord; that he is the light and the truth; and that it is through him you may obtain the forgiveness of your sins.'

Diocletian, highly enraged at these words, ordered him to be most inhumanly beaten with clubs, and afterward to be put into the hands of Plautian, the prefect of the praetorium, that he might compel him to sacrifice. Palutian commanded him to be put on the rack, where he was torn with iron hooks for a considerable time, and then burnt with torches. The martyr endured these torments with constancy, and persisted crying out, 'There is no other Lord of the universe besides him whom I have seen. Him I adore and serve, and to him I will adhere, though I should suffer a thousand deaths for his sake. No torments shall remove Jesus Christ from my heart or mouth. I regret exceedingly my former errors, and that I once detested his holy name, and came so late to his service. At length his head was struck off.

¶ Alban Butler, *The Lives of the Saints* (Dublin, 1833), vol. II, pp. 329–30

Marcellus
30th October 298

In the city of Tingis, while Fortunatus was governor, the date for celebrating the Emperor's birthday came round. While everyone was feasting at banquets and sacrificing, a certain Marcellus, a centurion from the Trajan legion, deeming those banquets to be pagan, threw down his soldier's belt in front of the legion's standards in the camp. Then he called out in a loud voice, 'I serve Jesus Christ the eternal king. From now on I stop serving your Emperors, and I refuse to worship your wooden and stone gods, which are deaf and dumb idols. If these are the terms of service, I renounce the standards, and refuse to serve.'

Agricolan said, 'What possessed you to throw away the emblems of your allegiance and to speak as you did?'

Marcellus answered, 'There is no madness in those who fear the Lord. It is wrong for a Christian, who serves the Lord Christ, to serve the cares of the world.'

Agricolan announced the following sentence: 'Marcellus must be put to death by the sword.'

When Marcellus was being led out to be executed he said to Agricolan, 'May God bless you! For a martyr should leave this world in this way.'

¶ E. C. E. Owen (trans.), *Some Authentic Acts of the Early Martyrs* (Oxford, 1927), pp. 122–4

Nicander and Marcian

Two soldiers, Nicander and Marcian were martyred, probably at the same time as Marcellus, probably at Dorostorum, in the Moesian province, which later became known as Bulgaria.

Governor of the province of Moesia, Maximus, said to Nicander and Marcian, 'If you are acquainted with the orders of the emperors, which require you to sacrifice to the gods, step up and obey the orders.'

'It is only required,' Nicander answered, 'of those who are willing to sacrifice. We are Christians, and cannot be bound by such a requirement.'

'You need only honour the gods with a grain of incense,' the governor pleaded.

Nicander replied, 'How can a Christian man worship stocks and stones, and forsake the everlasting God whom we worship, who made all things of nothing, and who is able to save both me and all who trust in him?'

Nicander's wife, Daria, was present. Even though Nicander had been away at war for a long time Daria, with the intensity of a Christian woman's love, set herself to encourage her husband in his resolution, and said, 'My lord, take good heed that you do it not. Take good heed, my lord, that you deny not our Lord Jesus Christ. Look up to heaven, and you will there see him to whom you are bound in loyalty and conscience. He is your helper.'

Maximus, the governor, heard some of these remarks. 'You bad woman,' he exclaimed, 'why do you want your husband to die?'

'That he may live with God,' she replied, 'and never die.'

'No, no,' said the governor, 'it is nothing of the sort. You want to be married to a better husband, and so are in a hurry to rid yourself of your present husband.'

'If you imagine that I think such a thing, and that I plan to do as you say,' replied the brave woman, 'kill me first for Christ's sake.'

'I shall certainly not do as you wish,' replied Maximus, 'but you shall be put in prison.'

All this time Marcian had been silent and unquestioned. The governor now addressed him: 'What do you say, Marcian?' he inquired.

'I say the same as my fellow-soldier,' he replied.

Maximus answered, 'You shall be thrust into prison together, then, and shall assuredly suffer the penalty.'

Later, Maximus pronounced the death penalty on them both. On their way to their execution, they were accompanied by their friends. Nicander's wife was there, and with her a man called Papian, whose brother Pasicrates had suffered martyrdom recently. Papian carried in his arms Nicander and Daria's young child. Marcian's wife and their child were also there, but Marcian's wife was either a heathen or a nominal Christian. She tore her clothes and shouted aloud, 'I told you in the prison that it would come to this. Look at your darling little son. Turn your face towards us, and do not disown us. Why are you in such a hurry? Where are you going? Why do you hate us? You have been carried off like a sheep to the slaughter.'

Marcian did eventually turn to the poor woman, and said, 'How long has Satan blinded your mind and soul? Go your way and let me go mine. Allow me to perfect my martyrdom for God.'

A Christian called Zoticus clasped Marcian's hand, and encouraged him, saying, 'Be of good courage, the Lord be with you, you have fought the good fight. How can we weak ones have such faith? Remember the promises which the Lord has made, and which he will so soon pay. Perfect Christians are you indeed: blessed are you.'

The unhappy wife was still following with her cries, attempting to hold Marcian back. 'Hold my wife,' said Marcian to Zoticus, and Zoticus did so.

When they came to the place for the execution, the spirit of the martyr relented a little. Looking around, Marcian called his wife to him. He kissed her, and said, 'Depart in the Lord. You cannot bear to see me celebrate my martyrdom, with your mind beguiled by the evil one.' Marcian kissed his child, and looking up to heaven said, 'Lord God Almighty, take Thou care of him.' Then the two martyrs embraced one another, and stepped a few paces apart to be put to death.

At that moment, however, Marcian saw Nicander's wife vainly attempting to push through the crowd to her husband.

'God be with you,' said the husband.

'Be of good cheer, good my lord,' said his wife. 'Show them how you can strive. I spent ten years at home without you, and there was not a moment when I was not wishing to God that I might see you. Now I have seen you, and I am glad that you are setting out for the land of life. I shall sing louder now. How proud I shall be, to be a martyr's wife! Be of good courage, my lord. Bear your witness to God, that you may deliver me also from everlasting death.'

The Christians then had such great confidence in the power of a martyr's prayer. Handkerchiefs were bound round the eyes of Nicander and Marcian, and in a moment the skilled stroke of the sword sent them where they desired to be.

¶ Ruinart, *Acta Primorum Martyrum Sincera,* quoted by A. J. Mason, *The Historic Martyrs of the Primitive Church* (Longmans, 1905), pp. 214–6

Cassian
3rd December 298

When Aurelius Agricolan was acting as deputy for the Prefects of the Praetorian Guard, as he was preparing to hear the case of the holy martyr Marcellus, the blessed Cassian was the secretary. When Marcellus, one of the centurions of Asta, was brought into court at Tingis on 30th October, Aurelius Agricolan, acting as judge, threatened Marcellus as he attempted to deflect him from standing for Christ. But the blessed Marcellus was so unswerving that everyone thought of him as the judge's judge, as he testified that he was Christ's soldier and that he could not serve the cares of the world. This made Aurelius Agricolan speak in great anger.

Cassian was recording the proceedings, but when he saw that Aurelius Agricolan, defeated by the martyr's great devotion, pronounced the death sentence, he vowed that he would write nothing more down. He threw the pen and note book onto the ground. To the astonishment of the staff, and as Marcellus laughed, Aurelius Agricolan, trembling, leapt up from the bench and demanded to know why Cassian had thrown his notebooks down with an oath. Blessed Cassian replied that Agricolan had handed down an unjust sentence. To avoid being contradicted any more, Agricolan ordered Cassian to be taken away at once and to be thrown into prison.

The blessed martyr Marcellus had laughed because, through the Holy Spirit, he knew what was going to happen, and he rejoiced that Cassian would be his companion in martyrdom.

¶ E. C. E. Owen (trans.), *Some Authentic Acts of the Early Martyrs* (Oxford, 1927), pp. 125–6

Julius

Maximus was capable of recognising excellence, and, at the start of Julius' trial he was anxious to befriend Julius.

MAXIMUS: Julius, I see that you are a sensible and serious man. Take my advice therefore, and sacrifice to the gods.

JULIUS: I will not do as you desire, nor run into sin and eternal punishment.

MAXIMUS: If you think that sin, let it be laid to my charge. I will apply force to you, that it may not look as if you had complied willingly. Then you can go home with no further anxiety.

The offer was all the more seductive because it was so kindly intended; but Julius saw behind the indulgent governor the evil power which spoke through him.

JULIUS: You cannot draw me away from my eternal Lord. I cannot deny God. Give sentence against me, therefore, as a Christian.

MAXIMUS: Unless you will be obedient to the imperial orders and sacrifice I will cut your head off.

JULIUS: That is a good thought. I beseech you, religious governor, by the health of the emperors, to put it in execution, and give sentence upon me, that my desires may be fulfilled.

MAXIMUS: You are in such a hurry to die. You think that you will suffer for some praiseworthy object.

JULIUS: If I am permitted to suffer in this way everlasting glory will await me.

MAXIMUS: If you were suffering for your country and for the laws you would have everlasting praise.

JULIUS: It is indeed for the laws that I shall suffer, but the laws are God's laws.

MAXIMUS: Laws which are bequeathed to you by a dead man who was crucified. See what a fool you are, to make more of a dead man than of the live emperors.

JULIUS: He died for our sins that he might bestow on us eternal life, but he is God who endures for ever, and whoever confesses him shall have eternal life, and whoever denies him eternal punishment.

MAXIMUS: I am sorry for you and I advise you to sacrifice and live with us.

JULIUS: If I live with you it is death to me, but if I die, I live.

MAXIMUS: You have chosen death rather than life.

JULIUS: I have chosen death for the moment and then life everlasting.

The following sentence was then pronounced: 'Julius, who refuses to obey the orders of the emperors, is to receive capital punishment.'

Julius was taken out to be executed. His last words were, 'O Lord

Jesus Christ, for whose name's sake I suffer thus, vouchsafe to set my spirit among thy saints.' He was then beheaded.

¶ A. J. Mason, *The Historic Martyrs of the Primitive Church* (Longmans, 1905), pp. 218–19

Martyrs in Phrygia

Some people became martyrs as a result of war. The small town of Phrygia was surrounded by legions who then torched it and its whole population, men, women and children, because they were known to call on Almighty God. Everyone in the town had declared that they were Christians, including the Mayor and magistrates, and they refused to give way to worshipping idols.

The saintly Domnina from Antioch had two attractive unmarried daughters. They hid themselves as they feared that would be raped by the soldiers. When they were captured by the soldiers they quietly asked the soldiers to excuse them for a moment, and then they threw themselves into the river next to them and drowned themselves.

Tortures that make a hearer shudder were carried out in Pontus. Sharpened reeds were driven under the fingernails of both hands Others had the seething mass of molten lead poured over their backs and their bodies were roasted alive. Others had their bowels or private parts tortured by noble judges who were supposed to uphold the law.

¶ Eusebius, *The History of the Church*, Book VIII

Sebastian

'He was prepared for his second martyrdom.'

Sebastian was born at Narbonne, in Gaul, instructed in Christianity at Milan, and was later an officer in the Imperial Guard at Rome. He remained a Christian in the middle of idolatry, untainted by evil examples around him. He was informed against and betrayed; but being of rank too considerable to be put to death without the emperor's orders, Emperor Diocletian was acquainted with the persecution.

On hearing the accusation, he sent for Sebastian, and charged him with being an enemy of the gods of the empire. Sebastian replied that proof of his faithfulness was in praying to the only true God for the well being and prosperity of the emperor and the government. Incensed at this reply, the emperor ordered him to be taken to the Campus Martius, and there to be shot to death the arrows, which sentence was carried out. A few Christians attended the execution, in order to bury his body, and they perceived signs of life in him. They took him away and shortly he recovered and was prepared for his second martyrdom.

As soon as he was able to walk, he placed himself in the emperor's way as he was going to the temple. The appearance of a person supposed to be dead astonished the emperor, nor did the words of the martyr less surprise him, for he began to reprehend him for his cruelties, and for his prejudices against Christianity. Having overcome his surprise, he ordered Sebastian to be seized and beaten to death, and his body thrown into a common sewer.

¶ John Foxe, *The Book of Martyrs,* revised with notes and an appendix by W. Bramley-Moore (London, 1869), p. 30

Tarachus, Probus and Andronicus

While Maximus, Governor of Cilicia, was at Tarsus, three Christians were brought before him. Tarachus, the eldest, was asked by Maximus what he was. The prisoner replied, 'A Christian'. This reply offending the governor, he again made the demand, and was answered in a similar manner. The governor then told him that he ought to sacrifice to the gods, as the only way to promotion, riches, and honours; and that the emperors themselves did what he recommended him to perform. Tarachus answered that avarice was a sin, and gold itself an idol as abominable as any other. As for promotion, he desired it not, as he could not in conscience accept any place which would subject him to worship idols; and with regard to honours, he desired none greater than the honourable title of Christian. As to the emperors themselves, he added that they were deceived in worshipping idols, and misled by the devil himself. For this speech his jaws were broken. He was then scourged, loaded with chains, and thrown into a dungeon, to rmeain there till the trials of the other two prisoners.

Probus was then brought before Maximus, who asked his name. The prisoner answered, the most valuable name that he could boast of was that of a Christian. To this Maximus replied: 'Your name of Christian will be of little service to you; be therefore guided by me; sacrifice to the gods, engage my friendship, and the favour of the emperor. Probus answered that as he had relinquished a considerable fortune to become a soldier of Christ, it might appear evident that he neither cared for his friendship nor the favour of the emperor. Probus was then scourged; and Demetrius, the officer, observing how his blood flowed, advised him to comply; but his only answer was that those severities were agreeable to him.

'What!' cried Maximus. 'Does he still persist in his madness?'

To which Probus replied, 'That character is wrongly bestowed on one who refuses to worship idols.' After being scourged, he was committed to prison, and his feet and hands were stretched on the stocks.

Andronicus was next brought up, when being asked the usual questions, he said, 'I am a Christian, a native of Ephesus, and descended from one of the first families in that city.' He was ordered to undergo punishments similar to those of Tarachus and Probus, and then was remanded to prison. Having been confined some days, the three prisoners were brought before Maximus, who began to reason with Tarachus, expressing the hope that he would change his mind. Finding himself mistaken, Maximus ordered him to be tortured in a variety of ways: fire was placed in the palms of his hands; he was hung up by his feet; a mixture of salt and vinegar was poured into his nostrils; and in this state he was remanded to his dungeon.

Probus being called, and asked if he would sacrifice, replied: 'I come better prepared to die than before; for what I have already suffered has only confirmed me in my resolution. Employ your whole power on me, and you will find that neither you, nor your masters the emperors, nor the gods whom you serve, nor the devil, who is your father, shall oblige me to adore idols whom I know not.' The governor, however, pressed him to sacrifice to Jupiter; but Probus turned this casuistry into ridicule, and said, 'Shall I pay divine honours to Jupiter, to one who married his own sister to a debauchee, as he is even acknowledged to have done by your priests and poets?' Provoked at this speech, the governor ordered him to be struck on the mouth for uttering blasphemy. His body was then seared with hot irons; he was put on the rack, and scourged; his head was shaved, and red-hot coals placed on the crown of his head; and after all these tortures, he was remanded in prison.

When Andronicus was again brought before Maximus, the latter attempted to deceive him by pretending that Tarachus and Probus had repented of their obstinacy, and owned the gods of the empire. To this the prisoner answered, 'I cannot believe that they have renounced their hopes in our God, nor will I fall short of them in faith in our common Saviour. Thus armed, I neither own your gods nor your authority; fulfil your threats, employ every cruel art in your power; I am prepared to bear it for the sake of Christ.' For this answer he was scourged, and his wounds rubbed with salt.

These intrepid Christians were brought to a third examination, when they retained their constancy, were again tortured, and at length ordered to be executed.

¶ John Foxe, *The Book of Martyrs,* revised with notes and an appendix by W. Bramley-Moore (London, 1869), pp. 31–4

Martyrs at Nicomedia

Peter
In Nicomedia the rulers ordered a certain man to offer sacrifice. Because he refused, he was stripped, and tied up naked, and whipped with loaded whips which tore into his flesh. This was to continue until he agreed to sacrifice. As he did not give in to this his wounds were then bathed in salt and vinegar, especially where bones had been exposed. He treated these agonies scornfully and so he was put in a brazier that was already on fire and roasted very slowly until he eventually breathed his last, but remained immovable to the end. Such was the martyrdom of one of the imperial servants, whose name was Peter.

Hadrian
Twenty-three Christians had been brought before Galerius. He was

incensed at the way they answered his questions. He called his chief official to note down their names. Then another man, Hadrian, stepped forward and said, 'Make a note of my name with theirs.'

'Are you mad?' asked Galerius, 'do you want to throw away your life as well?'

'I am not mad, sir. Once I was mad, but now I have come into my right mind.'

'Do not speak,' said Galerius, 'but beg my pardon. Say in the presence of everyone that you have made a mistake. Then your answer will be erased from the minutes of this court.'

'No,' replied Hadrian, 'from now on I will ask pardon of God for my evil deeds and for the errors of my past life.'

Hadrian was thrown into prison with the other twenty-three Christians. He was visited by his wife, Natalia, whom he had been married to for just over a year. When Hadrian was before Galerius for trial, he carried the hobbyhorse on which he was to be tortured. Natalia was there to keep him true to his profession. Hadrian was also beaten. Galerius said to Hadrian, 'These other poor creatures are but peasants. You are a noble and are not like them. Acknowledge the gods and you will be freed.'

Hadrian would not be separated from his new friends, and said, 'I dare say that you know about my home and family and ancestors, but if you knew the family of these holy men, and their wealth, and the home that they are looking for, you would throw yourself instantly at their feet, and beg them to pray for you. Moreover, you would smash your gods with your own hands.'

Hadrian was turned over and beaten on his stomach. After a while, the emperor told the beaters to stop. The delicately nurtured body could not bear much more. 'You see,' said the emperor, 'how I wish to spare you. If you will only call on the gods with your voice' [he meant without performing any sacrificial act] 'I will have the doctors brought in to attend to your wounds and you will be with me in my palace today.'

Hadrian replied that he would do so, if the gods would promise with their own lips to do what Galerius had said they would do for him.

'What,' said the emperor, 'they cannot speak.'

'Why, then,' replied the Christian, 'do you sacrifice to things which cannot speak?'

Hadrian was thrown back in prison, where, along with some of the other twenty-three confessors, he had his wrists and ankles broken by an iron bar. Natalia held his poor hands on the wooden block while this was done. Mortification set in, and Hadrian died in his prison. Natalia was forced to flee from Byzantium to escape the attentions of the officer of the town, who wanted to marry her. She took with her, as her chief treasure, the hand of her martyred husband, embalmed, and wrapped in a purple covering, which she always kept at the head of her bed.

¶ A. J. Mason, *The Historic Martyrs of the Primitive Church* (Longmans, 1905), pp. 227–8

Tortures of the first Christian martyrs
8: Wild beasts

It was customary with the ancients in former days to condemn criminals, or Christians if it so happened, to the wild beasts.

a. Savage dogs: in the Acts of the holy martyr St Benignus, we read, 'The most wicked Emperor commanded him to be shut up in prison, and a great stone with a hole through it to be brought, and his feet to be fixed therein with molten lead, and red-hot bradawls to be stuck lengthwise into his fingers under the nails, and for six days neither food nor drink to be given him; moreover that twelve savage dogs should be imprisoned along with him, maddened with hunger and thirst, to the end these might tear him in pieces, and the gaol to be watched by soldiers.'
b. Martyrs were imprisoned in a net, and so exposed to be tossed by a savage bull.
c. Martyrs were wrapped in a wild beast's hide, and so left to be torn by animals.

¶ *Tortures and Torments of the Christian Martyrs, from the 'De SS. Martyrum Cruciatibus' of the Rev. Father Gallonio,* translated by A. R. Allinson (London and Paris, printed for the subscribers, 1903), pp. 159–61

Theodotus

In the reign of Emperor Maximin, Theodotus ran an eating-house in Ancyra, Galatia's capital city. He helped the church and the Christian cause in this way. Theotecnus had ordered that every item of food and drink that was sold in the city should be defiled by being offered to idols, or by coming into contact with something that had been offered. Theotecnus made sure that all bread and wine was treated in this way to hit out at the sacrament which he knew was the church's mainstay. But Theodotus managed to sell food to his Christian customers which had not been polluted, as he bought some of his food from Christian tradesmen.

Theodotus was brought before Theotecnus, who personally helped to torture him. All the usual horrors were tried. Eventually, as blazing torches were held under him, the martyr smelt his own flesh as it burned and tried to turn his nose away from the smell. Theotecnus stood beside him, looking for the slightest sign of weakness. He said, 'If you had not blasphemed the gods you would never have suffered like this. You should take my advice, for you are only a shopkeeper, and not say anything against the emperors who have power to shed your blood.'

The martyr's reply was enough to make Theotecnus order the executioners to knock out his teeth. Theodotus only answered, 'If you cut out my tongue, and all my speech organs, God can still hear a Christian who cannot speak.'

Theodotus was remanded in prison. The governor did this deliberately so that as he was led back through the market-place everyone would see how Christians were treated. Theodotus said to the people who crowded round him, 'It is fitting for those who believe in Christ to offer to him such sacrifices as I have offered, for he first suffered thus for each of us.' After five days in prison, fresh arguments and fresh tortures were applied to him. Theodotus was not insensible to the pain. 'O Lord Jesus Christ, hope of the hopeless,' he cried out, 'hear my prayer and assuage my agony, for it is for thy holy name that I suffer it.' He received grace to endure, praying to God that the violence of the enemy might come to an end in him, and that peace might be restored to the church.

¶ A. J. Mason, *The Historic Martyrs of the Primitive Church* (Longmans, 1905), pp. 238–9

Eustratius, Eugenius, Auxentius, Mardarius and Orestes

Emperor Diocletian placed turbulent Cappadocia in the hands of two special commissioners, Lysias and Agricola. Eustratius (who was also known as Cyrisices to his friends), as head registrar in Lysias' court, was forced to witness scenes which tormented him. One day it was his duty to cite in court the actions of a presbyter called Auxentius, who had already made a good confession before Lysias. As Eustratius did this, he was so overcome with admiration for the presbyter, that he announced in public that he himself was also a Christian, and had been once since his childhood. Eustratius was tried by fire, but instead of screaming, he merely smiled.

'Would you like me to dream up a different torture?' asked the angry magistrate. Eustratius welcomed the idea. 'Then bring some strong brine, mixed with vinegar,' ordered Lysias. 'Scrape his burns with a piece of broken pottery, and pour brine over the wound, until he can stand no more pain.' Eustratius bore this quietly.

'Perhaps,' said Lysias, 'your bodily exhaustion has affected your mind, and made you delirious. Put away your groundless hopes, and accept the salvation I offer you.' But Eustratius would have none of it.

His example was contagious. One of his underlings, Eugenius, now stood up and said aloud, 'I too am a Christian, and I curse your religion, and am determined to resist your wishes and the command of the emperors, as my superior Eustratius has done.' Eugenius was thrown in prison with Eustratius.

That night the magistrate set out for Nicopolis and made the Christian prisoners march along with him, with nails in their shoes. The next day they arrived in Auauraca, which happened to be the birthplace of both Eustratius and Eugenius. There, one man, Mardarius, took the opportunity to declare himself a Christian and considered it an honour being numbered with the prisoners.

Auxentius, the presbyter, who lived in Auauraca, was being examined. 'Do not trouble me any more, Auxentius,' ordered Lysias, 'pay yourself the favour of thinking yourself worthy of being saved. Tell us that you have now given up this silly and dangerous obstinacy.'

'I will tell you in a very few words,' answered the priest, 'I swear to you by the justice above us which takes account of all things, that I will not change my mind. I know and worship one God and one only.'

Lysias condemned him to be beheaded.

'Now,' said Lysias, 'bring in the person who has just attached himself to the others. We will soon give him the honour which he courts.'

Mardarius asked Eustratius, 'Pray for me, Cyrisices, and tell me how to reply to this wolf of a man. I am no scholar, and he will laugh at me.'

'Say nothing, brother,' replied Eustratius, 'except, "I am a Christian"; "I am a servant of Christ."'

Mardarius did as he was told. To all questions his answer was the same. The 'wolf' of a magistrate had him tied up head downwards, by a rope passed through the tendons of his heels, and hot irons placed on him. After a time, Mardarius expired, with thanksgiving on his lips, and Eugenius soon followed.

Lysias' troubles for the day were not yet over. He went out to review his troops in a nearby field. He was particularly struck by the looks of a tall, handsome soldier called Orestes. He was paying the man a compliment, when accidentally it came out that Orestes was a Christian. His belt was taken away at once and he was dismissed from the army and arrested. Orestes was executed by Lysias' brother-commissioner, Agricola, in Sebastia. Agricola tried to save Eustratius by suggesting that he should pretend in public to worship the gods, and seek forgiveness from his God afterwards. Eustratius naturally rejected this base suggestion with contempt, and died like a good Christian in the fire.

¶ A. J. Mason, *The Historic Martyrs of the Primitive Church* (Longmans, 1905), pp. 245–7

Claudius, Asterius, Neon, Domnina and Theonilla

Lysias, the president of the province of Cilicia, sat on the judgment-seat in the city of Aegae. The accused consisted of three boys, brothers, and two women with a baby. There was no need to find out whether the young man was a Christian; that was already ascertained.

LYSIAS: What is your name?

CLAUDIUS: Claudius.

LYSIAS: Do not throw away your young life by mad folly. Come this moment and sacrifice to the gods, according to the commandment of our lord the Augustus, and so escape the horrors prepared for you.

CLAUDIUS: My God does not require such sacrifices, but works of mercy and upright lives. But your gods are unclean devils, and that is why they are pleased with sacrifices of this kind, destroying for ever the souls of those who worship them. You will never persuade me to worship them.

Lysias ordered him to be prepared for the rods.

LYSIAS: 'I have instructions from the emperors to offer rewards and promotions to Christians who consent to sacrifice.

CLAUDIUS: Their rewards are temporal, but to confess Christ is everlasting salvation.

Claudius was placed on the hobby-horse and his feet were burnt. Part of his foot was cut off and shown to him.

CLAUDIUS: Fire and tortures cannot hurt those who fear God. It only helps them to everlasting salvation, because they suffer these things for Christ's sake.

The hooked talons tore his sides. Other tortures followed in succession. They only made him assert more confidently that torture was the way of salvation, and at last he was sent to prison, and his brother Asterius was called in.

LYSIAS: Torture his sides, and as you do so say to him, 'Even now obey and sacrifice.'

ASTERIUS: I am the brother of the one who answered you just now. He and I are of one mind, and make the same confession. Do what you can. You have my body in your power, but not my soul.

Fresh tortures were tried.

ASTERIUS: Fool! Madman! Why do you torment me? Do you not care about what the Lord will make you pay for this?

After further tortures, Asterius still did not give way.

ASTERIUS: Blind, completely blind. I only ask you to leave no part of my body untortured.

The third boy, Neon, came into court.

LYSIAS: My son, come and sacrifice to the gods, and escape torture.

NEON: If your gods have any power let them defend themselves from those who deny them, without wanting you to defend them. But if you are as bad as they are, I am much better than your gods and than you. I will not obey you. My God is the true God, who made heaven and earth.

LYSIAS: Hit him on the neck, and as you do that say, "Do not blaspheme the gods.'

NEON: Is it a blasphemy to tell the truth?

Neon's feet were stretched on the horse and hot coals were placed on him and his back was lashed.

NEON: What I know to be for my good and profitable for my soul, that I will do. I cannot change my mind.

LYSIAS: Let the brothers Claudius, Asterius, Neon, who are Christians, who blaspheme the gods, and refuse to sacrifice, be crucified outside the gate, and let their bodies be left to be torn to pieces by the birds.

The two women remained to be dealt with. Domnina was presented first.

LYSIAS: You see, my good woman, the tortures and the fire prepared for you. If you wish to escape them, come and sacrifice to the gods.

DOMNINA: I do not wish to fall into eternal fire and into everlasting torments. Therefore I worship God, and his Christ, who made heaven and earth and all things that are therein. Your gods are stone and wood, the work of men's hands.

Lysias ordered her to be stripped naked, and laid out flat, and beaten all over. This order was enough to kill her. Then came Theonilla. To her the same invitation was made, to which she replied in similar words as Domnina.

LYSIAS: Slap her face; throw her to the ground, tie her feet together and torture her well.

THEONILLA: Whether you think it good to torture a gentlewoman and a stranger like this, you know best. God sees what you do.

LYSIAS: Hang her up by her hair, and slap her face.

THEONILLA: Is it not enough that you have stripped me naked? I am not the only one that you have covered with shame, but your own mother and wife also through me, for all women are of the same nature.

LYSIAS: Are you married or are you a widow?
THEONILLA: hI have been a widow for twenty-three years. I have stayed a widow for my God's sake, fasting and watching in prayers ever since I forsook the unclean idols and knew my God.

Lysias responded by ordering the tormentors to shave her head with a razor to see if anything would make her ashamed, to put a girdle of wild briars on her, to tie her to four stakes, and to have her body beaten all over. The final torture was to be burning charcoal placed above and below her so that she could be left to die in these fumes.

But before the charcoal was brought, Theonilla, like Domnina, was mercifully released.

EXECUTIONER: Sir, she is no longer alive.
LYSIAS: Get a sack and put her body in it. Tie it tight and throw it into the sea.

¶ A. J. Mason, *The Historic Martyrs of the Primitive Church* (Longmans, 1905), pp. 252–4

Procopius

Procopius was born in Jerusalem, lived at Scythopolis, the Bethshan of the Bible, where he was reader and exorcist. He had lived an ascetic life from his youth, living on a diet of bread and water, sometimes fasting for seven days. Day and night he studied the scriptures and translated Greek books into Aramaic for the edification of his countrymen.

Along with other Christian confessors he was brought, at the beginning of the persecution to Caesarea. As soon as he arrived at the city gate, without even going to prison, he was brought before the governor and told to sacrifice to the gods. Procopius answered, 'There is only one God, the Almighty.' The governor did not argue with him but begged him, if he would not acknowledge the gods, to burn incense to the four emperors.

Procopius burst out laughing and replied with a quotation from the Iliad, where Homer says,

> It is not good to have lords many;
> Let One be Lord, One King.

The governor did not understand the spiritual meaning which the Christian put into this verse. He considered that Procopius' language was treasonable and condemned him to be beheaded.

¶ A. J. Mason, *The Historic Martyrs of the Primitive Church* (Longmans, 1905), pp. 285–6

Alphaeus and Zacchaeus

Many leading Christians from the neighbouring churches were soon called on to follow Procopius' example. Some failed from the first. Others passed from torture to torture, were scourged, racked, had their sides crimped, were loaded with heavy irons, so that some of them lost the use of their hands.

In many cases the officials were satisfied with an unreal appearance of success. One man was dragged to the altar, both his hands held fast by attendants on either side; some of the sacrificial meat was placed by force in his right hand, and he was dismissed. Another never even touched the sacrifice, but the bystanders shouted that he had sacrificed and he went free. Another was brought from prison in a fainting condition, and thrown on one side for dead. His chains were taken off and he was deemed to have sacrificed. Some others, who vehemently protested that they had neither sacrificed nor intended to do so, were struck on the mouth, and their cries were drowned by people shouting around them, and they were thus hustled out of court.

Out of all this group of people only two were put to death under governor Flavian, Alphaeus and Zacchaeus. Zacchaeus, a deacon from Gadara, was given his name by his friends because, like the tax collector from Jericho, he was very short and because he earnestly longed to see the Lord. He joyfully bore his testimony before the magistrate under torture, and was thrown into the stocks overnight.

Alphaeus, a reader and exorcist from Caesarea itself, tried hard to convince his feebler brethren not to comply with the command to sacrifice. This quickly brought him before the magistrate. There he spoke freely and eloquently about his beliefs, and after being tortured was thrown into the stocks like Zacchaeus. Three days later the two men were brought into the court. The magistrate told them to sacrifice to the emperors, but they answered, 'We know but one King, the King of all.' The two men were then sentenced and beheaded.

¶ A. J. Mason, *The Historic Martyrs of the Primitive Church* (Longmans, 1905), pp. 286–7

Agapius and Thecla

Urban succeeded Flavian as governor of Palestine and a man, Agapius, and a woman, Thecla, were killed.

As the great festival approached, Urban was determined to add special interest to the celebration, by announcing that, in addition to horse racing in the circus at Caesarea, a gala performance in the theatre, and other interesting spectacles, two Christians, Agapius and Thecla, along with some other Christians, would fight the beasts. The sensation throughout Palestine was immense, for such exhibitions were uncommon there. On the appointed day, six stalwart young men tied one another's hands tight behind their backs, ran as fast as they could up to Urban, just as he was entering the amphitheatre, and shouted aloud that they were Christians, and were not afraid of wild beasts.

One of the six, Timolaus, came from the distant province of Pontus; Tionysius came from Tripoli in Phoenicia; Romulus was a sub-deacon from Diospolis; Paesis and Alexander were Egyptians, and another Alexander came from Gaza. As soon as the governor and his attendants had recovered themselves they had the six men thrown into prison. There they were visited by a compassionate brother of the last-named Alexander, another Agapius from Gaza, and by another Christian called Dionysius, who looked after their needs. These two visiting Christians looked after the prisoners so well that Urban had them arrested as well. A few days later, all eight Christians were brought out together, condemned, and beheaded.

As soon as Thecla was thrown to the wild beasts she died, but Agapius survived. He languished in prison for two and a half years in Caesarea. At least three times during this time he had been led out with criminals to be executed. But, each time, the governor either had pity on him or lived in hope that he would recant, and had him thrown back into prison. But in November 306, the cruel emperor Maximin came to Caesarea to celebrate his birthday. On such occasions it was customary for the emperor to treat the crowds to a fine show of animals from a foreign country, or to acrobats or jugglers. But the only novelty Maximin had to offer was a pair of criminals to be given to wild beasts. In front of one of them a placard reading, 'Christian, Agapius' was carried. The other man was a slave who had murdered his master. No sooner were they presented before Maximin than the emperor, in the middle of shouts and applause crying for his clemency, bestowed a free pardon on the murderer.

Agapius was paraded around the amphitheatre and exposed to the derision of the spectators. The emperor asked him if he would abandon his Christianity, in which case he would be set at liberty. Agapius refused, callng on the crowd to witness that he had been condemned without committing any crime, except for his belief in the one Almighty God. For this belief Agapius said that he would gladly die, so that his endurance might encourage younger Christians to despise death for the sake of eternal life. The cages were then opened. Agapius ran and flung himself into the arms of a she-bear, which tore him, but did not kill him. He was returned to prison for one more night. On the following day they tied heavy stones to his feet and dropped him into the sea.

¶ A. J. Mason, *The Historic Martyrs of the Primitive Church* (Longmans, 1905), pp. 289–90

Apphian

Apphian was martyred at Caesarea under Urban.

A similar death [to that of Agapius] had been inflicted a little earlier upon one in whom the historian Eusebius was more deeply interested. A young man of nineteen, Apphian, who belonged to a distinguished family in Lycia, had been sent by his heathen parents to complete his education in Beirut. That city was famed for its luxurious vices and its schools, but Apphian surprised everyone by the purity and severity of his life. When his course had finished, he returned home; but during his absence he had embraced the Christian faith, and, finding the heathen atmosphere intolerable, he determined to run away. Casting himself wholly upon the providence of God, he found himself at Caesarea. It was the very place for the studious young Christian. There was the vast library of the learned Pamphilus, who had gathered round him a community of students, of whom Eusebius himself was one. Apphian was welcomed into the community, to which a brother of his already belonged, and threw himself with ardour into the teaching of Pamphilus, living, like his master, a life of stern asceticism.

Apphian had been in Caesarea for nearly a year when an edict was received, requiring the attendance of the whole population at sacrificial rites. Criers passed through the streets summoning men, women, and children to the temples, where military officers stood with lists of the inhabitants, calling them over, name by name. Urban, the governor, was himself in the very act of pouring a libation when the young Apphian, who had told no one what he intended to do, slipped through the band of soldiers and officials in attendance upon him, seized the governor by the right hand and bade him desist from the idolatrous proceeding. With gentle earnestness he warned him that it was not well to turn from the one true God and to sacrifice to devils.

Naturally the guards fell upon the audacious youth, and carried him off into the darkness of the prison, where they left him for the night with his legs in the torturing stocks. Next day he appeared before Urban. The governor bade him sacrifice, and he refused. Then began a dreadful series of tortures. Again and again the young man's ribs were laid open. Blows fell about his head and neck till his face was so swollen and disfigured that no one could have recognised him. Urban told them to soak some rags with oil, and wrap them around his legs, and set fire to them. The juices of his body exuded and dripped with the heat; but Apphian was undaunted. To all questions about himself, his origin, his lodging-place, he only replied that he was a Christian. Next day he was sentenced to death by drowning.

Eusebius eyewitnesses the sequel. An earthquake – no uncommon phenomenon in those parts – shook the city. A violent storm arose in the sea. Amidst the roaring and raging of the elements, the body of the young martyr was thrown up by the waves at the very gate of the city.

¶ A. J. Mason, *The Historic Martyrs of the Primitive Church* (Longmans, 1905), pp. 290–2

Irenaeus

Sirmium, on the Save, a little above its confluence with the Danube, was one of the main seats of the empire during Diocletian's reign. The bishop of Sirmium, at the height of the persecution, was a young man for his station, called Irenaus. Probus, the governor of Pannonia, summoned him.

PROBUS: Obey the divine ordinances.

IRENAEUS: The person who sacrifices to the god and not to God shall be utterly destroyed.

PROBUS: Our most gracious princes have ordered sacrifices to be carried out, or torture to be applied.

IRENAEUS: My orders are to submit to torture rather than to deny God and sacrifice to devils.

PROBUS: Sacrifice, or I must have you tortured.

IRENAEUS: I shall rejoice if you do, that I may take part in my Lord's suffering.

The torture was severely inflicted.

What do you say, Irenaeus – will you sacrifice?
I am sacrificing to my God by a good confession, as I have always done.

Irenaeus' mother and father, and wife and friends were then brought in and they cried in front of him, pleading with him that he was too young to die.

PROBUS: Let their tears deter you from your madness. Think of your youth and sacrifice.

IRENAEUS: I think about my eternal welfare when I decline to sacrifice.

Probus ordered Irenaeus to be thrown into prison where he endured many hardships. In the middle of one night Probus sent for him and ordered him to sacrifice, and so save himself from further troubles.

IRENAEUS: Do as you have been ordered, but you must not expect me to sacrifice. I have a God whom I have learned to worship since I was a child. I adore him. He comforts me in everything, and to him I offer sacrifice, but I cannot worship gods made with hands.

PROBUS: Have you a wife?

IRENAEUS: No.

PROBUS: Have you any children?

IRENAEUS: No.

PROBUS: Have you any mother and father?

IRENAEUS: No.

PROBUS: Then, who were the people crying who were brought into court?

IRENAEUS: One of Jesus Christ's commandments says, 'He that loveth father or mother, or wife or children or kinsfolk, more than me, is not worthy of me.'

Probus then sentenced Irenaeus to be executed with the sword. Irenaeus was led out to one of the bridges over the Save, where he took off his clothes, stretched out his hands towards heaven and prayed, 'O Lord Jesus Christ, who suffered for the salvation of the world, let thy heavens open that the angels may receive the spirit of your servant Irenaeus, who suffers for thy name and for thy people in thy catholic church of Sirmium. I beseech thee, and I entreat thy mercy, that thou receive me and confirm thy faith in them.' Then the sword fell and Irenaeus' body was thrown into the Save.

¶ A. J. Mason, *The Historic Martyrs of the Primitive Church* (Longmans, 1905), pp. 349–51

Quirinus

Quirinus was bishop of Siscia, in the province of Pannonia. He heard that Christians were being arrested so he left Siscia, seeking refuge elsewhere. But he was caught and brought before the local justice, Maximus.

MAXIMUS: Why are you trying to run away from Siscia?

QUIRINUS: I am only obeying the command, 'When they persecute you in one city, flee to another one.'

MAXIMUS: Whose commandment is that?

QUIRINUS: The commandment of Christ, the true God.

MAXIMUS: Do you not know that the emperor's commandments would find you wherever you were? He whom you call the true God cannot help you once you are caught, as you are discovering now.

QUIRINUS: The Lord whom we serve is always with us, and wherever we are, he is able to help us. He was with me when I was caught, and he is here to comfort me, and it is he who answers you through my mouth.

MAXIMUS: You talk a great deal and while you do so you are disobeying the orders of the emperors.

QUIRINUS: I will not listen to the bidding of your emperors because that is sacrilegious, as they command Christ's servants to sacrifice to your gods. I cannot serve them, as they are nothing. My God, whom I serve, is in heaven and earth, and in the sea and everywhere, but is above everything. Everything was made by him and in him everything lives.

MAXIMUS: You have lived too long and have picked up old wives' tales.

Maximus ordered Quirinus to be beaten with sticks.

MAXIMUS: Acknowledge that the gods whom the Roman empire serves are mighty gods. If you comply, you shall be made a priest of the great god Jupiter. If not, you shall be sent and tried by Amantius, the governor of Pannonia Prima. He will pass the death sentence on you which you deserve.

QUIRINUS: I am now discharging the office of priesthood. I am made a priest indeed, if I am allowed to offer my own body to the true God. As for my body being beaten, I like it. It does not hurt me. I am at your disposal for worse tortures so that others may follow me to eternal life which is easily reached by this road.

MAXIMUS: Put him in heavy chains and return him to prison.

QUIRINUS: I have no horror of prison, as God will be with me there.

Three days later Quirinus was taken in heavy chains from town to town along the Danube until he came to Sabaria [Stein-am-Anger] where Amantius was governor. Amantius said he was reluctant to have a man of Quirinus' age whipped. He told Quirinus to sacrifice so that he might spend the rest of his days in peace. Quirinus replied that, old as he was, faith would give him strength greater than all his tortures, that he had no great desire to live, and no fear of dying.

Quirinus was sentenced. Quirinus was to have a stone fixed to his neck and thrown into a river. The road to Scarabantia crossed the river Sibaris over a high bridge, from which the bishop was thrown.

¶ A. J. Mason, *The Historic Martyrs of the Primitive Church* (Longmans, 1905), pp. 360–2

Maxima and Donatilla

Christian women and girls in North Africa were as courageous as the Christian men. Anulinus, the proconsul of Africa, visited Thuburbo and sent off two officers to bring all the Christians there before him to sacrifice. When they arrived they were told to sacrifice or be painfully tortured.

A panic seized the unhappy crowd. Husbands who might have been willing to endure something themselves could not bear the thought of what might be done to their wives. Priests, deacons, people in lesser orders, gave way. Even the young men and virgins had not heart to stand out. All bowed down and worshipped the idols.

The proconsul was also told about two Christians girls, Maxima and Donatilla, who were not present. They were found and brought before Anulinus and they were questioned. He delivered them to be whipped.

Maxima told him that it was no great punishment to have their flesh beaten, when the spirit is saved and the soul is redeemed and comforted. Then the poor girls, with their bruised backs, were forced to lie on broken potsherds and glass. They told Anulinus that they had a great Physician who healed their wounds, and that while he, their judge, was being brought low, they were exalted in glory. They were placed on the hobby-horse. 'It is God's judgment that men should suffer for their Lord,' they said. When it seemed as if they must be exhausted from torture, with their throats parched, Anulinus ordered a drink to be given to them. 'You are foolish,' they said to him, 'have we not our God, the most high, for our refreshment?' The proconsul ordered hot coals to be placed on the hair on their heads. 'It is true,' they said, 'what is written in the law, "We went through fire and water, and came through into a place of refreshment."'

At last Anulinus ordered them to the amphitheatre. It was a joyful sound to them. 'Now our hour is coming,' they said, 'give what sentence you will.' The proconsul confessed that he was tired, and would be glad to be rid of them. 'Tired,' cried the undaunted girls, 'with one hour of it! You have only just come, and you are tired?' The proconsul gave word for a hungry bear to be let loose on them. 'Do as you are bidden,' said Donatilla to the keeper, 'do not fear.'

'In the name of our Lord Jesus Christ we shall conquer you today,' they cried to Anulinus. The bear, as so often happened, only growled and licked Maxima's feet. Then Anulinus read the final judgment from his tablet: 'We order Maxima and Donatilla, to be punished with the sword.' They answered, 'Thanks be to God,' and suffered without further delay. Their bodies were buried within the precincts of the amphitheatre itself.

¶ A. J. Mason, *The Historic Martyrs of the Primitive Church* (Longmans, 1905), pp. 392–4

Theodota
c. 318, Greece

Towards the end of the reign of Licinius a persecution arose in Philippopolis, in Thrace, Greece. Agrippa the prefect, on Apollo's festival, ordered that the whole city should offer a great sacrifice with him. Theodota, who had formerly been a harlot, was accused of refusing to conform, and being called on by the president, answered him, that she had indeed been a grievous sinner, but could not add sin to sin, nor defile herself with a sacrilegious sacrifice. Her constancy encouraged 750 men, probably a troop of soldiers, to step forth, and, professing themselves Christians, to refuse to join in the sacrifice.

Theodota was thrown into prison for twenty days, where she prayed continually. Being brought to the bar she entered the court and burst into tears, and prayed aloud that Christ would pardon the crimes of her past life, and arm her with strength that she might bear with constancy and patience the cruel torments she was to going to suffer. In her answers to the judge she confessed that she had been a harlot, but declared that she had become a Christian, though unworthy to bear that sacred name. Agrippa commanded her to be cruelly scourged. The president ordered her to be hoisted upon the rack, and her body to be torn with an iron comb. Under these torments she earnestly prayed to Christ, and said: I adore you, O Christ, and thank you, because you have made me worthy to suffer this for your name.'

The judge, enraged at her resolution and patience, said to the executioner: 'Tear her flesh again with the iron comb; then pour vinegar and salt into her wounds.'

She said, 'So little do I fear your torments, that I entreat you to increase them to the utmost, that I may find mercy and attain to the greater crown.' Agrippa then commanded the executioners to pluck out her teeth, which they violently pulled out one by one with pincers. The judge at length condemned her to be stoned. She was led out of the city, and, during her martyrdom, prayed thus: 'O Christ, as you showed favour to Rahab the harlot, and received the good thief; so turn not your mercy from me.'

¶ Alban Butler, *The Lives of the Saints* (Dublin, 1833), vol. II, pp. 522–3

Felix

Felix was bishop of Tibiuca, a town near Carthage. The curator sent an official to fetch him. 'Bishop Felix,' he said respectfully, 'give me any books or parchments you possess.'

'I have some,' he answered firmly, 'but I will not give them.'

'What the emperors have commanded,' said the curator, 'must come before what you say. Give me the books, to be burnt with fire.'

The bishop answered, 'I would prefer to be burnt with fire myself than have the sacred Scriptures burnt. It is good to obey God rather than men.'

The curator could only repat his saying, that the emperor's command must come before what the bishop chose to say.

'The commandment of the Lord', answered Felix, 'comes before the commandment of men.'

The magistrate gave him three days to reflect. On the third day he asked him the result of his reflections. 'What I said before', Felix answered, 'I say again now, and I shall say the same before the proconsul.'

'You shall go to the proconsul, then,' said the curator, 'and shall there give your account.'

The bishop was brought to the bar of the proconsul. Anulinus asked him why he had not given up his 'useless books'. Perhaps he intended to give the bishop a hint how to escape from the situation. But Felix was too straightforward to resort to any subterfuge. There was only one end to such determination. 'Slay Felix with the sword,' said Anulinus. Felix cried aloud, 'Thanks be to thee, O Lord, who hast vouchsafed to deliver me.' At the place of execution, he lifted his eyes to heaven, and said, 'Thanks be to thee, O God. I have lived fifty-six years in this world. I have kept my virginity. I have preserved the Gospels. I have preached faith and truth. O Lord God of heaven and earth, O Jesus Christ, I bow my neck as an offering to thee, who abidest for ever, to whom be glory and majesty, for ever.'

¶ A. J. Mason, *The Historic Martyrs of the Primitive Church* (Longmans, 1905), pp. 405–6

Sabas the Goth
372

The faith of Christ erected its trophies not only over the pride and sophistry of the heathen philosophers, and the united powers of the Roman empire, but also over the kings of barbarous infidel nations; who, though in every other thing the contrast of the Romans, and enemies to their name, yet vied with them in the rage with which they sought, by every human stratagem, and every invention of cruelty, to depress the cross of Christ: but they finger of God was sore visible in the propagation of hs faith. Even among the Goths, his name was glorified by the blood of martyrs. Athanaric, king of the Goths, in 370, started to persecute the Christians. The Greeks commemorate fifty-one martyrs who suffered in that nation. The two most illustrious are Nicetas and Sabas.

Sabas was born a Goth, but was converted in his youth and became a faithful imitator of the obedience, mildness, humility, and other virtues of the apostles. He was affable to all men, yet with dignity; a lover of truth, an enemy to all dissimulation or disguise, intrepid and modest. He often spent a whole day or all night in prayer. He burned with an ardent desire in all things to glorify Jesus Christ.

The princes and magistrates of Gothia began, in 370, to persecute the Christians, by compelling them to eat meats which had been sacrificed to idols. In 371 a commissary of the king arrived at Sabas' town in search of Christians. Some of the inhabitants offered to swear that there were no Christians in the place. Sabas appeared, and stepping up to those who were going to take that oath, said: 'Let no man swear for me: for I am a Christian.' The commissary asked the by-standers what wealth he had: and being told he had nothing besides the clothes on his back, the commissary despised him.

The next year Atharidus, son of one that enjoyed a petty sovereignty in that country, entered Sabas' town in the middle of the night, and hauled Sabas from his bed without allowing him to put on his clothes, and dragged him naked over thorns and briars, forcing him along with whips and staves. The persecutors did not have a rack so they took the axle-tree of a cart, laid it on Sabas' neck, and stretching out his hands, fastened them to each end. They fastened another in a similar way to his feet. He was tortured through most of the night in this position. The next morning Atharidus had Sabas' hands tied and had him hung up on a beam of the house. Then he ordered meats that had been sacrificed to idols to be served before him, but Sabas said, 'This pernicious meat is impure and profane, as is Atharidus himself who sent it.' One of the slaves of Atharidus, incensed at these words, struck the point of his javelin against the saint's chest with such force that all present believed that he had been killed.

But Sabas said, 'Do you think you have killed me? Know that I felt no more pain than if the javelin had been a lock of wool.' Atharidus, being informed of these particulars, gave orders that he should be put to death. Sabas was then thrown into the River Musaeus where he drowned.

¶ Alban Butler, *The Lives of the Saints* (Dublin, 1833), vol. I, pp. 459–60

Alban

The city of St Albans derives its name from the first English martyr, the proto-martyr. In 304 a Roman soldier, Alban, was stationed at Ver-ulamium, a Roman town which subsequently changed its name to St Albans. During persecutions during the reign of Emperor Severus, a priest called Amphibalus, from Caerleon, was on the run and arrived in Verulamium looking for shelter. Alban took Amphibalus into his home, even though Alban was not a Christian himself. Alban took note of the hours the priest spent in prayer. He then asked Amphibalus to instruct him in his faith and was quickly earmarked as a protector of Christians and was denounced for this. Soldiers were sent to search his house, but Alban heard they were on the way. So he gave Amphibalus his clothes and let him out of his house through a secret door. Alban just had time to put on the priest's clothes before the soldiers arrived. He was taken before a judge where his disguise was quickly unmasked. In an attempt to make Alban deny his new faith he was ordered to make a sacrifice to the gods, by sprinkling a handful of incense on an altar. As a Christian Alban felt he could not do this. When asked to offer sacrifices to Jupiter and Apollo, Alban replied, 'I confess Jesus Christ, the son of God, with my whole being. Those whom you call gods are idols; they are made by hands.' Alban further enraged the court when he refused to disclose where Amphibalus had escaped to. He was then scourged. Partly because he bore this terrible punishment so patiently he was then sentenced to death.

He was taken across the river Ver, to the top of a nearby hill, which overlooked the city. On the way there the soldier who had been instructed to carry out the execution refused to do this as he himself also followed in Alban's footsteps and embraced Christianity. This resulted in Alban and this Roman soldier both being beheaded. The date for this is now thought to be 22nd June 309 and the abbey marks it annually.

Tradition says that Amphibalus was brought to Redbourne, near Verulamium, where he was terribly tortured before being executed.

¶ Robert Backhouse, *The SPCK Book of Pilgrimages* (forthcoming)

PART THREE

MARTYRS FROM THE 5TH – 15TH CENTURIES

An Old English Martyrology

From an early period, the Christian church endeavoured to keep alive and to celebrate the memory of its martyrs. They compiled martyrologies and remembered martyrs, usually on the anniversary of their death. This English Martyrology is compiled from manuscripts in the libraries of the British Museum and of Corpus Christi College, Cambridge.

The figures in brackets are the age of the martyrs.

DECEMBER

25	Anastasia*	Rome	A glorious martyrdom
26	Eugenia	Rome	Died in prison
26	Stephen	Jerusalem	Stoned to death

JANUARY

3	Anteros	Rome	Suffered martyrdom for Christ
20	Faianus	Rome	Suffered martyrdom for Christ
20	Marius	Rome	Suffered martyrdom for Christ
21	Agnes*	Rome	Suffered martyrdom for Christ (13)
22	Anastasius*	Persia	Beheaded
23	Emerentiana*	Rome	Beheaded
24	Babyllas*	Antochia	Beheaded

– A gap in the manuscripts for several pages now occurs –

MARCH

7	Perpetua* & Felicitas*	Carthage	Suffered martyrdom for Christ
23	Theodoretus	Antioch	Beheaded

APRIL

9	Seven Women*	Sirmium	Suffered martyrdom for Christ
14	Valerianus & Tiburtius*	Rome	Beheaded
18	Eleutherius & Anthia*	Rome	Killed with a sword
25	Mark	Alexandria	Dragged by a rope around his neck
28	Vitalis*	Vicolongo	Burned alive
28	Christophorus	Samos	Beheaded

MAY

3	Alexander*	Rome	Stabbed to death
8	Victor*	Milan	Beheaded
12	Pancratius*	Rome	Beheaded (15)
14	Victor* & Corona	Rome	Beheaded
20	Basilla	Rome	Killed with the sword

JUNE

2	Marcellinus & Petrus	Rome	Beheaded
2	Arthemius	Rome	Killed with the sword
16	Ferreolus & Ferrucius	Besançon	Killed with the sword
17	Nicander & Blastus	Rome	Burned to death
18	Marcus & Marcellinus*	Rome	Beheaded
19	Gervasius & Protasius	Milan	Beaten to death; beheaded
22	James the Less*	Jerusalem	Killed by a weaver's beam
22	Alban	St Albans	Beheaded

JULY

7	Procopius	Caesarea	Beheaded
7	Marina	Antioch	Beheaded
10	Seven brothers*	Rome	Killed by different tortures
10	Rufina & Secunda	Rome	Drowned in River Tiber
14	Phocas	Pontus	Thrown into a burning oven
17	Speratus	Carthage	Beheaded
19	Christina	Tyrus	Drowned at sea

AUGUST

2	Theodota	Nicea	Burned to death
9	Romanus	Rome	Suffered martyrdom for Christ
10	Lawrence	Rome	Roasted alive
12	Euplius*	Catania	Beheaded
13	Hipploytus	Rome	Dragged behind wild horses
17	Mommos	Caesarea	Stoned to death
22	Symphorianus	Autun	Beheaded
25	Bartholomew*	India	Flayed alive
29	John the Baptist		Beheaded
30	Felix*	Venusia	Beheaded

SEPTEMBER

11	Protus* & Hycinthus*	Rome	Beheaded
21	Matthew the apostle		Stabbed with a sword from behind
24	Andochius & Thyrsus	Gaul	Necks broken with cudgels

OCTOBER

8	Dionysius	Paris	Beheaded
24	Sixteen soldiers	Fidenae	Beheaded
31	Quintinus	Rome	Beheaded

NOVEMBER

8	Quattuor Coronati	Rome	Drowned in a locked lead chest
28	Saturninus*	Toulouse	Dragged by a wild bull
30	Andrew	Patras	Crucified

DECEMBER

| 13 | Lucia | Rome | Beheaded |
| 21 | Thomas | India | Stabbed with sword, pierced with spears |

¶ George Herzfeld, *An Old English Martyrology* (Kegan Paul, Trench, Trubner, 1900)

*The following entries give the details about some of the people featured in this old English Martyrology:

December 25 **Anastasia**

On the same day as Christ's birth the churches of God celebrate the birth of St Anastasia the holy lady. She was very noble in the sight of the world and much better before God. The heathen emperor Diocletianus delivered her to his prefect that he might terrify her with tortures, so that she abjured Christ and sacrificed to the idols. The prefect ordered her to be locked up in the dungeon sixty days and nights. After a glorious martyrdom she gave up this present life, and her body rests now in the town of Rome.

January 21 **Agnes**

The passion of the holy virgin St Agnes is on the twenty-first of January. She suffered martyrdom for Christ when she was thirteen years old. Symphronius, a prefect of the town of Rome, tried to compel the virgin by threats to become his son's wife. When she refused this, he commanded her to be led naked to a brothel. When the son of the town prefect was about to ravish her he died, and so the Romans said that she was an enchantress and a sorceress, and a sword was thrust into her throat. Thus she yielded up her spirit to God, and her body rests near the town of Rome on the road called Numentana.

January 22 Anastasius
The holy man Anastasius was at first a sorcerer in the country of Persia, but afterwards he believed in Christ. Cosroas, king of Persia, ordered him to be hung up by one hand and urged him to forswear the belief in God. As he would not consent to this, the king ordered him to be beheaded.

January 23 Emerentiana
Emerentiana was brought up by Agnes, and very boldly reproached the pagans at Rome with their folly, and she was stoned by them, until she sent forth her spirit.

January 24 Babyllas
Babyllas was holy bishop in the town of Antiochia. This bishop defended the door of the church with Christian folks against Numerianus, the heathen emperor. Babyllas said to the emperor, 'Do thou not enter into the house of God, thou hast polluted hands and thou art a devilish wolf.' The emperor commanded him to be beheaded and his three servants with him, one of whom was twelve years, the second nine years, and the third seven years; the names of the servants were Urbanus, Prilidianus, and Epolonius.

April 9 Seven Women
Seven women suffered martyrdom for Christ at Sirmium in Pannonia. Their names are: Saturnina, Hilarina, Dominando, Rogantina, Serotina, Donata, Paulina.

April 14 Valerianus and Tiburtius
The brothers Valerianus and Tiburtius were urged under tortures by Almachius, prefect of Rome, to abjure Christ. As they would not submit to this, he commanded them to be beheaded. The man who saw them beheaded believed in God, and he was scourged to death for Christ's sake; his name was Maximus.

April 18 Eleutherius and Anthia
Eleutherius was bishop of Mechania in Apulia, but later suffered martyrdom at Rome for Christ's sake. The emperor Hadrianus urged him by threats to renounce Christ. As he refused to do this, the emperor ordered four horses to be hitched to a cart, and for Eleutherius to be

placed in fetters and dragged behind the cart, so that the wild horses might run over rough paths in the desert and break all his limbs. Then the emperor ordered him to be killed with a sword. Then Eleutherius' mother, Anthia, threw herself on to her son's body. The emperor ordered Anthia to be martyred also, and praising God she gave up her spirit.

April 28 Vitalis

The body of Vitalis rests at Vicolongo, that is, in the long town. Vitalis was first a soldier of the emperor under the consul Paulinus in the town of Ravenna, but then he believed in Christ and converted other people to the Christian faith. The consul grew angry at this and forced him to worship idols. As he would not submit to it, the consul commanded men to dig a deep hole and to put him into it alive, and to fill it from above with earth and stones, until he gave up his spirit.

May 3 Alexander

On the third day of the month is the martyrdom of the young pope Alexander in Rome and of two priests with him who were called Eventius and Theodolus. The prefect Aurelianus who killed the Christians there urged them to forswear Christ. As they would not submit to this, he commanded them all three to be thrown into a burning oven. As the fire would not burn them, he ordered the priests to be beheaded and the pope to be stabbed to death.

May 8 Victor

This Victor was of Moorish descent, and he was a soldier of the heathen emperor Maximianus, but he was a Christian. The emperor advised him to give up the faith of Christ. As he would not agree to this he was threatened with tortures. He commanded molten lead to be poured on him, but that did not harm him any more than cold water. Then he bade his jesters lead him to a wood and behead him there.

May 12 Pancratius

The noble youth Pancratius was only fifteen years old when he suffered death for the Christian faith. He was was born in the country of Phrygia of an illustrious family, his father's name was Clendonius, and his mother's name Cyriada, and he was baptised at Rome by the pope Cornelius. Then the pagan emperor Diocletianus advised him to forswear Christ, and declared that he then would make him as wealthy as if he were his own son. As he would not consent to this, he ordered him to be beheaded on the road at Rome called Aurelia.

May 14 Victor and Corona

This Victor came from the country of Cilicia. He was a soldier of the emperor Antoninus, yet he believed in Christ. Sebastian, the heathen prefect of Egypt, tried to compel him to worship idols. As he would not assent to this, he bade a certain sorcerer give him meat that was poisoned with the strongest poison, and that did not hurt him. Then he ordered him to be flayed alive.

There was the wife of another soldier, Corona by name, who was young and had been married one year and four months. She said to Victor, 'Blessed art thou, Victor, and thy holy works are blessed. I see two crowns coming from heaven, the larger one is thine, and the smaller mine.' On account of this apparition the woman believed in Christ, and then the prefect ordered them both to be martyred.

June 18 Marcus and Marcellinus

These illustrious men were brothers and both were Christians. The emperor Diocletian commanded that they should sacrifice to the idols, or else be beheaded. As they went to the execution, their father and mother and their two wives with many children came to meet them and implored them to forsake the faith of Christ. When their mind turned to the worship of idols, St Sebastian, the Christian hero, heard of this and began to show them how insignificant and how shameful a man's life is in this world, and how long and how fearful the eternal punishment, and how glorious the eternal happiness, until their hearts turned to Christ again; and they kissed each other and were martyred for Christ's sake.

June 22 James the Less

On the twenty-second day of the month is the commemoration of the apostle and messenger of God who in Scripture is called James the son of Alpheus. After the Lord's ascension he was bishop in Jerusalem. He never ate meat nor drank wine nor used woollen garments, but only linen ones, nor did he care for bathing, nor did he shorten his locks with scissors nor clip his beard with a knife; but he always earnestly prayed to God, so that his skin grew hard on the knees as the knees of a camel are. This James was killed by the Jewish scribes with a weaver's beam because they hated Christ.

August 12 Euplius

Euplius carried Christ's gospel in a case on his shoulders wherever he went. He came into the town of Catania and went into the courthouse, where the judge Calvisianus was in a large assembly with heathen folks. There Euplius uncovered Christ's gospel and told the people what the four evangelists said about the terrible judgment of God. For that reason the judge became angry and ordered him to be beheaded, and when he was led to his martyrdom, heaven was opened, and he saw our Lord in his glory.

August 25   Bartholomew

The apostle Bartholomew was Christ's messenger in India. In this country he destroyed the images that had been worshipped before. The king of that nation received baptism and his queen and all the people that belonged to his dominion. The heathen bishops then went and complained about this to the king's brother, who was in another kingdom and was older than he was. The older brother therefore ordered Bartholomew, the servant of Christ, to be flayed alive. Then the believing king came with a strong army and took his body and brought it away with great glory and buried it in a wonderful large church.

September 11   Protus and Hyacinthus

Protus and Hyacinthus were servants of the noble virgin Eugenia, and they received baptism with her. In the days of Gallienus, Nicetius, the town-reeve of Rome, ordered them to be brought to the idol of Mars and bade them worship it. When they offered a prayer to God, the idol fell down at their feet and was entirely broken. The reeve ordered them to be beheaded for this, and they were made Christ's martyrs.

November 28   Saturninus

Saturninus lived in Toulouse and because of the bishop's sanctity all the idols that were worshipped in the town were silent. Therefore the heathen townspeople became angry with him and bound the holy bishop by his feet to a bull and made it fierce, so that it rushed over stony ground and crushed the bishop's head: all his limbs were torn, and he gave up his spirit to Christ.

¶ These entries and the Old English Martyrology have been compiled from the following four manuscripts: British Museum, Add. MS. 23211 and Cod. Cotton. Julius A X; Corpus Christi College, Cambridge, nos. 196 and 41. They illustrate what particular details of the martyr's life and martyrdom were originally thought worth remembering.

Martyrs of Najran

While Jews and Christians were battling for control over Arabia, before the rise of Islam, a widespread persecution of Christians by Jews took place from about 520, which was centred on the Arab city of Najran. When Ethiopia conquered South Arabia it resulted in its Christian evangelisation.

The following extracts are summaries of a 'Letter' by Simeon of Beth-Arsham, regarded as a primary source, recording these persecutions and martyrdoms.

Paul

After the Jews captured the Christians in the city of Najran they ordered them to show them the bones of their martyrs. They brought the bones of their bishop, Paul, who had been consecrated the first bishop of Najran by Philoxenos, the bishop of Hierapolis. Paul had won his martyr's crown by being stoned by Jews from Tiberias.

Martyrs and church burnt

The Jews made a great heap of all the bones of Christian martyrs in the centre of the church. Then they crammed the church full of two thousand Christians, including readers, deacons, sons of the covenant and daughters of the covenant, presbyters and subdeacons. The Jews then encircled the church with wood and set fire to the wood and to the inside of the church.

Some women who had not been caught, but who were companions to those inside the church, saw the church on fire. They ran to the church, shouting to each other, 'Come, companions,' as they ran into the fire and were also burnt.

Elizabeth

Elizabeth, the sister of the former bishop Paul, had been hidden in a house by Christians. When she found out that the church, the bones of her brother and the sons of the covenant were being burnt, she left her place of hiding and went to the burning church, saying, 'I go with you all to Christ.' With that she went into the church's court where the Jews saw her and seized her. The Jews thought that she had escaped from the burning church and concluded that she must be a witch. Elizabeth protested that she came from outside the church and that she wanted to die inside the church with her companions, saying, 'I want to be burnt in the church where I served, along with my brother's bones and with my companions.' She was forty-seven years old.

But the Jews tied her up with thin ropes after making her bend her head and knees like a camel. They tortured her with ropes on her legs, arms, breasts and temples. Then they placed a crown of mud on her head, and mocked her, saying, 'Take your crown, servant of the carpenter's son.' Then they poured boiling oil on her head, before taking her outside the city, where they stripped her naked and tied her legs with ropes which were then attached to a wild camel. These ropes had wooden bells on them so the camel ran off into the desert, and so the blessed Elizabeth received her crown.

A child of eight

An eight-year-old boy was found by the Jews wandering among the corpses from the burnt church. They took him to their king who asked the boy, 'Who were you looking for among the corpses?' The boy replied that he was searching for his father, so that he might die with him. He said, 'I am not going to leave you until you kill me as you killed my father and my mother. I do not want them to go to Christ without me.' The king responded by ordering the boy's execution by being beheaded.

¶ Irfan Shahid, *The Martyrs of Najran: New Documents* (Brussels: Société des Bollandistes, 1971), pp. 46, 47, 49–51, 61

Anastasius
Persia, 628

St Anastasius was a trophy of the holy cross of Christ, when it was carried away into Persia by Chosroes, in 614, after he had taken and plundered Jerusalem. The martyr was a Persian, son of a Magian, instructed in the sciences of that sect, and a young soldier in the Persian troops. Upon hearing the news of the taking of the cross by his king, he became very inquisitive concerning the Christian religion. Its sublime truths made such an impression on his mind, that when he returned to Persia from an expedition into the Roman empire, he left the army and went to Hierapolis. In Hierapolis he stayed with a devout Christian, who was a silversmith. He went to Jerusalem to be baptised and changed his Persian name of Magundat, to that of Anastasius, meaning according to the signification of that Greek word, that he was raised from death to a new and spiritual life. In 621 he became a monk in a monastery five miles from Jerusalem, where the abbot, Justin, had his hair cut off, and put him in monastic habit.

On a visit to Garizim, seven years later, which was then under the control of the Persians, Anastasius saw Persian soothsayers from the garrison occupied in their abominable superstitions in the streets. Anastasius spoke boldly against them and was arrested by the Persian magistrate, on suspicion of being a spy. Anastasius informed them that he had once enjoyed the dignity of Magian with them, and had renounced it to become a humble follower of Christ. Upon this confession he was thrown into prison. Marzabanes, the governor of the city commanded him to be chained by the foot to another criminal, and his neck and one foot to be also linked together by a heavy chain, and condemned him in this condition to carry heavy stones.

Anastasius was later transferred to Barsaloe in Assyria, six miles from Discartha, near the Euphrates, where the king was. There he was beaten with staves for three days, then laid on his back, and a heavy beam placed on his legs, which crushed his flesh and bones. Then he was hung up for two hours by one hand, with a great weight at his feet. The judge, despairing to overcome him, went to the king for his orders, which were, that Anastasius should be executed. The sixty-eight other Christian prisoners were strangled one after another, on the banks of the river, in front of Athanasius. All the time the judge urged Athanasius to return to Persian worship, and to escape so disgraceful a death, promising, in case of compliance, that he should be made one of the greatest men in the court. Anastasius, with his eyes lifted up to heaven, gave thanks to God for bringing his life to so happy a conclusion. He was accordingly strangled, and after his death he head was cut off. This was in 628, the seventeenth of the emperor Heraclius, on 22nd January.

¶ Alban Butler, *The Lives of the Saints* (Dublin, 1833), vol. I, pp. 95–6

Kilien

Kilien was born in Ireland, and received from his parents a pious and Christian education. In the course of time he crossed the sea, with eleven other people, in order to make converts on the Continent. On arriving at the city of Wurtzburg, they found the people in general, with their governor Gozbert, to be pagans, but conceived great hopes of converting them to the gospel faith. Gozbert directed the attention of his heathen subjects to the preaching of the prelate; and the greater part of them became Christians in less than two years.

Gozbert had married his brother's widow; Kilien entreated him, as the proof of his sincerity, to quit the person whom he had looked up as his wife, as he could not retain her without sin. Gozbert, surprised at the proposal, told the bishop this was the hardest test he had ever exacted from him. 'But,' he said, 'since I have renounced my own inclinations and pleasures in so many particulars for the love of God, I will make the work complete by complying with your advice in this too.'

His wife, however, determined to take revenge on those who had persuaded Gozbert to adopt such a resolution. She accordingly sent to the place where they were assembled, and had them all beheaded. Kilien and his companions submitted without resistance, the former telling them that they need not fear those who had no power over the soul, but could only kill the body, which in a short time would perish in the course of nature. This happened in 689, and the martyrs were privately buried in the night, together with their books, clothes and all that they had.

¶ John Foxe, *The Book of Martyrs,* revised with notes and an appendix by W. Bramley-Moore (London, 1869), pp. 54–5

The Hewalds

Bede records that after Willibrord preached in Frisia many people were converted to Christ resulting in his companions the Hewalds being martyred, in 692.

Egbert, the man of God, perceived that God did not wish him to go and preach to the heathen, so he sent Willibrord and twelve of his companions to preach in western Frisia. Many turned from worshipping idols to believing in Christ. Two more English priests followed in their wake and preached in the province of the Old Saxons. These priests both had the same name, but due to their very different coloured hair, one was called Hewald the Black, and the other Hewald the White. Both men were devout and religious and sang psalms and said prayers and brought holy cups and a consecrated table to serve as an altar for their daily sacrifice of the Saviour to God.

When the Old Saxons realised that the Hewalds practised a different religion from them they began to fear them. They were afraid that they might ask their God to convert them to their religion and so the whole province would go over to the new religion. They suddenly attacked them. They put Hewald the White to the sword at once, but made Hewald the Black suffer a lingering death, as they tore him apart, limb by limb. Their bodies were then thrown into the Rhine, on 3rd October.

¶ *The English Martyrs under Henry VIII and Elizabeth 1535–1583* (Catholic Truth Society, 1901), pp. 280–2

Christian martyrs in Muslim Spain

Between 850 and 859 forty-eight Christians were decapitated in the Spanish town of Cordoba for religious offences against Islam. All these martyrdoms were recorded by Eulogius, a Cordoban priest, so that he could write up passions which would perpetuate the memory of these Christian martyrs through his martyrology.

Isaac
The first of these forty-eight martyrs was Isaac. Due to his noble birth he rose to the highest rank in the local government that a non-Muslim was allowed, that of secretary of the covenant (*katib adh-dhimam*). He gave all this up and went to live in a monastery close to Cordoba, in Tabanos. Isaac visited Cordoba three years later to ask a judge about some details of Islamic law. This official spoke about Muhammad's life and this launched Isaac into a full scale attack on Islam in

which he affirmed that its prophet was being tormented in hell for misleading the Arabs.

The judge was amazed at this outburst and concluded that Isaac must be either drunk or mad. But Isaac assured the judge that he was compelled to so outspoken because of the 'zeal of righteousness'. Isaac was promptly arrested, sentenced. His decapitated body was left hanging for all to see.

Sanctius

Two days after Isaac's martyrdom Sanctius, a young Christian soldier, was also decapitated, for the same reason. It is not clear if Isaac's example had inspired Sanctius, but it is known that six more Christians were so greatly influenced by Sanctius' example that Cordoba had six more dead Christians within forty-eight hours of Sanctius' death.

Six more martyrs

The deacon Walabonsus and the priest Petrus came to study in Cordoba. Two monks, Sabinianus and Wistremundus from the monastery at St Zoylus, were also visiting Cordoba. Habentius, who came from Cordoba and the founder of a monastery at Tabanos, and Hieremia, made up the last two of this group of six Christians. All six went before the judge together and made their intentions very plain when they said that they confessed the same faith as Isaac and Sanctius. They boldly stated that Christ was God and that Muhammad was the antichrist. They were speedily executed.

Helios, Paulus and Isidorus

On 16th April 856, a priest from western Spain, Helios, and two monks, Paulus and Isidorus, committed blasphemy in the eyes of the Muslims and were also speedily dispatched.

Aurea

Aurea's father was a Muslim, but Aurea had lived with her mother as a nun in a convent, without any of her Muslim relatives finding out. Aurea had witnessed the martyrdom of her two brothers, Joannes and Adulphus, as well as three people from her convent, Maria, Walabonsus and Petrus. When some of Aurea's relatives discovered Aurea they brought her before the judge. Aurea was given the choice of renouncing her Christian faith or being executed. Aurea chose the former. But her conscience plagued her and she continued to live as a Christian, until she met up with her family, who ensured that she was imprisoned and executed for being a follower of Christ.

Five Friars Minor, 1220

Berardus, Peter, Acursius, Adjutus and Otto were sent by St Francis to preach to the Muslims in the west, while he went in person to those of the east. They preached first to the Moors of Seville, where they suffered much for their zeal, and were banished. Passing on from there to Morocco, they began to preach Christ there, and being banished returned again. The infidel judge had them scourged until their ribs appeared bare. He then ordered burning oil and vinegar to be poured into their wounds, and their bodies to be rolled over sharp stones and potsherds. At length the king brought them before him, and taking his scimitar, clove their heads asunder in the middle of their foreheads, on the 16th of January, 1220.

¶ Alban Butler, *The Lives of the Saints* (Dublin, 1833), vol. I, p. 72

Thomas à Becket

'We rejoice and mourn in the death of martyrs. We mourn, for the sin of the world that has matyred them; we rejoice, that another soul is numbered among the Saints in Heaven, for the glory of God and for the salvation of men' (T. S. Eliot, Murder in the Cathedral).

The year 1170 saw the fateful killing of Archbishop Thomas Becket by Henry II's knights, on the steps leading up to the cathedral's high altar. Less than three years later Becket was declared a saint and pilgrims flocked to his grave in their thousands. Today the spot of Becket's murder is marked by a six-inch-square stone. On a wall nearby the following words are carved:

Thomas Becket
Archbishop. Saint. Martyr.
Died here
Tuesday 29th December
1170

In the struggle between State and Church it was not possible for Becket to be neutral. From the moment of his consecration all Becket's efforts were directed against the power of the King, Henry II. By 1164 the breach was complete and Becket went into exile in France for six years, calling himself Brother Dearlove. Henry took out his rage on Becket's friends and followers and it was probably this, more than anything else, which brought all England to Becket's side.

Early in 1170, the King and the Archbishop patched up their quarrel near Freteval and on 1st December Becket returned to England. But Becket knew that his life was in danger. The day after his return he preached in the chapter house on the text, 'Here we have no abiding city, but we seek one to come'. On Christmas Day, he preached his famous sermon in Canterbury Cathedral, using the familiar text, 'I come to die among you.' The clash between monarch and archbishop over the immunity of the clergy from secular jurisdiction could not be resolved. In Becket's absence Henry II had arranged for his son Henry to be crowned as his successor and colleague by the Archbishop of York, assisted by the Bishops of London and Salisbury. Since Augustine's day the crowning of monarchs had always been performed by the Archbishop of Canterbury, so Becket procured letters from the Pope against the these three men. They went to see Henry in France and told him, 'As long as Thomas Becket lives you will have neither good days, nor peaceful kingdom, nor quiet life.' These words produced the following outcry from Henry, 'A fellow that I have loaded with benefits; a fellow who came to court on a lame horse, with a cloak for a saddle, sits without hindrance on the throne itself. What sluggard wretches, what cowards have I brought up in my court! Not one will deliver me from this low-born priest.' Henry then rushed from the room. Among the courtiers to hear this outburst were four knights, Hugh de Moreville, Richard de Bret, Reginal Fitzurse and Sir William Tracy. They crossed over to England and surprised Becket by suddenly appearing in his room in Canterbury on the morning of 29th December 1170. They felt repulsed by the determined words of the archbishop and they withdrew to arm themselves so they could arrest him. The primate's servants then locked all the gates, but Randulf del Broc, whom the four knights were staying with, being the King's custos of the see of Canterbury, was able to guide the knights back to Becket's rooms, by way of the orchard. Becket's monks had advised him to flee, but as he would not, they hastily guided the archbishop into the church, by way of the cloisters. But the knights caught up with Becket as he passed the north transept and was going up the steps leading to the choir. The presence of the four armed knights made everyone except three men desert Becket's side: Robert Canon of Merton, William Fitzstephen the historian, and Edward Grim, a clerk who later wrote up an accurate account of the event.

Reginald Fitzurse seized Becket by his pall, intending to drag him back across the church, but the archbishop managed to cling to a pillar, so one of the other knights struck him with the flat of his sword. Then Becket shouted: 'Touch me not, Reginald Fitzurse! Why should you treat me thus? I have granted you many favours. You are my man, and owe fealty and obedience – you and your fellows.' Fitzurse replied, 'I owe you no fealty inconsistent with that I owe to my lord the King.' Becket was then wounded in the head by a blow that might have killed him had not his faithful clerk, Edward Grim, cushioned the blow by using his own arm. Richard le Bret then struck Becket with such force that the point of his sword, after striking Becket, was broken off. (This broken piece of sword was later preserved as a relic of the martyrdom.)

Richard le Bret's thrust proved fatal, but was followed by a despicable deed, carried out by Hugh of Horsea, a subdeacon. He placed his own foot on the neck of the archbishop, as he lay on the ground, and with his sword drew out Becket's brains, scattering them over the pavement, exclaiming, 'Let us be off. He will rise no more!' Only one of the four knights had struck no blow, Hugh de Moreville, a man of gentle disposition, who kept the crowds from becoming involved by preventing them from going beyond the transept where the murder took place. The knights then left: 'with a savage burst of triumph they ran, shouting as if in battle the watchword of the kings of England, "The king's men! The king's men!",' wounding a servant of the archdeacon of Sens for lamenting this horrific murder.

When Becket's body was finally lifted, it was discovered that he was wearing an extremely coarse horse-hair shirt. The medieval people were quick to respond to the tragedy. Becket had been the first Englishman to defy autocratic power. His supporters knew that they were fighting against evil actions. Because Becket stood out as a burning light in the dark struggle against tyranny, tens of thousands of people visited his shrine from all over the world.

¶ Robert Backhouse, *The SPCK Book of Pilgrimages* (forthcoming)

Seven Friars Minor
1221

Seven zealous priests from the Franciscan order, Daniel, the provincial of Calabria, Samuel, Angelus, Donulus, Leo, Nicholas, and Hugolin, sailed to Africa in 1221, to announce Christ to the Muslims. They arrived at Ceuta where they preached for three days in the suburbs of the city, where Christians lived. Then they went into the heart of the city where the infidels lived and preached Christ to them. The populace hearing them immediately took fire, covered them with mire and filth, and carried them before the king, whose name was Mahomet. From their rough habits and shorn heads he took them for madmen, but sent them to the governor of the town. By him, after a long examination, they were remanded to the king, who condemned them to be beheaded. They suffered with great joy in 1221, on 10th October.

¶ Alban Butler, *The Lives of the Saints* (Dublin, 1833), vol. II, p. 655

Antony, John and Eustachius
Lithuania, 1342

Antony, John and Eustachius were three noblemen from Lithuania. Antony and John were brothers. In Lithuania they were called Kukley, Mihley, and Nizilo. They were all chamberlains to Olgerd, the great duke of Lithuania, who governed there from 1329 to 1381. They also attended on the great duchess, and were worshippers of fire, according to the idolatrous superstition of that country, till they had the happiness to be converted to the Christian faith, and baptised by a priest called Nestorius.

For refusing to eat forbidden meats on fastdays, they were cast into prison, and, after many trials, put to death by order of Olgerd, the great duke: John, the eldest, on 24th April, his brother Antony on 14th June, and the youngest Eustachius, on 13th December. Eustachius endured many tortures before his execution. He was beaten with clubs, had his legs broken, the hair and skin of his head violently torn off, because he would not allow his hair to be shaved, according to the custom of the heathen. They suffered at Vilna, about 1342, and were buried in the church of the Holy Trinity, of the Russian-Greek rite, united in communion to the Roman Catholic church.

¶ Alban Butler, *The Lives of the Saints* (Dublin, 1833), vol. I, p. 467

Ramon Lull

'I desire to be a fool that I may give honour and glory to God, and I will have no art nor device in my words by reason of the greatness of my love' (Ramon Lull, Blanquerna, chapter 79).

Ramon Lull, who delighted to call himself the Fool of Love, was an influential writer and missionary in the Middle Ages. He was martyred in 1315 or 1316.

The aged 83-year-old 'white-bearded old apostle' was more successful in his third African mission in Tunis than his previous two. One chronicler relates that among his converts were some of the most influential and learned Moors of the city. This may have been the reason why people stopped being tolerant towards him. From Tunis, Lull went to Bugia where, throwing caution to the winds, the Fool of Love went out boldly into the streets, proclaiming in a loud voice the truth of the religion for which he had spent his life. A hostile crowd gathered round him. Without putting up any resistance the aged Lover of Christ allowed the cruel stones to crash into his frail body. The moment of his departure had come, a moment which he had looked forward to since as a young convert he had written in his *Book of Contemplation,* 'Thy servant and subject, O Lord, hath very great fear of dying a natural death for he would fain have his death the noblest that is, namely, death for thy love.' Lull had his wish and he died a Christian martyr.

Joan of Arc

'If I were to say that God had not sent me, I would be damning myself, for it is true that God did send me' (Joan of Arc).

Joan of Arc was burned by the English on 29th May 1431 at Rouen, and while not officially recognised as 'a martyr of the church' in the Roman Catholic calender, is regarded as the national saint of France, and 489 years after her death, was canonised, in 1920.

On 8th May 1429, Joan of Arc, dressed in white armour, successfully led the French army against the English siege of Orleans. A few days later Joan inflicted a crushing defeat on the English on the Loire, resulting in Charles being crowned king on 17th July at Rheims, flanked by Joan, holding her standard. However, when Joan was captured by the Burgundians at Compiègne on 23rd May 1430, King Charles never lifted a finger to help her, even after she had been sold by the Duke of Burgundy to the English on 21st November.

All the English wanted to do with Joan of Arc was to pass sentence on her as a heretic and a sorceress. Joan endured six public and nine private sessions which all amounted to a most biased trial. Joan admitted quite categorically during her trial that 'God sent a voice to guide me'. She was told that her voices, inner convictions and visions all emanated from the devil and only a heretic would place her voices above the teaching and wisdom of the church. Wearing men's clothes was used as corroborating evidence that Joan was evil.

Joan suffered a terrible imprisonment. She was denied all the comforts of the Church as she was denied a place in the ecclesiastical prison and was thrown into a common cell, where she was chained to a block of wood, and denied a bed. Joan was condemned for being apostate, a heretic and a sorceress. But, just after she was excommunicated and pronounced a heretic, Joan broke down. For a brief time, she agreed to follow the Church in everything and she no longer insisted that she had received visions and revelations and heard voices. Joan's relapse was short-lived. When Bishop Cauchon visited her cell she told him that her voices had started again and had told her, 'They told me that through them God sent me his pity of the betrayal to which I consented in making the abjuration and revocation to save my life and that in saving my life I was damning myself. If

I were to say that God had not sent me, I would be damning myself, for it is true that God did send me.' This statement sent Joan to her death. On 29th May 1431 Joan was condemned as a relapsed heretic and on Wednesday 30th May at 8.00 a.m. was burned by the British at the stake at Rouen. Joan died a teenager, nineteen years of age.

The Waldenses

Pope Innocent VIII, in 1488, determined to persecute the Waldenses (named after Peter Waldo of Lyons who opposed some of the teachings of the Pope). To this end he sent Albert de Capitaneis, Archdeacon of Cremona, to France. The lieutenant readily granted his assistance, but when they arrived in the valley, they found that it had been deserted by the inhabitants, who had fled to the mountains, and hid themselves in dens and caves of the earth. The archdeacon and lieutenant immediately followed them with their troops, and catching many, threw them over precipices, resulting in them being dashed to pieces. Several, however, hid in the innermost parts of the caverns, where they were able to remain concealed. The archdeacon and lieutenant not being able to find them, ordered the mouths of the caves to be filled with faggots, which being lighted, those inside were suffocated. On searching the caves, numerous children were found suffocated, either in their cradles or in their mothers' arms; and a total of about 3,000 men, women, and children were destroyed in this persecution.

¶ John Foxe, *The Book of Martyrs,* revised with notes and an appendix by W. Bramley-Moore (London, 1869), pp. 60–2

PART FOUR

MARTYRS FROM THE REFORMATION ERA

John Huss

Under the story of John Huss Bunyan wrote in his copy of Foxe's
Book of Martyrs *that he had with him during his own 12-year*
imprisonment:

> *Heare is John hus that you may see,*
> *Uesed in deed with all crulity;*
> *But now leet us follow and look one him,*
> *whear he is full field in deed to the brim.*

'Christianity has stayed faithful, with no pope – who is only a man, *because it has Jesus Christ at its head. Christ is its guide. The life of grace is its heartbeat, from which flow the seven gifts of the Holy Spirit. It is to Christ, wretched though I am, that I flee, in the sure hope that he will guide me with his life and help. I trust that he will deliver me from my sins and from my existing wretched life and will give me the reward of infinite joy'* (Letter from Huss to two of his *friends).*

John Huss was a Bohemian by birth, and born in the village of Hussinetz, in about 1380. His parents gave him the best education they could bestow, and, having acquired a tolerable knowledge of the classics at a private school, he was then sent to Prague University.

As pastor of the church of Bethlehem in Prague, and rector of the university, Huss soon became famous for his preaching and bold proclamation of the truth which quickly attracted the notice and excited the malignity of the Pope and his followers.

The principal reason which aroused Huss's indignation was a bull published by Pope John XXIII which promised remission of sins to everyone who joined his forces against Ladislaus, King of Naples. When the bull was published in Prague Huss did not refrain from preaching against it as repugnant to the spirit of the Christian faith. The Pope summoned Huss to Rome, and, upon his refusing to comply, excommunicated him, and forbade divine service to be performed in all the churches in Prague, except for one, so long as Huss remained in the city. To avoid disturbances, Huss moved to Hussinetz.

The teachings of the English reformer, Wycliffe, were eagerly received in Bohemia by many people, especially by John Huss and his friend and fellow-martyr, Jerome of Prague.

The Pope summoned Huss to appear before the court at Rome to answer the accusations levelled against him about his preaching. Eventually three proctors appeared for Dr Huss before Cardinal Colonna: they pleaded an excuse for Huss's absence, and said they were ready to answer on his behalf. But the cardinal declared him contumacious, and, accordingly, excommunicated him. Notwithstanding such a severe decree, and an expulsion from his church in Prague, he moved again to Hussinetz, where he continued to promulgate the truth, both from the pulpit and with the pen.

In November 1414 a general council assembled at Constance in Germany to resolve the dispute between three people contesting for the papal throne: John, supported by the Italians; Gregory, supported by the French, and Benedict supported by the Spaniards. John Huss was summoned to appear before this council together with a certificate of safe conduct, but, according to the maxim of this same council, that 'faith is not to be kept with heretics,' when Huss entered the city he was arrested, and imprisoned in the palace.

While Huss was in prison the council acted like the inquisitors. They condemned all the teaching of Wycliffe and ordered his remains to be exhumed, and burned to ashes, which was carried out.

When Huss was brought before the council he was accused of twenty-six heresies. The council pronounced him a heretic condemning him to be burned as such, unless he recanted. Huss was then thrown into a filthy prison, where, during the day, he was so laded with chains that he could hardly move, and at night was fastened by his hands to a ring on the prison wall.

Soon after Huss had been condemned four bishops and two lords were sent by the emperor to the prison, in order to prevail on Huss to recant. But Huss called God to witness, with tears in his eyes, that he was not conscious of having preached or written anything against God's truth, or against the faith of his orthodox church. The deputies then represented the great wisdom and authority of the council: to which Huss replied, 'Let them send the meanest person of that council, who can convince me by argument from the word of God, and I will submit my judgment to him.' The deputies, finding they could not make any impression on him, departed, greatly astonished at the strength of his resolve.

On 4th July Huss, for the last time, was brought before the council. After a long examination he was commanded to abjure, which, without hesitation, he refused to do. The Bishop of Lodi then preached a sermon concerning the destruction of heretics, from the text, 'Let the body of sin be destroyed.' The council then censured him for being obstinate and incorrigible, and ordained that he should be degraded from the priesthood, his books publicly burnt, and himself delivered to the secular powers.

Huss received the sentence without the slightest emotion; and then knelt down, lifted up his eyes towards heaven, exclaiming, with the magnanimity of a primitive martyr, 'May thy infinite mercy, O my God! pardon this injustice of mine enemies. Thou knowest the injustice of my accusations: how deformed with crimes I have been represented; how I have been oppressed with worthless witnesses, and a false condemnation; yet, O my God! let that mercy of thine, which no tongue can express, prevail with thee not to avenge my wrongs.'

But these excellent sentences were received as so many expressions of treason, and only tended to inflame his adversaries. Accordingly, the bishops appointed by the council stripped him of his priestly garments, degraded him, and put a paper mitre on his head, on which they painted three devils, with this inscription: 'Heresiarch' [Heretic]. This mockery was received by the martyr with an air of unconcern, and seemed to give him dignity rather than disgrace. A serenity appeared in his looks, which indicated that his soul was approaching the realms of everlasting happiness; and when the bishop urged him to recant, he turned to the people and addressed them thus.

> These lords and bishops do counsel me that I should confess before you all that I have erred; which thing, if it might be done with the infamy and reproach of men only, they might, peradventure, easily persuade me to do; but now I am in the sight of the Lord my God, without whose great displeasure I could not do that which they require. For I well know that I never taught any of those things which they have falsely accused me of, but I have always preached, taught, written, and thought contrary thereunto. Should I by this my example trouble so many consciences, endued with the most certain knowledge of the Scriptures and of the gospel of our Lord Jesus Christ? I will never do it, neither commit any such offence, that I should seem to esteem this vile carcass appointed unto death more than their health and salvation.

At this most godly word he was forced again to hear that he did obstinately persevere in his pernicious errors.

After the ceremony of degradation the bishops delivered him to the emperor, who handed him over to the Duke of Bavaria. His books were burnt at the gates of the church; and on 6th July he was led to the suburbs of Constance to be burnt alive.

Having reached the place of execution, he fell on his knees, sung several portions from the Psalms, and looked steadfastly towards heaven, saying, 'Into thy hands, O Lord! do I commit my spirit: thou hast redeemed me, O most good and faithful God.'

As soon as the chain was put around him at the stake, he said, with a smiling countenance, 'My Lord Jesus Christ was bound with a harder chain than this for my sake: why, then, should I be ashamed of this old rusty one?' Then he prayed: 'Lord Jesus Christ, it is for the sake of the gospel and the preaching of the word that I patiently undergo this ignominious death.'

When the faggots were piled around him, he said, 'I never preached any doctrine of an evil tendency; and what I taught with my lips I now seal with my blood.' He then said to the executioner, 'You are now going to burn a goose (the meaning of Huss's name in Bohemian), but in a century you will have a swan whom you can neither roast nor boil.' If this were spoken in prophecy, he must have alluded to Martin Luther, who came about a hundred years after him, and had a swan for his arms.

As soon as the faggots were lighted, the martyr sang a hymn, with so cheerful a voice, that he was heard above the cracklings of the fire and the noise of the multitude. At length his voice was interrupted by the flames, which soon put an end to his existence. His ashes were collected, and, by order of the council, thrown into the Rhine, lest his adherents should honour them as relics.

¶ John Foxe, *The Book of Martyrs,* revised with notes and an appendix by W. Bramley-Moore (London, 1869), pp. 152–9

Jerome of Prague

This hero in the cause of truth was born and educated at Prague, where he soon became distinguished for his learning and eloquence. Having completed his studies, he travelled over a great part of Europe, and visited many of the seats of learning, particularly the universities of Paris, Heidelberg, Cologne, and Oxford. At Oxford he became acquainted with the works of Wycliffe, and being a person of uncommon application, he translated many of them into his own language, having made himself master of English. On his return to Prague, Jerome openly professed the doctrines of Wycliffe, and finding that they had made considerable progress in Bohemia, from the industry and zeal of Huss, he became his assistant in the work of reformation.

On 4th April 1415, Jerome went to Constance, about three months before Huss's death. He entered the town privately, and consulting with some of the leaders of his party, was convinced that he could render his friend no service. The council at Constance wanted to seize Jerome, so he left there for Bohemia, but at Hirsaw, on officer under the command of the Duke of Sultzbach seized Huss. The Duke of Sultzbach immediately wrote to the council in Constance who told him to send his prisoner to them. The Duke of Sultzbach then put Huss in irons and set off for Constance. On his way he met the Elector Palatine who had a long chain fastened to Jerome, by which he was then pulled along, like a wild beast, to the cloister, where, after some insults and examinations, he was taken to a tower and tied to a block, with his legs in stocks. He remained like this for eleven days and nights until he became so dangerously ill that he had to be untied. He remained in prison until the martyrdom of his friend Huss. Then he was brought out and threatened with torture, and, in a moment of weakness, he forgot his resolution, abjured his doctrines, and confessed that Huss deserved his fate, and that both he and Wycliffe were heretics. As a result of this his chains were taken off and his harsh treatment was suspended. He was kept in prison, but hoped to be released every day. But his enemies suspected his sincerity and proposed another form of recantation to him. He refused to answer this, except in public, and was accordingly brought before the council, when, to the astonishment of his hearers he renounced his recantation and asked permission to plead his own cause. This was refused and he vented his indignation thus.

What barbarity is this? For 340 days have I been confined in a variety of prisons. The cause I now plead is not my own, it is the cause of men: it is the cause of Christians: it is a cause which is to affect the rights of posterity, however the experiment is to be made in my person.

At the end of Jerome's trial Jerome received the same sentence as had been passed on Huss, and was delivered over the secular power; but, being a layman, had not to undergo the ceremony of degradation. They had, however, prepared for him a paper cap painted with red devils, which, being put on his head, he said, 'Our Lord Jesus Christ, when he suffered death for me, a most miserable sinner, did wear a crown of thorns upon his head; and I, for his sake, will wear this cap.'

They delayed his execution for two days, hoping that he would recant; during which time the Cardinal of Florence used all his powers to win him over, but all proved ineffective. Jerome had resolved to seal his teaching with his blood.

On his way to the place of execution he sang several hymns; and on arriving at the place where Huss had suffered, the knelt down and prayed fervently. He embraced the stake with great cheerfulness; and when the executioner went behind him to set fire to the faggots, he said, 'Come here and kindle it before my eyes; for had I been afraid of it, I would not have come here, having had so many opportunities to escape.' When the flames enveloped him he sang a hymn; and the last words he was heard to say were: 'Hanc animam in flammis affero, Christe, tibi!' ('This soul in flames I offer, Christ, to thee!')

¶ John Foxe, *The Book of Martyrs,* revised with notes and an appendix by W. Bramley-Moore (London, 1869), pp. 159–65.

Persecution in Bohemia

A secret order was issued by the emperor Ferdinand for apprehending all noblemen and gentlemen who had been principally concerned in supporting the Protestant cause, and in nominating Frederick, Elector Palatine of the Rhine, to be King of Bohemia. Fifty of these were suddenly seized in one night, and brought to the castle of Prague; while the estates of those who were absent were confiscated, themselves made outlaws, and their names fixed upon a gallows as a mark of public ignominy.

The high court of the reformers later tried those who had been apprehended, and two apostate Protestants were appointed to examine them. As none of the prisoners would renounce their faith, or acknowledge themselves in error, they were all pronounced guilty; the sentence was, however, referred to the emperor. When that monarch had read their names, and the accusations against them, he passed judgment on all, but in a different manner; his sentences being of our kinds: death, banishment, imprisonment for life, and imprisonment during pleasure.

Twenty of them being ordered for execution. The morning of the execution having arrived, a cannon was fired as a signal to bring the prisoners from the castle to the principal market-place, in which scaffolds were erected, and a body of troops drawn up to attend. The prisoners left the castle, and passed with dignity the cheerfulness through soldiers, Jesuits, priests, executioners, and a prodigious concourse of people assembled to see the exit of these martyrs.

The following are among the principal who suffered on this occasion.

Lord Schilik

Lord Schilik, a nobleman about 50 years old. On being told that he was to be quartered, and his parts scattered in different places, he smiled, and said, 'The loss of a sepulchre is but a trifling consideration.' A gentleman who stood by, crying, 'Courage, my lord.' Lord Schilik replied, 'I possess the favour of God, which is sufficient to inspire anyone with courage: the fear of death does not trouble me. I have faced him in fields of battle to oppose Antichrist.' After repeating a short prayer, he told the executioner he was ready, who cut off his right hand and head, and then quartered him. His hand and head were placed on the high tower of Prague, and his quarters distributed in different parts of the city.

Viscount Winceslaus

Another victim was Viscount Winceslaus. This venerable 70-year-old nobleman was noted equally for his piety, learning and hospitality. He was so little affected by the loss of worldly riches, that on his house being broken open, his property seized, and his estates confiscated, he only said, with great composure, 'The Lord hath given, and the Lord hath taken away.' As he approached the block, he stroked his grey beard, and said, 'Venerable hairs, the greater honour now attends you; a crown of martyrdom is your portion.' Then laying down his head, it was severed from his body, and afterwards placed upon a pole in a conspicuous part of the town.

Sir Gasper Kaplitz

This 86-year-old nobleman, as he came to the place of execution, addressed the principal officer thus: 'Behold a miserable ancient man, who hath often entreated God to take him out of this wicked world, but could not till now obtain his desire; for God reserved me till these years to be a spectacle to the world, and a sacrifice to himself; therefore God's will be done.'

An officer told him, that out of consideration of his great age, if he would only ask pardon, he would immediately receive it. 'Ask pardon!' he exclaimed. 'I will ask pardon from God, whom I have frequently offended, but not of the emperor, whom I never offended. No. I die innocent, with a clear conscience. I would not be separated from my noble companions in the faith.' So saying, he cheerfully resigned his neck to the block.

Simon Sussickey

Simon Sussickey, not being of noble birth, was ordered to be hanged. He appeared impatient to go, saying, 'Every moment delays me from entering the kingdom of Christ.'

Nathaniel Wodnianskey

This gentleman was hanged for having supported the Protestant cause. At the gallows the Jesuits used all their persuasions to make him renounce his faith, but without effect. His own son then approached the gallows, and said, 'Sir, if life should be offered to you on condition of apostasy, I entreat you to remember Christ.'

To this the father replied, 'It is very acceptable, my son, to be exhorted to constancy by you, but suspect me not; rather endeavour to confirm in their faith your brothers, sisters, and children, and teach them to imitate my constancy.' He had no sooner concluded these words than he received his fate with great fortitude.

¶ John Foxe, *The Book of Martyrs*, revised with notes and an appendix by W. Bramley-Moore (London, 1869), pp. 147–51

Thomas Bilney

Thomas Bilney was brought up at Cambridge. On leaving the university, he went to several places and preached; and in his sermons spoke with great boldness against the pride and insolence of the clergy. This was during Cardinal Wolsey's ministry, who upon hearing of Bilney's attacks, imprisoned him. Overcome with fear, Bilney abjured, was pardoned, and returned to Cambridge in 1530.

Here he fell into great horror of mind in consequence of his denial of the truth. He became overwhelmed with shame, and bitterly repenting of his sin, resolved to make some atonement by a public confession of his sentiments. To prepare himself for the task, he studied the Scriptures with deep attention for two years, at the end of which he left the university and went to Norfolk, where he preached up and down that country against idolatry and superstition. He openly confessed his own sin of denying the faith; and, taking no precautions as he travelled, was soon seized by the bishop's officers, condemned as a relapse, and degraded.

Parker, later Archbishop of Canterbury, was an eyewitness of his sufferings, which he bore with great fortitude and resignation, and continued very cheerful after his sentence. He ate up the poor provisions that he was given, saying he must keep up a ruinous cottage till it fell. He often quoted these words from Isaiah: 'When thou walkest through the fire, thou shalt not be burned.' By burning his finger in a candle, he prepared himself for the fire, and said it would only consume the stubble of his body, and would purify his soul.

On 10th November he was taken to the stake, where he repeated the Creed, as a testimony that he was a true Christian. He then prayed earnestly, and with the deepest feeling repeated these words, 'Enter not into judgment with thy servant.' Dr Warner, who attended, embraced him, shedding many tears, and wishing he might die in as good a frame of mind as Bilney then was. The friars requested him to inform the people that they were not instrumental to his death, which he did, so that the his last act was full of charity.

The officers then put the reeds and faggots around his body, and set first to the first, which made a great flame and disfigured his face; he held up his hands, and struck his chest, crying sometimes, 'Jesus!', sometimes, 'Credo!' But the flame was blown away from him several times, by a strong wind, until eventually the wood caught fire and the flame grew stronger and he gave up his spirit.

His body shrank and leaned down on the chain, until one of the officers with his halbert struck out the staple from the chain behind him, so that his body fell down to the base of the fire, where they heaped wood over it to consume it.

¶ John Foxe, *The Book of Martyrs,* revised with notes and an appendix by W. Bramley-Moore (London, 1869), pp. 227–9

John Frith

Frith was a young man well known for his learning and the first in England to write against the bodily presence in the sacrament. He followed Zwingli's teaching on these grounds: Christ received in the sacrament gave eternal life, but this was given only to those who believed, from which he inferred that he was received only by faith. These reasons he put in writing, which falling into the hands of Sir Thomas More, were answered by him; but Frith never saw his publication until he was in prison; and then, though he was loaded with irons, and had no books, he replied.

For these offences he was seized in May 1533, and brought before Stokesly, Gardiner, and Longland. They accused him with not believing in purgatory and transubstantiation. He gave his reasons that made him see neither of these as articles of faith; but thought that neither the affirming nor the denying them ought to be determined positively. The bishops seemed unwilling to proceed to sentence; but he continuing resolute, Stokesly pronounced it, and delivered him to the secular power, at the same time desiring that his punishment might be moderated, so that the rigour might not be too extreme, nor yet the gentleness of it too much mitigated – a piece of hypocrisy which deceived no one.

Frith, with fellow martyr Hewitt, were taken to the stake at Smithfield on 4th July 1533. On arriving there, Frith expressed great joy, and hugged the faggots with sheer delight. A priest called Cook, who stood by, told the people not to pray for them more than they would do for a dog: at this Frith smiled, and prayed God to forgive him. The fire was then kindled, and consumed the martyrs to ashes.

¶ John Foxe, *The Book of Martyrs,* revised with notes and an appendix by W. Bramley-Moore (London, 1869), p. 231

John Lambert

I answer with Augustine that 'this is the body of Christ after a certain manner.'

John Lambert was born in Norfolk and educated at Cambridge University. After being converted by Bilney he became disgusted at the corruption of the church; and apprehensive of persecution, he crossed the sea and joined Tyndale and Frith. He was appointed chaplain to the English at Antwerp. But the persecuting spirit of Sir Thomas More reached him, and on the accusation of a man called Barlow, was taken from Antwerp to London. He was put on trial in Lambeth and then in Oxford before Archbishop Warham. Warham died the following year and Lambert was released.

Lambert argued that when Christ said, 'This cup is the new testament,' these words do not change either the cup nor the wine corporeally into the new testament. Using the same argument he said that Christ's words spoken about the bread do not turn it corporeally into the body of Christ.

On account of this teaching he was summoned for trial by Archbishop Cranmer and forced to defend himself, for Cranmer, who later became a fervent believer in the reformed doctrines on the sacrament, still favoured the Roman view. At his trial King Henry VIII asked him, 'Answer as touching the sacrament of the altar. Dost thou say that it is the body of Christ, or dost thou deny it?'

LAMBERT: I answer with Augustine that 'this is the body of Christ after a certain manner'.
THE KING: Answer me neither out of Augustine nor any other authority; but tell me plainly, do you believe it is the body of Christ or not?
LAMBERT: Then I deny that it is the body of Christ.
THE KING: Mark well, for now thou shalt be condemned by Christ's own words: 'Hoc est corpus meum' ('This is my body').

On the appointed day Lambert was taken to Smithfield to be executed. The manner of his death was dreadful; for after his legs were burned up to the stumps, and his wretched tormentors had withdrawn the fire from him, so that only a small one was left under him, two soldiers who stood on either side of him hoisted him on their halberts as far as the chain would go, while he, lifting up such hands as

he had, cried unto the people: 'None but Christ, none but Christ.'
Then he was let down again from the soldiers' pikes, fell into the fire,
where he expired.

¶ John Foxe, *The Book of Martyrs,* revised with notes and an appendix by
W. Bramley-Moore (London, 1869), pp. 238–40

William Tyndale

'Lord, open the King of England's eyes!'

William Tyndale was born around the borders of Wales, and brought
up in the University of Oxford, where he studied the liberal arts and
the Scriptures. He then moved to Cambridge, and then to Gloucester-
shire where he became tutor to a knight called Welch. To this gentleman's table several abbots, deans, and other beneficed men used to
go, with whom Tyndale talked about learned men, especially Luther
and Erasmus, and about questions concerning the Scriptures.

Not long after, Tyndale happened to be in the company of a certain
divine, and in their discussion pressed him so hard that the doctor
burst out with these blasphemous words: 'We were better to be without God's laws than the Pope.'

Tyndale, full of godly zeal, replied: 'I defy the Pope and all his
laws.' He added that if God spared him life, ere many years, he would
cause a boy who drives the plough to know more of the Scriptures
than he did.

Tyndale left Mr Welch's service, under pressure from disapproving
priests, and on arriving in London he was recommended to Tunstall,
Bishop of London, by Sir Henry Guildford. But Tyndale found no
favour in the bishop's eyes. He remained in London for nearly a year,
greatly distressed with the pomp, pride, and ignorance of the clergy,
so that he realised that not only was there no room in the bishop's
house for him to translate the New Testament, but that there was no
room for him to do this in all England.

He left for Germany and then moved on to the Netherlands and
stayed most of the time in Antwerp. There he pondered how he might
best help his countrymen understand God's word. He realised that the

cause for people's blindness in England, and the reason for the errors and superstitions of the church was ignorance of the Scriptures. The truth was entombed in a dead language, while the priests spent their energy on preventing people from enquiring about the oracles of God. With these considerations in mind Tyndale felt moved, by God's Spirit, to translate the Scriptures into his mother tongue for the benefit of the uneducated people in England. He started with the New Testament in around 1527. His books were published and sent over to England, and became like holy fire from the altar, to give light in the night season.

Tyndale then translated the first five books of the Old Testament and sailed to Hamburg, intending to print them in that city, when one of those mysterious providences happened to him which are beyond human reason. On his voyage he was shipwrecked, and lost all his manuscripts, and almost everything he possessed. However, he started his work again in Hamburg with a man called Coverdale, in a house belonging to Miss Emmerson, in 1529. The English church leaders had persuaded the king to issue a proclamation which condemned and forbad Tyndale's translation of the New Testament. Not content with this they plotted to see how they could kill the author.

Tyndale had returned to Antwerp and was betrayed there by a man called Philips. Tyndale was taken to Filford castle, eighteen miles from Antwerp, where he remained until his death.

At last, after eighteen months, and must fruitless arguments, Tyndale was condemned by a decree issued from Augsburg by the emperor. Tyndale was taken to be executed and as he was being tied to the stake, he cried with a loud and earnest voice, 'Lord, open the King of England's eyes!' He was then strangled, and his remains burnt to ashes. Such was the power and excellence of this truly good man, that during his imprisonment he converted the jailor, and his daughter, and others in his employment. Several of them who came into contact with him during his imprisonment said of him, that if he were not a good Christian, they did not know whom to trust; and the procurator-general left this testimony about him, that he was 'a learned, a good, and a godly man.'

¶ John Foxe, *The Book of Martyrs*, revised with notes and an appendix by W. Bramley-Moore (London, 1869), pp. 278–84

Four views on the Holy Communion

The four views which have unhappily divided the Christian world on the subject of the sacrament [i.e., Holy Communion, the Lord's Supper or the Mass] are the following:

1. The Romish doctrine, or transubstantiation. This maintains the absolute change of the elements into the actual body and blood of Christ; so that though the elements of bread and wine remain present to the senses, they are no longer what they seem, being changed into the body, blood, and divinity of Christ.

2. The Lutheran view, called consubstantiation. This maintains that after consecration the body and blood of Christ are substantially present, but nevertheless that the bread and wine are present, unchanged.

3. The Anglican view – that Christ is present in the sacrament only after the spiritual manner, and that his body and blood are eaten by the faithful after a spiritual, and not after a carnal manner, to the maintenance of their spiritual life and their growth in grace.

4. The Zwinglian, which declares the sacrament to be no channel of grace, but only a commemorative feast, admitting only a figurative presence of Christ's body and blood.

Alas! that prisons should have been peopled, and thousands immolated on the pyre, for the sake of opinions; and that nothing but death could atone for the horrible crime of individual judgment, instead of allowing each to stand or fall to their own master.

¶ John Foxe, *The Book of Martyrs,* revised with notes and an appendix by W. Bramley-Moore (London, 1869), p. 369

John Fisher

John Fisher, Cardinal and Bishop, takes the first place among the martyrs of the sixteenth century in dignity, example, and the influence of his name. He was born in 1459, at Beverley, and studied when young with a priest of that collegiate church. Afterwards he spent many years at Cambridge with distinction, and was made Bishop of

Rochester in 1504, being forty-five years of age. No one was more vigilant against the poison of Luther's doctrines creeping into England. The book which earned for Henry VIII from the Pope the title of Defender of the Faith was written by his advice, if not indeed by his hand. Fisher was considered the most learned, pious and inflexible of the English bishops, and Cardinal Pole regards him as the model of a perfect prelate.

The time, however, came when his virtue and adherence to the faith were imputed to him as crimes. The king, tired of his wife, and in love with Anne Boleyn, affected to have scruples about his marriage. Wolsey, from political motives, wished a divorce, and knew that if Fisher could be gained over, little opposition need be feared from the clergy. But the holy bishop, being sent for, at once advised his majesty with all speed to lay aside those thoughts: 'and for any peril,' he added, 'that may happen to your soul thereby, let the guilt rest on mine.' When after long delay, the cause of divorce was before the Papal Legates' Court, as Queen Catherine's chief defender 'there stood forth John Fisher, the light not only of England, but of Christendom, to demonstrate that their marriage could not be dissolved by any power, divine or human. He declared that for this opinion he was ready to lay down his life, adding that as John the Baptist, in olden times, regarded death glorious in a cause of matrimony, and it was not so holy then as it has now become by the shedding of Christ's blood, he could not encourage himself more, or face any peril with greater confidence than by taking the Baptist for his own example.'

Fisher was brought before Cranmer, the Archbishop of Canterbury, who told him, 'You must answer directly, whether you will, or you will not subscribe' [to the supremacy of the Church of England being vested in the king of England, his heirs and successors].

Then said the Bishop of Rochester, 'If you will needs have me answer directly, my answer is, that, forasmuch as my own conscience cannot be satisfied, I absolutely refuse the oath.'

A verdict of guilty was soon recorded, and the Lord Chancellor asked the bishop if he had any more to say for himself. The persecuted bishop replied, 'Truly, my lord, if that which I have before spoken be not sufficient, I have no more to say, but only to desire Almighty God to forgive them that have thus condemned me, for I think they know not what they have done.'

Bishop John Fisher's reply when sentenced

My lords, I am here condemned before you of high treason for denial of the king's supremacy over the Church of England, but by what order of justice I leave to God, who is the searcher both of the king his majesty's conscience and yours; nevertheless, being found guilty, as it is termed, I am and must be contented with all that God shall send, to those who I wholly refer and submit myself. And now to tell you more plainly my mind, touching this matter of the king's supremacy, I think indeed, and always have thought, and do now lastly affirm, that his grace cannot justly claim any such supremacy over the church of God, as he now taketh upon him; neither has it ever been, or heard of, that any temporal prince, before his days, hath presumed to that dignity; wherefore, if the king will now adventure himself in proceeding in this strange and unwonted case, so no doubt but he shall deeply incur the grievous displeasure of the almighty, to the great damage of his own soul, and of many others, and to the utter ruin of this realm committed to his charge, whereof will ensue some sharp punishment at his hands; wherefore, I pray God his grace may remember himself in good time, and hearken to good counsel for the preservation of himself and his realm, and the quietness of all Christendom.

On 22nd June 1535 he was upon the scaffold at about ten of the clock, when the executioner, being ready to do his office, kneeled down to him, as the fashion is, and asked him forgiveness. 'I forgive thee,' said he, 'with all my heart, and I trust thou shalt see me overcome this storm lustily.'

Then was his gown and tippet taken from him, and he stood in his doublet and hose, in sight of all the people, whereof was no small number assembled to see his execution. There was to be seen a long, lean, and slender body, having on it little other substance besides skin and bones, insomuch as most part of the beholders marvelled much to see a living man so far consumed, for he seemed a very image of death; and as it were death in a man's shape, using a man's voice; and therefore it was thought the king was some- thing cruel to put such a man to death, being near his end, and to kill that which was dying already, except it were for pity sake to rid him of his pain. When the innocent and holy man was come upon the scaffold, he spake to the people to the following effect:

Christian people, I am come hither to die for the faith of Christ's holy Catholic church, and I thank God hitherto my stomach hath served very well thereunto, so that yet I have not feared death; wherefore I desire you all to help and assist with your prayers, that at the very stroke and instant of death's stroke, I may stand stedfast, without fainting in any one point of the Catholic faith, free from any fear.

Then he knelt down and prayed the Te Deum Laudamus, ending with the words, 'In Thee, O Lord, have I hoped'. Then came the executioner, and bound a handkerchief about his eyes; and so this holy Father, lifting up his hands and heart towards heaven, said a few prayers, which were not long, but fervent and devout; which being ended, he laid his head down on the middle of a little block, when the executioner, being ready with a sharp and heavy axe, cut asunder his slender neck at one blow, which bled so abundantly that many wondered to see so much blood issue out of so slender and lean a body.

¶ E. H. Burton and J. H. Pollen, *Lives of the English Martyrs, vol. 1, 1583–1588* (Longman, 1914), pp. 10–15

Sir Thomas More

'I die the King's good servant, but God's first' (More, from the scaffold).

Acts of Parliament, passed in November 1534, sealed More's fate. Firstly, the Act of Supremacy rejected any foreigners having any authority in ecclesiastic matters and declared that the King was the supreme head of the English Church. Secondly, the Treason Act now made it a treasonable offence to deny any of his titles, specifically being Supreme Head of the English Church. Thirdly, Fisher, along with five other non-juring clergymen, and More were cited in the Act of Attainder.

More still refused to say whether or not he accepted the King as supreme head in religious matters. So at his state trial in Westminster Hall a false witness had to be resorted to. He declared that he had heard More say in prison, 'No more than Parliament could make a law that God were not God could Parliament make the King Supreme Head of the Church.' This was enough to convict More. Lord Chancellor Audley, More's successor, asked More if he wanted to say anything. More replied, 'I verily trust that though your Lordships have now here on earth been judges to my condemnation, we shall yet in heaven merrily all meet together to our everlasting salvation.' Later, More stated his true position about the king being the Supreme Head of the Church. He said, 'In as much as this indictment is based on an Act of Parliament directly repugnant to the laws of God and his holy Church, the supreme Government of which, or of any part whereof, may no temporal Prince presume by any law to take upon him, as rightfully belonging to the See of Rome, a spiritual preeminence by the mouth of our Saviour himself, personally present on earth, only to St Peter and his successors, bishops of the same See, by special prerogative granted, it is therefore in law, amongst Christian men, insufficient to charge any Christian man.'

More's Trial and Execution

When at last the judge called on the jury, they brought in a verdict of death against him. Thereupon he said, frankly, 'I have by the grace of God been always a Catholic, never out of the communion of the Roman Pontiff, but I had heard it said at times that the authority of the Roman Pontiff was certainly lawful and to be respected, but still an authority derived from human law, and not standing on a divine prescription. Then when I observed that public affairs were so ordered that the sources of the power of the Roman Pontiff would necessarily be examined, I gave myself up to a most diligent examination of that question for the space of seven years, and found that the authority of the Roman Pontiff, which you rashly – I will not use stronger language – have set aside, is not only lawful, to be respected, and necessary, but also grounded on the divine law and prescription. That is my opinion, that is the belief in which by the grace of God I shall die.' He had hardly ended his answer when they all cried out that More was a traitor and a rebel.

Sentence was therefore passed upon him, and he was led back to the Tower. He was met at the Old Swan Stairs by his son who with tears in his eyes asked his blessing. His daughter Margaret placed herself at the Tower wharf and received his blessing upon her knees; then she forced her way through the guard, and embracing her father, ceased not for some time from kissing him, and exclaiming 'My father! O my father!' Sir Thomas comforted her, and they separated. But a second time she rushed through the throng, and hung upon his neck; Sir Thomas then shed some tears; all around were overcome, and even the guards could not refrain from weeping.

As More was led to the scaffold he had a joke with the Master Lieutenant, and said to him, 'I pray you, Master Lieutenant, see me safe up, and for my coming down, let me shift for myself.' More was allowed to say little. He simply asked for the prayers of the spectators, and that they should pray for the King, recited Psalm 51, and assured the crowd that he died for the Catholic faith and that he died 'the King's good servant, but God's first.' To the executioner he said, 'Thou wilt do me this day a greater benefit than ever any mortal man can be able to do me; pluck up thy spirit, man, and be not afraid to do thy office; my neck is very short, take heed therefore that thou strike not awry, for saving they honesty.' The executioner severed More's head from his body in a single blow.

¶ *The English Martyrs under Henry VIII and Elizabeth* (Catholic Truth Society, 1891), pp. 20–1

Twelve Carthusian Monks

Every means which dissimulation and cruelty could devise had been ineffectually resorted to in order to induce the religious of the Charterhouse Priory to stifle the dictates of their consciences, subscribe to the oath of supremacy, and in fine, acknowledge the legality of all the king's proceedings. Lay governors were appointed over them, who treated them with the utmost severity and daily insults. They were scarcely allowed sufficient food for the sustenance of life, while the intruders feasted and drank.

All these means, however, failing, four of these holy men, who were considered to have the greatest influence in the house, were removed to distant convents in the country, where the monks had conformed to the will of the king and his Vicar-General, Cromwell.

Blessed John Rochester was one of the four monks who were forcibly removed from the Charterhouse. He was sent to a convent of his Order, near Hull, in Yorkshire, on 4th May 1536. Blessed James Walworth was the companion of Rochester in all his sufferings. Like Rochester he resisted every overture to break his monastic vows, or to

Faith of sixteenth-century monks

There entered others to pry into the liberty of the monks, searching forth the cause of their courage and constancy, and inquiring how they, above all others, durst stoutly resist the king's command, and what the weapons were wherewith they feared not to bid combat unto such a king. And when they found that the weapons, wherewith they defended themselves and their doctrine, were the sword of the spirit, which is the Word of God, and the frequent reading of the divine Scriptures and ancient fathers, being always ready to give satisfaction to every one that demanded an account of the faith and hope which was in them, therefore they took away all the books they could find in their cells, that by this means disarmed, they might be the more easily overcome. But neither could they thus prevail, for, although some armed with shield of learning did fight valiantly, notwithstanding others more confounded and pierced the hearts of the adversaries with their innocent simplicity; wherewith being well armed they would by no means pass over the bounds which their forefathers had set down for them, nor depart from the doctrine of our holy mother the church.

Then the time of trial came to show how every man's affections were inclined; whether to God or the devil, or the flesh and the world; because every one might do what he would, and the liberty of the one might do what he would, and the liberty of the flesh, which is the very slavery and thraldom of the devil, was granted to all that would depart out of the house. But thanks be to God, there was so much holiness of life, such constancy of mind, such modesty of words, such gladness in their countenance, such joy in their doings, and the moderation in all things, that all were troubled and confounded that saw them; for although they were deprived of a Prior, and made orphans without a father, yet every one was a prior unto himself, directing and instructing themselves prudently in all things.

swerve from the faith of his forefathers. A nobleman, who resided in the neighbourhood of the monastery, informed Cromwell of their constancy, and the impracticability of overcoming their resolution. Whereupon the Vicar-General gave him authority to proceed against their lives. They were accordingly conducted to York, and in the presence of the Duke of Norfolk, the nobleman commanded them to be put to death. So little were the forms of law and justice attended to by the men who professed to bring about a reformation in religion.

The command was immediately put into execution, and the courageous champions of the faith were suspended upon a gallows, in chains, where their bodies were left hanging until, after the lapse of many years, their bodies fell to the ground.

Ten more names were yet to be added to the roll of Carthusian martyrs. Of these three were priests, Blessed Richard Bere, Blessed Thomas Johnson, and Blessed Thomas Green. One was a deacon, Blessed John Davy, and six were lay-brothers, BB. William Greenwood, Thomas Scryven, Robert Salt, Walter Pierson, Thomas Redyng, and William Horne. It was judged impolitic to put these ten monks publicly to death, so they were dragged, towards the end of May 1537, from their convent, and committed close prisoners to Newgate. The king's intention was to destroy them privately by severe treatment; and to effect his purpose, they were confined, with their hands tied behind them to the walls of their dungeon, so that they could in no way render any service to each other, or even assist themselves. All communication with them was strictly forbidden, and their prison was rendered insupportable by the stench and filth which surrounded them.

In this deplorable condition they must have perished in a few days had their sufferings not come to the knowledge of the virtuous and intrepid Margaret Clement. This lady was the wife of a learned and pious physician, the friend of Sir Thomas More. She bribed the gaolers and so obtained daily entrance into the prison, disguised as a milk woman, with a pail upon her head, and supported the famishing religious, with the milk that she brought with her. She also cleansed, as far as she was able, their place of confinement, and carried away the filth in her pail. This charitable office she pursued for some days, until the king inquired if the monks were all dead? Being answered in the negative, he expressed his surprise, and gave orders that their confinement should be rendered still more rigorous. The keeper, being then fearful for his own personal safety, would no longer permit Mrs Clement to gain admittance into the prison. How long each of these persecuted men were able to bear such inhuman treatment is not known, but it appears that they died by mid June 1537.

¶ E. H. Burton and J. H. Pollen, *Lives of the English Martyrs, vol. 1, 1583–1588* (Longman, 1914), pp. 146–8

The Duke of Somerset

On 22nd January 1552, King Edward's uncle, the Duke of Somerset, was brought out of the Tower of London, and delivered up to the sheriffs of the city, who were accompanied by a great number of armed men and guards. When brought upon the scaffold, he maintained the utmost serenity; and kneeling down, he lifted up his hands, and commended his soul to God.

After having offered up a few short prayers, he arose and turned round, apparently quite undismayed at the sight of the executioner and his axe; but with the most perfect cheerfulness and composure addressed the people, in almost the following words:

> Dearly beloved friends, I am brought here to suffer death, although I have never offended, by word or deed, against the king; and have been as true and faithful a subject as any man in this realm. Nevertheless, as the law has sentenced me to death, I acknowledge that I, as well as any other man, have no appeal from it. Therefore, to show my obedience to the laws, I have come here to die, heartily thanking God for having allowed me this time for repentance, instead of cutting me off by sudden death.

> There is yet something, beloved friends, regarding the Christian religion, which I must put you in mind of; and which, when I was in authority, I always set forth to the utmost of my power. Not only do I not repent of my actions, but I rejoice in them, since now the forms of our Christian religion have come nearer to the order of the primitive church; which I look upon as a great benefit unto you and me, and exhort you all with thankfulness to accept and embrace what is so purely set forth before you, and to show the same in your lives, which, if you do not, greater calamity and mischief will surely follow.

Just as he concluded these words, the assembly was suddenly alarmed by a loud and extraordinary noise. To some it appeared as the sound of a great tempest, to others as the explosion of gunpowder, and to others as if a multitude of horsemen were rapidly approaching; but though all heard the noise, no one could see any cause for it. The terrified people ran in all directions; some falling into ditches and puddles, other hastening into the houses; other, falling down upon the ground, cried out to Jesus to save them. Those who remained in their places scarcely knew where they were, so great was the general panic. I, among the rest, was so alarmed by this hurbly, that I stood still amazed. During this commotion the people espied Sir Anthony Brown riding under the scaffold, which raised a fresh tumult, for all hoped that the king had sent his uncle pardon by this messenger; and throwing their caps up in the air, with great rejoicings, they cried, 'Pardon, pardon is come; God save the king!' Thus the duke saw before his death what a popular favourite he was, and few dukes ever had more tears shed for them, for all men saw in his fall the ruin of England.

Somerset meanwhile remained standing quietly in his place. At length, making a sign to the crowd with his hand to maintain silence, he thus addressed them:

> Dearly beloved friends, there is no such matter here in hand as you vainly hope or believe. It seemeth thus good unto Almighty God, whose ordinance it is meet and necessary that we all be obedient unto. Wherefore I pray you all to be quiet, and to be contented with my death, which I am most willing to suffer. And let us now join in prayer unto the Lord for the preservation of the king's majesty.
>
> If there be any who hath been offended and injured by me, I most humbly require and ask him forgiveness; but especially Almighty God, whom throughout all my life I have most grievously offended. And all other, whatsoever they be, that have offended me, I do with my whole heart forgive them. Now I once again require you, dearly beloved in the Lord, that you will keep yourselves quiet and still, lest through your quietness I shall be much more composed.

After this, he again knelt down, and called out, 'Lord Jesus, save me!' As the name of Jesus was on his lips, the fatal blow was struck.

¶ John Foxe, *The Book of Martyrs,* revised with notes and an appendix by W. Bramley-Moore (London, 1869), pp. 288–94

John Hooper

When Mary ascended the throne Hooper was one of the first who were summoned to London. His friends, warning him of his danger, entreated him to leave the country, but he refused, saying, 'Once did I flee, and take me to my feet, but now, because I am called to this place and vocation, I am thoroughly persuaded to remain, and to live and die with my sheep.' He was commanded to appear before the queen and her council. On coming before them, Gardiner received him very opprobriously, railing at him, and accusing him of his religion. He answered boldly and freely, but was, notwithstanding, committed to ward, being told that it was not for his religion, but for certain sums of money which he owed the queen, that he was imprisoned. In March following, he was again called before Gardiner, and deprived of both his bishoprics (Worcester and Gloucester), not being permitted to plead his own cause.

On 4th February 1555 Bonner degraded Hooper, with all the usual pomp and pride of the Romish church. The same night his keeper gave him a hint that he would probably be sent to Gloucester to be burned. This greatly rejoiced Hooper, who, raising his hands to heaven, praised God for sending him to suffer death among the people over whom he was pastor. Immediately he sent word to his servant, to bring him his boots, spurs, cloak, that he might be in readiness to ride whenever the order came. At four o'clock the following morning, the keeper, accompanied by some others, came and searched him, to see whether he had concealed any papers. He was then led by the sheriff to a place previously appointed, where he was met by six of the queen's guard, who had orders to take him to Gloucester. The guard took him first to the Angel Inn, where he breakfasted. At break of day he cheerfully mounted his horse to proceed on the journey to Gloucester. His head was covered with a hood, placed under his hat, that he might not be recognised, and care was taken always to stop to bait or lodge at a different inn to the one the bishop was accustomed to stay at when he travelled. On Thursday they reached Cirencester, a town fifteen miles from Gloucester. Here the party halted at the house of a woman who knew the bishop, and had always hated him and the truths he had so boldly declared. When she saw the manner in which he was now being led to death, she lamented his case with tears, confessing that she had always believed that if put on his trial he would remain firm.

About a mile from Gloucester great numbers of people had congregated to meet their bishop, and they loudly bewailed his sad fate. Accordingly a strong body of men were sent to the gate, with weapons, and the people were ordered to remain in their houses. During the first part of the night Hooper slept soundly, and afterwards remained engaged in prayer until the morning.

Sir Anthony Kingston, a former friends of the bishop's, had been appointed to attend at his execution. As soon as he saw the bishop he burst into tears. Hooper did not at first recognise him, when Sir Anthony said:

'Why, my lord, do not you know me – an old friend of yours – Anthony Kingston?'

'Yes, Sir Anthony, I do know you well, and am glad to see you in health, and praise God for the same.'

'But I am sorry, my lord, to see you in this case, for, as I understand, you are come hither to die. But, alas! Consider that life is sweet, and death is bitter, therefore, seeing life may be had, desire to live, for life hereafter may do good.'

'Indeed, it is true, Sir Anthony; I am come hither to end this life, and to suffer death here, because I will not gainsay the truth that I have heretofore taught among you in this diocese and elsewhere, and I thank you for your friendly counsel, although it be not as I could have wished it.'

Sir Anthony then took leave of him, not without shedding bitter tears, and tears also ran down the face of the good bishop.

At eight the next morning, the commissioners who were appointed to witness the execution arrived, accompanied by a large band of men. On seeing such a strongly armed guard, Hooper said, 'I am no traitor, neither needed you to have made such a business to bring me to the place where I must suffer; for if you had allowed me, I would have gone alone to the stake, and troubled none of you.'

Having been strictly forbidden to speak, he went in silence to the appointed place, smiling cheerfully on any whom he knew; he walked with difficulty, as he was suffering much from sciatica, which he had caught in prison. Upwards of 7,000 people congregated to see the last scene, the boughs of the trees in the square being used as seats. Three iron hoops had been prepared to fasten him to the stake, and he had three bags of gunpowder tied to him. When he had been secured, he pointed out how the faggots should be placed, and even arranged some with his own hands. There was a strong wind, and the greater part of the faggots being green, it was a long time before they caught fire. Three times were they lighted before they really began to burn up, and even when the gunpowder exploded it did him no good. He was heard to pray aloud, 'Lord Jesus, have mercy upon me! Lord Jesus, receive my spirit!' These were the last words he was heard to utter; but when he was black in the mouth, and his tongue so swollen that he could not speak, yet his lips were seen to move. In three quarters of an hour his body fell forwards, and he was released from his sufferings.

¶ John Foxe, *The Book of Martyrs,* revised with notes and an appendix by W. Bramley-Moore (London, 1869), pp. 379–83

Thomas Tomkins

This plain honest Christian was by trade a weaver, and lived in the parish of Shoreditch, till he was summoned before the inhuman Bishop Bonner, and, with many others who had renounced the errors of Popery, was confined in a prison in that tyrant's house at Fulham.

During his ocnfinement, the treatment which he received at the bishop's hands was not only disgraceful to the character of the latter as a prelate, but even as a man; for Bonner's viollence was such, because Tomkins would not assent to the erroneous doctrine of transubsantiation, that his lordship struck him in the face, and plucked out the greatest part of his beard. Alas! that the outrages of Caiaphas' hall, Herod's palace, and Pilate's praetorium should thus have been reproduced in modern times by those who called themselves the disciples of the lowly Jesus.

On another occasion, because our martyr remained inflexible, and would not deviate in the least point from the uncorrupted truths of the gospel, Bonner, in the presence of several of his visitors at his seat at Fulham, took the poor weaver by the fingers, and held his hand over the flame of a wax candle, having three or four wicks, supposing that, being terrified by the smart of the fire, he would abjure the doctrine which he then maintained.

Tomkins, expecting nothing but immediate death, commended himself unto the Lord, saying, 'O Lord, into thy hands I commend my spirit.' When relating the incident to one James Hinse, Tomkins declared that his spirit was so entranced in God, that he did not feel the pain. And yet that burning was so severe, that the veins shrunk, and the sinews burst, and the water spurted in Mr Harpsfield's face, insomuch that Harpsfield, moved with pity, desired the bishop to stay, saying that he had tried him enough.

When he had been in prison for half a year, about 8th February he was brought with several others before Bishop Bonner, in his consistory, to be examined; to whom first was brought forth a certain bill or schedule, subscribed (as appeareth) with his own hand, the fifth day of the same month, containing these words:

> Thomas Tomkins, of Shoreditch, and of the diocese of London, hath believed and doth believe, that in the sacrament of the altar, under the forms of bread and wine there is not the very body and blood of our Saviour Jesus Christ in substance, but only a token and remembrance thereof, the very body and blood of Christ being only in heaven and nowhere else.

> By me, THOMAS TOMKINS

Whereupon he was asked whether he acknowledged the same subscription to be his own. He admitted it to be so. The bishop then endeavoured to persuade him with fair words, rather than with reasons, to relinquish his opinions, and to return to the unity of the Catholic Church, promising, if he would do so, to absolve him from the past. But he constantly refused.

Having been declared an obstinate heretic by the bloody tribunal of bishops, they delivered him up to the secular power, and he was burned in Smithfield, 6th March 1555, triumphing in the middle of the flames, and adding to the noble company of martyrs who had preceded him through the path of the fiery trial to the realms of immortal glory.

¶ John Foxe, *The Book of Martyrs*, revised with notes and an appendix by W. Bramley-Moore (London, 1869), pp. 85–8

John Rogers

Jesus said, 'No-one who has left home or wife or brothers or parents or children for the sake of the kingdom of God will fail to receive many times as much in this age and, in the age to come, eternal life' (Luke 18:29–30 NIV).

While Mr Rogers remained in prison, he expressed his sentiments, in a bold and manly strain, upon the evils and abuses brought into the country, and threatened its rulers with the vengeance that had fallen, in different ages, upon the enemies of truth.

'I am an Englishman born,' said he, 'and, God knoweth, do naturally wish well to my country. I have often proved that the things which I have much feared should come to pass have indeed followed. I pray God I may fail of my guessing in this behalf.

'The apostles were beaten for their boldness, and they rejoiced that they suffered for Christ's cause. Ye have also provided rods for us, and bloody whips; yet when ye have done that which God's hand and counsel hath determined that ye shall do, be it life or death, I trust that God will so assist us by his Spirit and grace, that we shall patiently suffer, and praise God for it. And whatsoever become of me and others, which now suffer for speaking and professing the truth, yet be ye sure that God's Word will prevail and have the upper hand, when your bloody laws and wicked devices, for want of sure foundation, shall fall in the dust.'

He was asked if he would recant his opinion. He answered that what he had preached he would seal with his blood. 'Then,' said the sheriff, 'thou art a heretic.'

To which the unshaken hero of God replied, 'That shall be known at the day of judgment.'

'Well,' said the sheriff, 'I will never pray for thee.'

'But I will pray for you,' said Mr Rogers.

All the way to the stake he was singing psalms; all the people were rejoicing at his constancy. On the way he was met by his wife and his eleven children, one an infant in her arms. This sad sight did not move him, but he cheerfully and patiently went on his way to Smithfield, where he was burnt to ashes in the presence of a great number of people, and his soul ascended in a chariot of fire to that Redeemer of whom he was worthy, inasmuch as he loved him more than wife and children, yea, even than his own life also.

¶ John Foxe, *The Book of Martyrs*, revised with notes and an appendix by W. Bramley-Moore (London, 1869), pp. 326–7

Rowland Taylor

The little town of Hadley first heard the pure gospel of Christ from the lips of the Rev. Thomas Bilney, who preached there with great earnestness, and whose work was greatly blessed, with many men and women gladly embracing the faith as it is in Christ Jesus. After Bilney's martyrdom Dr Rowland Taylor was appointed vicar of the parish.

When Mary succeeded to the crown, dark clouds gathered round Taylor and all others who were like-minded, and an opportunity was soon seized of bringing him into trouble. Two men in Hadley, Clark and Foster, the one a tradesman and the other a lawyer, determined to have mass publicly performed in the parish church, according to the rites of the Romish priests. They accordingly persuaded the minister from a neighbouring parish to come over and perform the service during Passion week. Dr Taylor, hearing the bells ringing at an unusual hour, hastened to the church to inquire the cause. Finding the large doors fastened, he entered through the chancel, and was astonished to see a priest in Romish vestments preparing to celebrate mass, and guarded by a body of armed men. Dr Taylor, as vicar, demanded of him what right he had to be there without his consent, to which the lawyer, Foster, insolently replied, 'Thou traitor! how darest thou to intercept the execution of the queen's orders?' But the doctor undauntedly denied the charge of traitor, and asserted his mission as a minister of Christ, and delegation to that part of his flock, commanding the priest, as a wolf in sheep's clothing, to depart, nor infect the pure church of God with Popish idolatry.

In January 1555, Dr Taylor was summoned to appear before the Bishops of London, Durham, Norwich, Salisbury, and Winchester, and required to give a determinate answer to the charge of heresy made against him, either to abjure his errors or receive the sentence of condemnation. He boldly answered that he would not depart from the truth he had preached nor submit to the authority of the Pope, and that he thanked God for his graciousness in counting him worthy to suffer for his name. On this the bishops at once proceeded to read the sentence of death on him.

At Chelmsford Dr Taylor was delivered to the sheriff of Suffolk, and conducted by him to Hadley. When they arrived there, and were riding over the bridge, there was a poor man waiting with five children: and when he saw Dr Taylor, he and his children fell down upon their knees, and holding up their hands, cried with a loud voice, 'Oh, dear father and good shepherd, God help and succour thee, as thou hast many a time succoured me and my poor children!' Such witness had this servant of God of his virtuous and charitable life. The streets of Hadley were crowded with men and women of the town and country, who waited to see him; and on beholding him led to death, with weeping eyes and lamentable voices they cried one to another, 'Ah, good Lord! There goeth our good shepherd from us, who so faithfully hath taught us, so fatherly hath cared for us, and so religiously hath governed us!'

Coming to the alms-houses, which he well knew, he cast money to the poor people, which remained out of what had been given him during his imprisonment. As for his living, they took it from him at his first committal to prison, so that he was supported all the time of his confinement by the alms of his visitors.

On arriving at Aldham Common, the place where he should suffer, seeing a great multitude, he asked, 'What place is this, and what meaneth it that so much people are gathered hither?'

It was answered, 'It is Aldham Common, the place where you must suffer: and the people are come to behold you.'

Then, said he, 'Thanked be God, I am even at home.'

On alighting, he desired leave of the sheriff to speak; but the latter refused it. Dr Taylor, perceiving that he would not be allowed to speak, sat down, and seeing one named Soyce, he called him, and said, 'Soyce, I pray thee come and pull off my boots, and take them for thy labour: thou hast long looked for them, now take them.' Then he rose up and pulled off his clothes unto his shirt, and gave them away; which done, he said with a loud voice, 'Good people, I have taught you nothing but God's holy Word, and those lessons that I have taken out of God's blessed book, the Holy Bible: and I am come hither this day to seal it with my blood.'

With that Holmes, yeoman of the guard, who had used Dr Taylor very cruelly all the way, gave him a great stroke upon the head. Then, seeing that they would not allow him to speak, Dr Taylor knelt down and prayed, and a poor woman who was among the people stepped in and prayed with him; but they thrust her away, and threatened to tread her down with their horses: notwithstanding this, she would not move, but remained and prayed with him. When he had prayed he went to the stake and kissed it, and placed himself in a pitch-barrel, which they had set for him to stand in, and so stood with his back upright against the stake, with his hands folded together, and his eyes towards heaven, and kept praying continually.

Sir John Shelton standing by, as Dr Taylor was saying the psalm Miserere in English, struck him on the lips. 'You knave,' said he, 'speak Latin; I will make thee.' At last they kindled the fire; when the martyr, holding up his hands, called upon God, and said, 'Merciful Father of heaven, for Jesus Christ my Saviour's sake, receive my soul into thy hands.' He then folded his hands together, and bore his sufferings without a murmur. Soyce, seizing a halbert, struck him such a blow on the head, that his brains were knocked out, and his body fell lifeless into the flames.

¶ John Foxe, *The Book of Martyrs*, revised with notes and an appendix by W. Bramley-Moore (London, 1869), pp. 334–7

Robert Farrar

Robert Farrar was bishop of St David's and was burned at Carmarthen, 30th March 1555.

This excellent and learned prelate had been promoted to his bishopric by the Lord Protector, in the reign of Edward; but after the fall of his patron, he also had fallen into disgrace, through the malice and false accusations of several enemies, among whom was George Constantine, his own servant. Fifty-six articles were preferred against him, in which he was charged with many negligences and contumacies of the church government. These he answered and denied. But so many and so bitter were his enemies, that they prevailed, and he was in consequence thrown into prison. He was now prosecuted on different charges – namely, such as related to doctrine; and he had been called up in company with the glorious martyrs, Hooper, Rogers, Bradford, and Saunders, on 4th February, and with them would have been condemned; but his condemnation was deferred, and he was sent to prison again, where he remained till 14th February. As much of the examination and answers as could be collected we here present to our readers.

At his first appearance before the lord chancellor, Stephen Gardiner,

Bishop of Winchester, and the Bishops of Durham, Bath (Dr Bourne) and Worcester, the lord chancellor said unto him, 'Now, sir, have you heard how the world goeth here?'

FARRAR: If it please your honour, I know not.

WINCHESTER: Lo! What a froward fellow is this!

FARRAR: It is please your lordship, how should I know anything abroad, being a prisoner?

WINCHESTER: Have you not heard of the coming in of the lord cardinal?

FARRAR: I know not my lord cardinal; but I have heard that a cardinal was come in, but I did not believe it, and I believe it not yet.

WORCESTER: I pray your lordship tell him yourself, that he may know what is done.

WINCHESTER: The queen's majesty and the Parliament hath restored religion to the same state it was in at the beginning of the reign of our King Henry VIII. Ye are in the queen's debt, and her majesty will be good unto you, if you will return to the Catholic Church.

FARRAR: In what state I am concerning my debts to the queen's majesty, in the Court of Exchequer, my lord treasurer knoweth: and the last time that I was before your honour, and the first time also, I showed you that I had made an oath never to consent nor agree that the Bishop of Rome should have any power or jurisdiction within this realm: and further I need not rehearse to your lordship; you know it well enough.

BOURNE: You were once abjured for heresy at Oxford.

FARRAR: That I was not.

BOURNE: You were.

FARRAR: I never was; it is not true.

BOURNE: You went from St David's to Scotland.

FARRAR: That did I never; but I went from York to Scotland.

BOURNE: Ah! so said I; you went with Barlow.

FARRAR: That is true, but never from St David's.

BOURNE: You carried books out of Oxford, to the Archbishop of York, L. Lee.

FARRAR: I did not; but I carried old books from St Oswald's to the Bishop of York.

BOURNE: You supplanted your master.

FARRAR: That did I never in my life.

BOURNE: By my faith you did.

FARRAR: Forsooth, I did not, never in my life; but did shield and save my master from danger, and that obtained of King Henry VIII, for my true service, I thank God therefore.

BOURNE (To my lord chancellor): My lord, he hath an ill name in Wales, as ever had any.

FARRAR: That is not so. Whosoever saith so, they shall never be able to prove it.

BOURNE: He hath deceived the queen in diverse sums of money.

FARRAR: That is utterly untrue; I never deceived the king nor queen of one penny in my life, and you shall never be able to prove that you say.

WINCHESTER: Thou art a false knave.

Then Farrar stood up unbidden, for all that while he kneeled, and said, 'No, my lord; I am a true man, I thank God for it. I was born under King Henry VII, I served King Henry VIII and King Edward VI truly, and have served the queen's majesty that now is, truly with my poor heart and word: more I could not do, and I was never false, nor shall be, by the grace of God.'

WINCHESTER: How sayest thou? wilt thou be reformable?

FARRAR: My lord, I have an oath to God, and to King Henry VIII, and also to King Edward, and in that to the queen's majesty, the which I can never break while I live, to die for it.

DURHAM: You have made another oath before.

FARRAR: No, my lord, I never made another oath before.

DURHAM: You made a vow.

FARRAR: That did I not.

WINCHESTER: You made a profession to live without a wife.

FARRAR: No, my lord, that did I never: I made a profession to live chastely; but not without a wife.

WORCESTER: You were sworn to him that was master of your house.

FARRAR: That was I never.

WINCHESTER: Well, you are a froward knave: we will have no more to do with you, seeing that you will not come; we will be short with you, and that you shall know within this seven-night.

FARRAR: I am as it pleaseth your honour to call me; but I cannot break my oath, which your lordship yourself made before me, and gave in example, the which confirmed my conscience. Then I can never break the oath whilst I live, to die for it.

DURHAM: Well, saith he, he standeth upon his oath; call another.

My lord chancellor then rang a little bell; and Mr Farrar said, 'I pray God save the king and queen's majesties long to continue in honour to God's glory and their comfort, and the comfort of the whole realm; and I pray God save all your honours,' and so departed.

After these examinations, Bishop Farrar remained in prison uncondemned, till 14th February, and then was sent down to Wales, to receive sentence of condemnation. Morgan pronounced the definitive sentence against him, contained in writing: by which sentence he denounced him as a heretic excummunicate, and to be given up forthwith to the secular power. Thus this godly bishop, being condemned and degraded, was committed to the secular power, and not long after was brought to the place of execution in the town of Carmarthen, where he, in the market-place on the south side of the cross, on 30th March, most patiently sustained the torments of fire.

¶ John Foxe, *The Book of Martyrs,* revised with notes and an appendix by W. Bramley-Moore (London, 1869), pp. 338–41

John Bradford

'I pray you stretch out your gentleness that I may feel it, for hitherto I have not.'

John Bradford determined to devote his life to the Scriptures, and the ministry of the Word. In order to carry out his plan, he went to Cambridge University, where he was befriended by Martin Bucer, who strongly urged him to use his talents in preaching. Bradford replied that he could not preach, as he did not consider himself qualified for such an office; to which his friend would answer, 'If thou hast not fine wheat bread, yet give the poor people barley bread, or whatsoever else the Lord hath committed unto thee.'

Bradford was appointed by Dr Ridley as a prebendary of St Paul's, where he laboured diligently for three years, after which he was called upon to show his allegiance to his Saviour by following him to prison and to death.

It was in the first year of Queen Mary's reign that the Bishop of Bath, Dr Bourne, preached at Paul's Cross on the merits of Popery, which raised the indignation of the people to such a pitch, that they would have pulled him out from the pulpit by force, had not the bishop, seeing the danger, called to Mr Bradford, who was standing near, to come forward and take his place. Bradford obeyed the request, and so greatly was he respected and beloved, that he soon quelled the rising tumult, and dismissed the people quietly to their homes. Within three days he was summoned before the queen's council, and accused of having put himself forward to preach in the bishop's stead; being found guilty, he was committed to the Tower.

For two years he remained closely confined there; and then he was brought before the lord chancellor, and other councillors, to be examined on the accusation of seditious behaviour at Paul's Cross.

On entering the council room, the chancellor told him he had been justly imprisoned for his arrogancy in preaching without authority; 'but now,' he said, 'the time for mercy has come, and the queen's highness hath by us sent for you, to declare and give the same, if you will with us return; and if you will do as we have done, you shall find as we have found.'

To this Bradford answered, 'My lords, I know that I have been long imprisoned, and – with humble reverence be it spoken – unjustly, for that I did nothing seditiously, falsely, or arrogantly, in word or fact, by preaching or otherwise, but rather sought truth, peace, and all godly quietness, as an obedient and faithful subject, both in going about to serve the present Bishop of Bath, then Mr Bourne, the preacher at the Cross, and in preaching for quietness accordingly.'

The chancellor angrily made answer: I know thou hast a glorious tongue, and goodly shows thou makest; but all is lies thou speakest. And again, I have not forgot how stubborn thou wast when thou wast before us in the Tower, whereupon thou wast committed to prison concerning religion.'

The conversation continued as follows:

BRADFORD: My lord, I stand as before you, so before God, and one day we shall all stand before him; the truth then will be the truth, though now ye will not take it so. Yea, my lord, I dare say that my lord of Bath, Mr Bourne, will witness with me, that I sought his safeguard with the peril of mine own life. I thank God, therefore.

BISHOP BONNER: That is not true, for I myself did see thee take upon thee too much.

BRADFORD: No; I took nothing upon me undesired, and that of Mr

Bourne himself, as, were he present, I dare say he would affirm. For he desired me both to help him to pacify the people, and also not to leave him until he was in safety.

The councillors and bishops then began to question him on religious opinions, that they might find some reason to sentence him to death.

In about a week he was again brought before the council, when the chancellor continued, endeavouring to clear himself from the charge of seeking to shed innocent blood, stating that Bradford's act at Paul's Cross was arrogant and presumptuous, and a taking upon himself to lead the people, which could not but tend to much disquietness. He then accused him of having written seditious letters when in the Tower, and of having endeavoured to pervert the people, and finally questioned him closely as to his belief in the presence of Christ in the sacrament.

At seven the next morning, Mr Thomas Hussey came into the room where he was confined, and, saying that he came to see and speak to him through love, said, 'So wonderfully did you behave yourself before the chancellor and other bishops yesterday, that even the greatest enemies you have say they have no matter against you; therefore I advise you to desire a time, and men to confer with, so by that means you may escape danger, which is otherwise nearer to you than you suppose.'

Bradford refused to make any such request, which would give occasion to people to think that he doubted the doctrine he confessed. While they were still talking Dr Seton entered the room, and began to speak of Ridley and Latimer, who, he said, were unable to answer anything, and had desired to confer with others, hinting that Bradford had better follow their example. Bradford, however, refused his suggestions as he had Mr Hussey's, whereupon they both became enraged, calling him arrogant and vain-glorious.

Soon after they had quitted his cell, the prisoner was again brought before his judges, when, after a long discussion, during which he displayed as much gentleness as they did ferocity, the sentence of excommunication was read, when he knelt down and thanked God that he was thought worthy to suffer for his sake. He remained in prison nearly five months; then he suffered death by being burnt alive, in company with a young man only twenty years of age, being joyful to the last moment of his life that he was thought worthy to die for his Saviour.

¶ John Foxe, *The Book of Martyrs,* revised with notes and an appendix by W. Bramley-Moore (London, 1869), pp. 339–46

Laurence Saunders

Laurence Saunders was one of the Puritans executed in 1555 as part of Queen Mary's great persecution of Protestants.

'If the Devil were wise enough and would stand by in silence and let the Gospel be preached, he would suffer less harm. For when there is no battle for the Gospel it rusts and it finds no cause and no occasion to show its vigour and power. Therefore, nothing better can befall the Gospel than that the world should fight it with force and cunning' *(Martin Luther).*

Laurence preached and in the afternoon returned to the church to deliver the customary second sermon. But the Bishop's officer arrived to escort him to Fulham Palace where he was charged with 'treason for breaking the Queen's proclamation, heresy and sedition for his sermon'. The bishop ordered him to write out his rejection of the Catholic doctrine of the mass. Laurence did so, realising that he was writing his own death warrant. 'My Lord, you do seek my blood,' Laurence said as he handed the paper to Bonner, 'and you shall have it. I pray God that you may be so baptised in it that you may thereafter loathe blood-sucking and become a better man.'

After a fifteen-month imprisonment, Laurence was taken to Coventry, where he arrived on 7th February 1555. He spent the night in the common gaol among other prisoners, where he passed the time praying. Next morning he was led to the place of execution outside the city, dressed in an old gown and a shirt, barefooted. Near the stake an officer asked Laurence to recant his heresies in exchange for a royal pardon: 'If not, yonder fire is prepared for you.'

Laurence remained steadfast. 'It is not I nor my fellow-preachers of God's truth that have hurt the Queen's realm, but yourself and such as you are, which have always resisted God's holy Word. I hold no heresies; but the blessed gospel of Christ, that I hold; that have I taught, and that will I never revoke.'

With that the tormentor cried, 'Away with him!'

'And away,' Foxe wrote, 'went Saunders with a merry courage towards the fire. He fell to the ground and prayed; he rose up again and took the stake in his arms and kissed it saying, 'Welcome the cross of Christ. Welcome everlasting life.'

Martyrdoms of Ridley and Latimer

'Be of good comfort, Mr Ridley, and play the man! We shall this day light such a candle, by God's grace, in England, as I trust never shall be put out' (Latimer's words to Ridley as a faggot was set on fire at his feet).

Ridley

On 17th October 1555, those two pillars of Christ's church, Dr Nicholas Ridley, Bishop of London, and Mr Hugh Latimer, sometime Bishop of Worcester, were burnt in one fire at Oxford – men ever memorable for their piety, learning, and incomparable ornaments and gifts of grace, joined with no less commendable sincerity of life.

Dr Ridley was first brought to a knowledge of Christ and his gospel by reading Bertram's book on the sacrament; and his conference with Archbishop Cranmer, and with Peter Martyr, did much to confirm him in that belief. Being now, by the grace of God, thoroughly converted to the true way, he was as constant and faithful in the right knowledge which the Lord had revealed unto him, as he was before blind and zealous in his old ignorance, and so long as the power and authority of the state defended the gospel, and supported the happiness of the church, his influence was mighty for spiritual good. But after it pleased God (in his wise providence) to bereave us of our stay, it taking from us King Edward, the whole state of the Church of England was left desolate and open to the enemy's hand: so that Bishop Ridley, after the accession of Queen Mary, was one of the first upon whom they laid their hands, and sent to prison: first in the Tower, and from there conveyed, with the Archbishop of Canterbury [Cranmer] and Mr Latimer, to Oxford, and with them confined in the common prison of Bocardo.

Letter from Bishop Ridley

The following letter from Bishop Ridley and his fellow-prisoners was written in 1554 to Mr Bradford and his fellow-prisoners in the King's Bench prison:

As for the rumours that have or do go abroad, either of our relenting or massing, we trust that they which know God and their duty towards their brethren in Christ, will not be too light of belief. For it is not the slanderer's evil tongue, but a man's evil deed, that can with God defile a man; and, therefore, with God's grace, you shall never have cause to do otherwise than you say you do, that is, not to doubt but that we will, by God's grace, continue. Like rumours as you have heard of our coming to London have been here spread of coming of certain learned men prisoners hither from London; but as yet we know no certainty which of these rumours is or shall be more true. Know you that we have your in our daily remembrance, and wish you and all the rest of our foresaid companies well in Christ.

My lord of Worcester passed through Oxford, but he did not visit us. The same day our restraint began to be more close, and the book of the communion was taken from us by the bailiffs, at the mayor's command, as the bailiffs did report to us. Blessed be God, with all our evil reports, grudges, and restraints, we are merry in God; all our care is and shall be, by God's grace, to please and serve him, of whom we look and hope, after there temporal and momentary miseries, to have eternal joy and perpetual felicity with Abraham, Isaac, and Jacob, Peter and Paul, and all the heavenly company of the angels in heaven, through Jesus Christ our Lord. As yet there has not learned man, nor any scholar, been to visit us since we came into Bocardo, which now in Oxford may be called a college of quondams [people who had previously held office]. For as you know we are no fewer than three, and I dare say every one well contented with his portion, which I do reckon to be our heavenly Father's fatherly, good, and gracious gift. Thus fare you well. We shall, by God's grace, one day meet together, and be merry. That day assuredly approacheth apace; the Lord grant that it may shortly come. For before that day come, I fear the world will wax worse and worse. But then all our enemies shall be overthrown and trodden under foot; righteousness and truth then shall have the victory, and bear the bell away, whereof the Lord grant us to be partakers, and all that love truly the truth.

We all pray you, as we can, to cause all our commendations to be made unto all such as you know did visit us and you when we were in the Tower, with their friendly remembrances and benefits. Mrs Wilkson and Mrs Warcup have not forgotten us, but ever since we came to Bocardo, with their charitable and friendly benevolence, have comforted us: not that else we did lack (for God be blessed, he hath always sufficiently provided for us), but that is a great comfort, and an occasion for us to bless God, when we see that he maketh them so friendly to tender us, whom some of us were never acquainted withal.

Yours in Christ, Nicholas Ridley.

Latimer

At the age of fourteen he was sent to Cambridge University. Latimer, like St Paul, was both zealous and misguided. He confesses that as a priest he was so servile an observer of the Romish decrees that in the celebration of mass his conscience was much troubled lest he had insufficiently mingled his wine with water; and, moreover, he believed that he should never be damned if he became a professed friar, with many other like superstitions. Mr Thomas Bilney, perceiving that Latimer had a great zeal, although, like that of some of the Judaising teachers, not according to knowledge, felt a brotherly pity towards him, and began to consider by what means he might expound to this ignorant brother the way of God more perfectly, even as Aquila and Priscilla did to Apollos.

Impressed with these feelings, after a short time he came to Mr Latimer's study, and asked him to hear his own confession; the result of which interview was, that Latimer's understanding was so enlightened by God's good Spirit, that immediately he forsook the study of the school doctors, and other such philosophers falsely so called, and became an earnest student of the Bible, and of that divinity which centres in the cross of Christ. He was a changed character, for he hated that which he had loved, and he now loved that which he had hated. Jesus, the Son of God, had been revealed to him, and, like the apostle, in faith and obedience he was now ready to ask, 'Lord, what wilt thou have me to do?'

After Latimer preached he gave the people certain cards out of the 5th, 6th, and 7th chapters of St Matthew, in the study of which they might, not only then, but at all other times, occupy their time. For the chief triumph [the word 'trump', as now used, is a corruption of 'triumph' – the 'triumph card'] in the cards he selected the heart, as the principal thing with which they should serve God, whereby he quite overthrew all hypocritical and external ceremonies, not tending to the furtherance of God's holy Word and sacraments. He added, moreover, to the praise of that triumph, that though it were ever so small, yet it would take up the best court card beside in the bunch, yea, though it were the king of clubs, meaning thereby how the Lord would be worshipped and served in simplicity of heart and verity, wherein consisteth true Christian religion, and not in the outward deeds of the letter only, or in the glittering show of man's traditions, or pardons, pilgrimages, ceremonies, vows, devotions, voluntary works, and works of supererogation, foundations, oblations, the

Pope's supremacy, and 'other such like things'. For the better attaining hereof, he wished the Scriptures to be in English, in order that the common people might be enabled to learn their duty to God and to their neighbours. As Latimer's sermons were so important in their consequences, we here present the reader with the following beautiful extract from one of them.

Extract from a sermon of Mr Latimer, in Cambridge, about the year 1529

'Tue quis es?' Which words are a much to say in English, 'Who art thou?' These be the words of the Pharisees, which were sent by the Jews unto St John the Baptist in the wilderness, to have knowledge of him who he was; which words they spake unto him of an evil intent, thinking that he would have taken on him to be Christ, and so they would have had him done by their good wills, because they knew that he was more carnal and given to their laws than Christ indeed should be, as they perceived by their old prophecies: and also, because they marvelled much at his great doctrine, preaching, and baptising, they were in doubt whether he was Christ or not; wherefore they said unto him, 'Who art thou?' Then answered St John, an confessed that he was not Christ.

Now then, according to the preacher, let every man and woman, of a good and simple mind, contrary to the Pharisees' intent, ask this question, 'Who art thou?' This question must be moved to themselves, what they be of themselves, on this fashion: 'What art thou of thy only and natural generation between father and mother, when thou camest into the world? What substance, what virtue, what goodness art thou of thyself?' Which question, if thou rehearse oftentimes to thyself, thou shalt well perceive and understand how thou shalt reply, which must be made like this: 'I am of myself, and by myself, coming from my natural father and mother, the child of anger and indignation of God, the true inheritor of hell, a lump of sin, and working nothing of myself, but all towards hell, except I have better help of another than I have of myself.' Now we may see in what state we enter into this world, that we be of ourselves the true and just inheritors of hell, the children of the ire and indignation of Christ, working all towards hell, whereby we deserve of ourselves perpetual damnation by the right judgment of God, and the true claim of ourselves: which unthrifty state that we be born unto is come unto us for our own deserts, as proveth well this example following:

Let it be admitted for the probation of this, that it might please the king's grace now being, to accept into his favour a mean man of simple degree and birth, not born to any possession; whom the king's grace favoureth, not because this person hath of himself deserved any such favour, but that the king casteth his favour unto him of his own mere motion and fancy: and because the king's grace will more declare his favour unto him, he giveth unto this said man a thousand pounds in lands, to him and his heirs, on this condition, that he shall take upon him to be the chief captain and defender of his town of Calais, and to be true and faithful to him in the custody of the same, against the Frenchmen especially above all other enemies.

This man taketh on him this charge, promising this fidelity thereunto. It chanceth in process of time, that by the singular acquaintance and frequent familiarity of this captain with the Frenchman, these Frenchmen give unto the said captain of Calais a great sum of money, so that he will be but content and agreeable that they may enter into the said town of Calais by force of arms, and so thereby possess the same unto the crown of France. Upon this agreement the Frenchman do invade the said town of Calais, only by the negligence of this captain.

Now the king hearing of this invasion, cometh with a great puissance to defend this his said town, and so by good policy of war overcometh the said Frenchmen, and entereth again into his town of Calais. Then he being desirous to know how these enemies of his came tither, maketh strict search and inquiry by whom this treason was conspired; but this search it was known, and found by his own captain to be the very author and the beginner of the betraying of it. The king, seeing the great infidelity of this person, dischargeth this man of his office, and taketh from him and his heirs this thousand pounds' possession. Think you not that the king doth use justice unto him, and all his posterity and heirs? Yes truly; the said captain cannot deny himself but that he had true justice, considering how unfaithfully he behaved himself to his prince, contrary to his own fidelity and promise. So likewise it was of our first father Adam: he had given him the spirit and science of knowledge, to work all goodness therewith; this said spirit was not given only to him, but unto all his heirs and posterity. He had also delivered him the town of Calais, that is to say, Paradise in earth, the most strong and fairest town in the world, to be in his custody: he, nevertheless, by the instigation of these Frenchmen, that is, the temptation of the fiend, did consent unto their desire, and so he broke his promise and fidelity, the commandment of the everlasting King, his master, in eating of the apple by him prohibited.

Now then, the King, seeing this great treason in his captain, dispossessed him of the thousand pounds of lands, that is to say, from everlasting life and glory, and all his heirs and posterity: for likewise as he had the spirit of science and knowledge for him and his heirs, so in like manner when he lost the same, his heirs also lost it by him, and in him. So now this example proveth that by our father Adam we had once in him the very inheritance of everlasting joy; and by him and in him again we lost the same.

And now the world standing in this damnable state, cometh in the occasion of the incarnation of Christ; the Father in heaven perceiving the frail nature of man, that he by himself and of himself could do nothing for himself, by his prudent wisdom sent down the second person in the Trinity, his Son Jesus Christ, to declare unto man his pleasure and commandment: and so at the Father's will Christ took on him human nature, being willing to deliver man out of this miserable way, and was content to suffer cruel passion in shedding his blood for all mankind; and so left behind, for our safeguard, laws and ordinances, to keep us always in the right path to everlasting life, as the gospels, the sacraments, the commandments etc, which if we keep and observe according to our profession, we shall answer better the question 'Who art thou?' that we did before: for before thou didst enter into the sacrament of baptism, thou wert but a natural man, or a natural woman; as I might say, a man, a woman; but after thou takest on thee Christ's religion, thou hast a longer name, for then thou art a Christian man, a Christian woman. Now then, seeing thou art a Christian man, what shall be the answer to this question, 'Who art thou?'

The answer to this question is, when I ask it of myself, I must say that I am a Christian man, a Christian woman, the child of everlasting joy, through the merits of the bitter passion of Christ. This is a joyful answer. Here we may see how much we are bound and indebted to God, that hath revived us from death to life, and saved us that were damned: which great benefit we cannot well consider, unless we remember what we were of ourselves before we meddled with him or his laws: and the more we know our feeble nature, and set less by it, the more we shall conceive and know in our hearts what God hath done for us; and the more we know what God hath done for us, the less we shall set by ourselves, and the more we shall love and please God; so that in no condition we shall either know ourselves of God, except we utterly confess ourselves to be mere vileness and corruption. Well, now it is come to this point, that we are Christian men, Christian women, I pray you, what does Christ require of a Christian man, or of a Christian woman? Christ requireth nothing else of a Christian man or woman but that they will observe his rule.

To relate the noise and alarm the preaching of these sermons occasioned at Cambridge would require too much time and space.

First came out the prior of Black Friars, named Buckenham, who attempted to prove that it was not expedient for the Scriptures to be in English, lest the ignorant and vulgar sort might be running into some inconvenience: as for example:

'The ploughman, when he heareth this in the gospel, "No man that layeth his hand on the plough and looketh back, is meet for the kingdom of God," might, peradventure, cease from his plough. Likewise a baker, when he hears that a little leaven corrupteth a whole lump of dough, may perchance leave our bread unleavened, and so our bodies shall be unseasoned. Also the simple man, when he heareth in the Gospel, "If thine eye offend thee, pluck it out, and cast if from thee," may make himself blind, and so fill the world with beggars.' Mr Latimer, being thus persecuted by the friars, doctors, and masters of that university, about the year 1529, continued, notwithstanding the malice of these adversaries, preaching in Cambridge for about three years. Mr Latimer and Mr Bilney conferred together so frequently, that the field wherein they walked was called 'The Heretics' Hill'.

Mr Latimer was, at length, cited before the cardinal for heresy. He was brought to London, where he was greatly molested, and detained a long time from his cure, being summoned thrice every week before the said bishops, to vindicate his preaching, and to subscribe to certain articles or propositions, devised by the instigation of his enemies. The following curious incident was related by himself, in a sermon preached at Stamford, 9th October 1550, and the following are his words:

> I was once in examination before five or six bishops, where I had much trouble: thrice every week I came to examinations, and many snares and traps were laid to get something. Now God knoweth I was ignorant of the law, but that God gave me wisdom what I should speak; it was God indeed, or else I had never escaped them. At last I was brought forth to be examined into a chamber hung with arras, where I was wont to be examined; but now at this time the chamber was somewhat altered. For now the fire was taken away, and an arras hung over the chimney, and the table stood near the fireplace.
>
> There was among the bishops who examined me one with whom I have been very familiar, and took him for my great friend, an aged man, and he sat next to the table's end.
>
> Then among all other questions, he put forth a very subtle and crafty one, and such a one, indeed, as I could not think so great danger in. And when I should make answer, 'I pray you, Mr Latimer,' said one, 'speak out; I am very thick of hearing, and here may be many that sit far off.' I marvelled at this, that I was bid to speak out, and began to suspect, and

give an ear to the chimney; and there I heard a pen writing in the chimney behind the cloth. They had appointed one there to write all mine answers, for they made sure that I should not start from them; and there was no starting from them. God was my good Lord, and gave me answer, else I could never have escaped.

Mr Latimer continued in his laborious episcopal functions until the passing of the Six Articles. Being then much distressed through the straitness of the times, he felt that the must either sacrifice a good conscience or else forsake his bishopric; accordingly he did the latter. When he visited London, he was imprisoned in the Tower, where he remained until King Edward came to the crown, when the golden mouth of this English Chrysostom was opened again. He often affirmed that the preaching of the Gospel would cost him his life, for which he was cheerfully prepared; for after the death of King Edward, and not long after Mary had been proclaimed queen, Mr Latimer was arrested and brought to London.

When Mr Latimer entered Smithfield, he merrily said that Smithfield had long groaned for him. He was then brought before the council, where he patiently bore all the mocks and taunts of the scornful Papists, and was again sent to the Tower.

Examination of Dr Ridley, September 1555

The Bishop of Lincoln, in a long oration, exhorted Dr Ridley to recant, and submit himself to the universal faith of Christ, endeavouring to prove the right of supremacy in the Church of Rome, charging him also with having formerly been favourable to their doctrine, and adducing many other arguments.

RIDLEY: I most heartily thank your lordship, as well for your gentleness as for your good and favourable zeal in this learned exhortation, in which I have marked especially three points, by which you sought to persuade me to leave my religion, which I perfectly know to be grounded, not upon man's imaginations and decrees, but upon the infallible truth of Christ's gospel.

The first point is this, That the see of Rome, taking its beginning from Peter, upon whom you say Christ hath built his Church, hath in all ages, lineally, from bishop to bishop, been brought to this time.

Secondly, That even the holy fathers from time to time have confessed the same.

Thirdly, That in that I was once of the same opinion, and together with you I did acknowledge the same.

First, as touching the saying of Christ, from whence your lordship gathereth the foundation of the Church upon Peter, truly the place is not to be understood as you take it, as the circumstance of the place will declare. For after Christ had asked his disciples whom men judged him to be, and they answered that some had said he was a prophet, some Elias, some one thing, some another, then he said, 'Whom say ye that I am?' Then Peter answered, 'I say that thou art Christ, the Son of God.' To whom Christ answered, 'I say thou art Peter, and upon this stone I will build my Church;' that is to say, Upon this stone, not meaning Peter himself, as though he would have constituted a mortal man so frail and brittle a foundation of his stable and infallible Church; but upon this rock-stone, that is, this confession of thine, that I am the Son of God, I will build my Church. For this is the foundation and beginning of all Christianity, with word, heart, and mind, to confess that Christ is the Son of God.

Here you see upon what foundation Christ's Church is built, not upon the frailty of men, but upon the infallible Word of God.

Now as touching the lineal descent of the bishops in the see of Rome, true it is that the patriarchs of Rome in the apostles' time, and long after, were great maintainers of Christ's glory, in which, above all other countries and regions, there especially was preached the true gospel, the sacraments most duly administered; and as, before Christ's coming, it was a city so valiant in power and martial affairs, that all the world was in a manner subject to it, and after Christ's passion diverse of the apostles there suffered persecution for the Gospel's sake, so after that the emperors, their hearts being illuminated, received the Gospel, and became Christians, the Gospel there, as well for the fame of the place, flourished most, whereby the bishops of that place were had in more reverence and honour, most esteemed in all councils and assemblies, not because they acknowledged them to be their head, but because the place was most reverenced and spoken of, for the great power and strength of the same. As now here in England, the Bishop of Lincoln, in sessions and sittings. As long as Rome continued to set forth God's glory I cannot but commend it. But after the bishops of the see, seeking their own pride, and not God's honour, began to set themselves above kings and emperors, challenging to them the title of God's vicars, the dominion and supremacy over all the world, I cannot but with St Gregory, a Bishop of Rome also, confess that place is the very true Antichrist, where St John speaketh by name of the whore of Babylon, and say, with the said St Gregory, 'He that maketh himself a bishop over all the world is worse than Antichrist.'

Now where you say I was once of the same religion as you are of, the truth is, I cannot but confess, the same. Yet so was St Paul a persecutor of Christ.

LINCOLN: Mr Ridley, we came here, not to dispute with you but only to take your answer to certain articles. These articles you shall now hear, and tomorrow, at eight o'clock, in St Mary's Church, we will require and take your answer, and then according to the same proceed.

The Articles which condemned Ridley and Latimer

In the name of God, Amen. We, John of Lincoln, James of Gloucester, and John of Bristol, bishops, etc.

1. We do object to thee, Nicholas Ridley, and to thee, Hugh Latimer, jointly and severally, first, that thou, Nicholas Ridley, in this high University of Oxford, in the year 1554, hast affirmed, and openly defended and maintained, and in many other times and places besides, that the true and natural body of Christ, after the consecration of the priest, is not really present in the sacrament of the altar.

2. That thou hast publicly affirmed and defended that in the sacrament of the altar remaineth still the substance of bread and wine.

3. That thou hast openly affirmed, and obstinately maintained, that in the mass is no propitiatory sacrifice for the living and the dead.

After examination upon the above articles, the Bishop of Lincoln concluded: 'Mr Ridley, I am sorry to see such stubbornness in you, that by no means you will be persuaded to acknowledge your errors, and receive the truth: but seeing it is so, because you will not suffer us to persist in the first, we must of necessity proceed to the other part of our commission. Therefore, I pray you, hearken to what I shall say.' And forthwith he read the sentence of condemnation, which was written in a long process; the substance of which was, that the said Nicholas Ridley did affirm, maintain, and stubbornly defend certain opinions, assertions, and heresies, contrary to the Word of God, and the received faith of the Church, and could by no means be turned from these heresies. They therefore condemned him as an obstinate heretic, and adjudged him presently, both by word and in deed, to be degraded from the degree of a bishop, from the priesthood, and all the ecclesiastical orders; declaring him, moreover, to be no member of the Church, and therefore they committed him to the secular powers, of them to receive the due punishment according to the temporal laws.

The last examination of Bishop Latimer before the Commissioners
LINCOLN: Recant, revoke your errors and turn to the catholic Church.
LATIMER: Your lordship often repeats the 'catholic Church', as though I should deny the same. No, my lord, I confess there is a catholic Church, to the determination of which I will stand, but not the church which you call catholic, which ought rather to be termed diabolic.

Christ made one oblation and sacrifice for the sins of the whole world, and that a perfect sacrifice; neither needeth there to be, nor can there be, any other propitiatory sacrifice.
LINCOLN: Recant, revoke your errors and false assertions.
LATIMER: I will not deny my Master, Christ.

The bishop then committed Mr Ridley to the mayor, saying, 'Now he is your prisoner, Mr Mayor.'

Ridley and Latimer's martyrdom, 16th October 1555
The place for their execution was chosen on the north side of Oxford, in the ditch over against Balliol College; and for fear of any tumult that might arise to hinder the burning of the servants of Christ, the Lord Williams and the householders of the city were commanded by the queen's letters to be prepared to assist if required.

Dr Ridley had on a black gown, furred and faced with foins, such as he used to wear when he was a bishop; a tippet of velvet, furred likewise, about his neck; a velvet night-cap upon his head, with a corner cap; and slippers on his feet. He walked to the stake between the mayor and the alderman.

After him came Mr Latimer, in a poor Bristow frieze frock, much worn, with his buttoned cap and kerchief on his head, and a new long shroud hanging down to his feet. The sight of these two martyrs stirred men's hearts to rue upon them, beholding, on the one hand, the honour they sometimes had, and on the other, the calamity into which they had fallen. They came to the stake. Dr Ridley, earnestly holding up both his hands, looked towards heaven; then shortly after, seeing Mr Latimer, with a cheerful look he ran to him and embraced him, saying, 'Be of good heart, brother, for God will either assuage the fury of the flame, or else strengthen us to abide it.'

He then went to the stake, and, kneeling down, prayed with great fervour, while Mr Latimer following, kneeled also, and prayed with like earnestness. After this, they arose and conversed together, and, while thus employed, Dr Smith began his sermon from Paul's epistle to the Corinthians, chapter 13: 'If I yield my body to the fire to be burnt, and have not charity, I shall gain nothing thereby.' Strange paradox, that this panegyric on love should have been so prostituted on this occasion.

At the conclusion of the sermon, which only lasted a quarter of an hour, Ridley said to Latimer, 'Will you answer, or shall I?'

Mr Latimer said, 'Begin you first, I pray you.'

'I will,' said Dr Ridley.

He then, with Mr Latimer, kneeled to my Lord Williams, the Vice-Chancellor of Oxford, and the other commissioners, who sat upon a form, and said, 'I beseech you, my lord, even for Christ's sake, that I may speak but two or three words.'

And while my lord bent his head to the mayor and vice-Chancellor, to know whether he might have leave to speak, the bailiffs and Dr Marshal, the vice-chancellor, ran hastily to him, and, with their hands stopping his mouth, said, 'Mr Ridley, if you will revoke your erroneous opinions, you shall not only have liberty so to do, but also your life.'

'Not otherwise?' said Dr Ridley.

'No,' answered Dr Marshal; 'therefore, if you will not do so, there is no remedy: you must suffer for your deserts.'

'Well,' said the martyr, 'so long as the breath is in my body, I will never deny my Lord Christ and his known truth. God's will be done in me.' With that he rose, and said, with a loud voice, 'I commit our cause to Almighty God, who will indifferently judge all.'

To which Mr Latimer added his old saying, 'Well, there is nothing hid but it shall be opened.' They were then commanded to prepare immediately for the stake.

They accordingly obeyed with all meekness. Dr Ridley gave his gown and tippet to his brother-in-law, Mr Shipside, who all the time of his imprisonment, although he was not suffered to come to him, lay there, at his own charges, to provide him necessaries, which he sent him by the sergeant in charge. Some other of his apparel he also gave away; the others the bailiffs took.

He likewise made presents of other small things to gentlemen standing by, divers of whom were weeping pitifully. To Sir Henry Lea he gave a new groat; to my Lord Williams' gentleman, some napkins; some nutmegs, some pieces of ginger, his watch dial, and all that he had about him, he gave to those who stood near. Some plucked the points off his hose, and happy was he who could get the least rag for a remembrance of this good man.

Mr Latimer quietly suffered his keeper to pull off his hose and his other apparel, which was very simple; and being stripped to his shroud, he seemed as comely a person as one could well see.

Then Dr Ridley, standing as yet in his truss, or trousers, said to his brother, 'It were best for me to go in my trousers still.'

'No,' said Mr Latimer, 'it will put you to more pain; and it will do a poor man good.'

Whereunto Dr Ridley said, 'Be it, in the name of God,' and so unlaced himself. Then, being in his shirt, he held up his hand, and said, 'Oh, heavenly Father, I give unto thee most hearty thanks that thou hast called me to be a professor of thee, even unto death. I beseech thee, Lord God, have mercy on this realm of England, and deliver it from all her enemies.'

Then the smith took an iron chain and placed it about both their waists; and as he was knocking in the staple, Dr Ridley took the chain in his hand, and, looking aside to the smith, said, 'Good fellow, knock it in hard, for the flesh will have its course.'

Then Dr Ridley's brother (Shipside) brought him a bag of gunpowder and tied it about his neck. Dr Ridley asked him what it was. He answered, 'Gunpowder'.

Then he said, 'I will take it to be sent of God, therefore I will receive it. And have you any,' said he, 'for my brother?' (meaning Mr Latimer).

'Yea, sir, that I have,' said he.

'Then give it him,' said he, 'in time, lest you come too late.'

So his brother went and carried it to Mr Latimer.

They then brought a lighted faggot, and laid it at Dr Ridley's feet; upon which Mr Latimer said, 'Be of good comfort, Mr Ridley, and play the man! We shall this day light such a candle, by God's grace, in England, as I trust never shall be put out.'

When Dr Ridley saw the fire flaming up towards him, he cried out, with an amazing loud voice, 'Into thy hands, O Lord, I commend my spirit: Lord, receive my spirit!' and continued often to repeat, 'Lord, Lord, receive my spirit!'

Mr Latimer cried as vehemently, 'O Father of heaven, receive my soul!' after which he soon died, seemingly with little pain.

But Dr Ridley, owing to the bad arrangement of the fire (the faggots being green, and piled too high, so that the flames were kept down by the green wood, and burned fiercely beneath), was put to such exquisite pain, that he desired them, for God's sake, to let the fire come to him; which his brother-in-law heard, but did not very well understand; so to rid him out of his pain (for which cause he gave attendance), and not well knowing what he did, in his own sorrow, he heaped faggots upon him, so that he quite covered him, which made the fire so vehement beneath, that it burned all Ridley's lower parts before it touched his upper, and made him struggle under the faggots. Ridley, in his agony, often desired the spectators to let the fire come to him, saying, 'I cannot burn.' Yet in all his torment he did not forget always to call upon God, 'Lord, have mercy upon me!' yet intermingling his cry with 'Let the fire come unto me, I cannot burn;' in which pain he laboured till one of the bystanders pulled the faggots from above with his bill, and where Ridley saw the fire flame up, he leaned himself to that side. As soon as the fire touched the gunpowder, he was seen to stir no more, but burned on the other side, falling down at Mr Latimer's feet, his body being divided.

The dreadful sight filled almost every eye with tears, for some pitied their persons, who thought their souls had no need thereof.

¶ John Foxe, *The Book of Martyrs*, revised with notes and an appendix by W. Bramley-Moore (London, 1869), pp. 413–71

Thomas Cranmer
21st March 1556

'I recant of my recantations.'

Archbishop of Canterbury and compiler of the Book of Common Prayer. In Queen Mary's reign he was tried and condemned to be executed for being a heretic. Before his execution, he signed recantations of the beliefs which were really his.

Thomas Cranmer was born at Aslacton, in Nottinghamshire, on 2nd July 1489. While he was at Cambridge, the vexed question of King Henry VIII's divorce with Lady Catherine of Aragon arose. The cardinals Campeggio and Wolsey had been appointed as Papal commissioners to decide the knotty point, but finding themselves beset with difficulties, from Henry's urgency on the one hand, and from the fact that Catherine was aunt to the Emperor Charles V, on the other, procrastinated matters, in the usual hope that time and the chapter of accidents would befriend them, and bring the desired solution. The king, however, became enraged at the delay. He accordingly dismissed Cardinal Campeggio, and visited Waltham Abbey, in Essex, where Cranmer was staying, because of the plague. At Waltham, Dr Gardiner, later Bishop of Winchester, and Fox, subsequently Bishop of Hereford, who were in attendance on the king, met Cranmer, and the conversation turned upon the pending controversy of the time.

In the course of conversation Cranmer suggested the expediency of 'trying the question by the Word of God'; and that the matter might be as well settled in England by the universities as in Rome, or in any foreign court. When Fox, who was Royal almoner, repeated the substance of the conversation to the king, the king swore 'that that man had the right sow by the ear'. Cranmer was accordingly summoned to court, received into favour, and, on the disgrace of Wolsey, promoted to the see of Canterbury.

In September 1555, Dr Brooks, Bishop of Gloucester, came with authority from Cardinal Pole to judge Cranmer. Brooks required Cranmer to appear before the Pope within eighty days. In February, 1556, Bonner and Thirleby were sent to degrade him for his contumacy in not going to Rome, although he was all the while kept in prison.

Cranmer denied that the Pope had any authority over him, and appealed from his sentence to a free general council.

But now many devices were set on foot to make him recant: both English and Spanish divines had many conferences with him, and great hopes were given him, not only of life, but of preferment, if he would do it; and these, at last, had a fatal effect upon him, for he signed a recantation of all his former opinions, and concluded it with a protestation that he had done it freely, for the discharge of his conscience. The queen, however, was resolved to sacrifice him to her resentments; and, she said, it was good for his own soul that he repented; but since he had been the chief spreader of heresy over the nation, it was necessary to make him a public example. Accordingly the writ was sent down to burn him. Dr Cole preached, and vindicated the queen's justice in condemning Cranmer; but magnified his conversion much, and ascribed it to God's Spirit. He gave him great hopes of heaven, and promised him all the relief that masses could bring.

All this time, with great grief, Carnmer stood hearing his sermon: one while lifting up his hands and eyes unto heaven, and then again, for shame, letting them down to earth, while the tears gushed from his eyes. Great commiseration and pity moved all men's hearts, that beheld so heavy a countenance, and such abundance of tears in an old man of so reverend dignity.

After Cole had ended his sermon, he called back the people to prayers that were ready to depart. 'Brethren,' he said, 'lest any man should doubt of this man's earnest conversion and repentance, you shall hear him speak before you, and, therefore, I pray you, Mr Cranmer, to perform that now which you promised not long ago – namely, that you would openly express the true and undoubted profession of your faith, that you may take away all suspicion from men, and that all men may understand that you are a catholic indeed.'

'I will do it,' said the archbishop, 'and that with a good will;' and rising up, and putting off his cap, he began to speak thus unto the people:

Cranmer's last words

Good people – my dearly beloved brethren in Christ, I beseech you most heartily to pray for me to Almighty God, that he will forgive me all my sins and offences, which are without number, and great above measure. But yet one thing grieveth my conscience more than all the rest, whereof, God willing, I intend to speak more hereafter. But how great and how many soever my sins be, I beseech you to pray to God of his mercy to pardon and forgive them all. [And here, kneeling down, he said the following prayer.]

'O Father of heaven, O Son of God, Redeemer of the world, O Holy Ghost, three persons and one God, have mercy upon me, most wretched caitiff and miserable sinner. I have offended both against heaven and earth more than my tongue can express. Whither, then, may I go, or whither shall I flee? To heaven I may be ashamed to lift up mine eyes, and in earth I find no place of refuge or succour. To thee, therefore, O Lord, do I run; to thee do I humble myself, saying, O Lord my God, my sins be great, but yet have mercy upon me for thy great mercy. The great mystery that God became man was not wrought for little or few offences. Thou didst not give thy Son, O heavenly Father, unto death for small sins only, but for all the greatest sins of the world, so that the sinner return to thee with his whole heart, as I do at this present. Wherefore have mercy on me, O God, whose property is always to have mercy; have mercy upon me, O Lord, for they great mercy. I crave nothing for mine own merits, but for thy name's sake. And now, O Father of heaven, hallowed be thy name.'

Every man, good people, desireth at the time of his death to give some good exhortation, that others may remember the same before their death, and be the better thereby; so I beseech God grant me that I may speak something at this my departing, whereby God may be glorified, and you edified.

First, it is a heavy cause to see that so many folk so much dote upon the love of this false world, and be so careful for it, that of the love of God, or the world to come, they seem to care very little or nothing. Therefore, this shall be my first exhortation: That you set not your minds over much upon this deceitful world, but upon God, and upon the world to come, and to learn to know what this lesson meaneth which St John teacheth, that the love of this world is hatred against God.'

The second exhortation is, That next unto God you obey your King and Queen, willingly and gladly.'

The third exhortation is, That you love altogether like brethren and sisters.'

The fourth exhortation shall be to them that have great substance and riches of this world, That they will well consider and weigh Luke 18:24,

1 John 3:17 and James 5:1–3. Let them that be rich ponder well these three sentences; for if they ever had occasion to show their charity, they have it now at this present, the poor people being so many, and victuals so dear.'

And now, forasmuch as I am come to the last end of my life, whereupon hangeth all my life past and all my life to come, either to live with my master Christ for ever in joy, or else to be in pain for ever with wicked devils in hell, and I see before my eyes presently either heaven ready to receive me, or else hell ready to swallow me up; I shall therefore declare to you my very faith how I believe, without any colour of dissimulation, for now is no time to dissemble, whatsoever I have said or written in times past.

First, I believe in God the Father Almighty, maker of heaven and earth etc. And I believe every article of the catholic faith, every word and sentence taught by our Saviour Jesus Christ, his apostles and prophets, in the New and Old Testament.

And now I come to the great thing, that so much troubleth my conscience, more than any thing that ever I did or said in my whole life; and this is the setting abroad of a writing contrary to the Truth; which now here I renounce and refuse, as things written with my hand, contrary to the truth which I thought in my heart, and written for fear of death, and to save my life, if it might be; and that is, all such bills and papers which I have written or signed with my hand since my degradation, wherein I have written many things untrue. And forasmuch as my hand offended, writing contrary to my heart, my hand shall first be punished therefore; for, may I come to the fire it shall be first burned.

[In two sentences that followed he abjured the Pope and stood by his former book on the sacrament.]

There was an immediate outcry at this unexpected recantation of his recantations, and he was pulled down from the stage and hustled along the street to the ditch opposite Balliol College, where Latimer and Ridley had been burned.

And when the wood was kindled, and the fire began to burn near him, stretching out his arm, he put his right hand into the flame, which he held so steadfast and immovable that all men might see his hand burned before his body was touched. His body did so abide the burning of the flame, with such constancy and steadfastness, that standing always in one place, without moving his body, he seemed to move no more than the stake to which he was bound: his eyes were lifted up unto heaven, and often times he repented his unworthy right hand, so long as his voice would suffer him: and using often the words of Stephen, 'Lord Jesus receive my spirit'; in the greatness of the flame he gave up the ghost.

¶ John Foxe, *The Book of Martyrs*, revised with notes and an appendix by W. Bramley-Moore (London, 1869), pp. 401–15

Persecutions in the Netherlands

In 1568 Scoblant, Hues and Coomans were arrested in Antwerp. In a letter from prison they wrote:

> Since it is the will of the Almighty that we should suffer for his name, we patiently submit; though the flesh may rebel against the spirit, yet the truths of the gospel shall support us, and Christ shall bruise the serpent's head. We are comforted, for we have faith; we fear not affliction, for we have hope; we forgive our enemies, for we have charity. Do not worry about us, we are happy because of God's promises and exult in being thought worthy to suffer for Christ's sake. We do not desire release, but fortitude; we ask not for liberty, but for the power of perseverance; we wish for no change but that which places a crown of victory on our heads.

Such were the noble sentiments of these three servants of God when subjected too the fiery furnace of martyrdom; the secret of their strength was because there was a fourth with them, even the Son of God.

Scoblant was the first to be put on trial. He persisted in his faith and was sentenced to death. On his return to prison he asked his jailor not to allow any friar to visit him, saying,

> They can do me no good, but may greatly disturb me; I trust that my salvation is already sealed in heaven, and that the blood of Christ, in which I firmly trust, has washed away my sins. I now throw off this mantle of clay, for robes of eternal glory. May I be the last martyr to Papal tyranny, that the church of Christ may have rest on earth, as she will hereafter.

On the day of execution he sang Psalm 40 and repeated the Lord's Prayer with great fervency as he was bound to the stake. Having commended his soul to God, the martyr soon perished in the flames.

Shortly after this Hues died in prison.

After the loss of Hues, Coomans wrote to his friends: 'I am now deprived of my companions: Scobland is martyred, and Hues is dead; yet I am not alone: the God of Israel is with me, who is my shield and my exceeding great reward.' When brought to trial, Coomans readily acknowledged himself to be of the reformed religion; and to every charge levelled against him explained his doctrine from the gospel.

'But,' said the judge, 'will you die for the faith you profess?'

'I am not only willing to die for the truth,' replied Coomans, 'but also to suffer the utmost stretch of inventive cruelty for the gospel's sake; after which my soul shall be received by God himself in the midst of eternal glory.' After this Coomans was sentenced to death. He went cheerfully to his execution, and perished with a holy resignation, as a result of an enlightened faith.

¶ John Foxe, *The Book of Martyrs,* revised with notes and an appendix by W. Bramley-Moore (London, 1869), pp. 165–7

London Separatists
1569

In 1569 John Nash was released from prison and on behalf of the London Separatists (members of the first Congregational churches) he wrote the following letter complaining about Christians being imprisoned.

In this your tyranye, you maynteyne and extoll them [the ceremonies] above the worde of God, in that you persecute and imprison some, to the death of the faythful servaunts of the Lord, those names here folowe.

1. Randall Partrag
2. giles fowler
3. Thomas Bowland
4. Mr Pattenson, preacher
5. John Kynge

6. Mr Fitz, preacher
7. John Lernarde
8. Margrett Racye
9. the wyffe of Mr Causlen

All thees were godlye and zealous christians and dyed by your tyrannous imprisonment and cruel tyrannye. These with all their companye abhorred all false sects and schismes, errors, herecyes, and all papistry, and all false and fayned religion and stoode faste to Chrystes institution and holye religion to the death, those that dyed departed constant Christians, even in your persecution.

¶ Albert Peel, *The Noble Army of Congregational Martyrs* (Independent Press, 1948), pp. 25–6

The Huguenots

Our attention is now turned to one of those more appalling massacres which dares claim a fiendish prominence in the annals of slaughter. We allude to the massacre of St Bartholomew. Charles IX of France and his mother Catherine, finding open persecution only excited the Huguenots to more obstinate resistance, determined to gain by subtlety what they failed to obtain by force. To make themselves more sure of their prey, they fixed on two plans: first, the king commanded Coligny to take his army into the Low Countries, so that he might find out the number and names of his followers: secondly, a marriage was proposed between the king's sister, Marguerite de Valois, and Henry of Navarre, the head of the Huguenot princes and the heir to the crown. All the leading Huguenot nobles were invited to Paris for this marriage which took place on 18th August 1572. The 24th August was fixed for the massacre. At 2 a.m. the bell of St Germain l'Auxerrois tolled, at which signal the Duke of Guise led his followers to Coligny's house: the duke remained below while his servants, headed by a young man named Besme, ascended to the admiral's room. On their entering his apartment, Coligny said, 'You ought to respect my grey hairs; but, do what you will, you can but shorten my life by a few days.' The admiral, on being wounded in both arms, immediately said to Maure, preacher to the Queen of Navarre, 'Oh, my brother! I now perceive that I am beloved of my God, seeing that for his name's sake I do suffer these wounds.' After stabbing him several times they threw him out of the window, when his head and arms were cut off by the rabble, and the body hung up by the feet on a gibbet. Besme later declared that he had never seen any person suffer death more courageously.

The martyrdom of this virtuous man had no sooner taken place than the armed soldiers ran about slaying all the Protestants they could find within the walls of the city. This continued for several days; but the greatest slaughter took place during the first three days, in which over 100,000 men and women of all ages are said to have perished.

These brutal deeds were not confined within the walls of Paris, but extended into other cities and quarters of the realm, especially to Lyons, Orleans, Toulouse, and Rouen, where the cruelties were unparalleled. Within one month 60,000 Protestants are said to have been slain in France alone. When news of the massacre was received in Rome, the greatest of rejoicings took place, and a medal was struck to commemorate this victory of the faith.

¶ John Foxe, *The Book of Martyrs,* revised with notes and an appendix by W. Bramley-Moore (London, 1869), pp. 130–2

Blessed Thomas Sherwood

Blessed Thomas Sherwood was born in London, of pious and Catholic parents, and by them brought up in the true faith and in the fear of God. Mr Sherwood frequented the house of Lady Tregony, a virtuous Catholic, who had a son named Martin, whose faith and manners were widely distant from those of his mother. This young spark suspected that Mass was sometimes privately said in his mother's house, and this as he imagined, by the means of Mr Sherwood; which was the occasion of his conceiving an implacable hatred against him; insomuch that, one day meeting him in the streets, he cried out, 'Stop the traitor! Stop the traitor!' and so causing him to be apprehended, had him before the next Justice of Peace. Where, when they were come, Mr Tregony could allege nothing else against Mr Sherwood, but that he suspected him to be a Papist. Upon which the Justice examined him concerning his religion; and in particular, what his sentiments were concerning the Queen's Church-headship, and the Pope's supremacy. To which Mr Sherwood candidly answered, 'That he did not believe the Queen to be the head of the Church of England; and that this preeminence belonged to the Pope.' Upon which he was immediately committed, and cast into a dungeon in the Tower.

In the Tower he was most cruelly racked, in order to make him discover where he had heard Mass. But he suffered all their tortures with a greatness of soul not unequal to that of the primitive martyrs, and would not be induced to betray or bring any man into danger. After this, he was thrust into a dark, filthy hole, where he endured very much from hunger, stench and cold, and the general want of all things, no one being allowed to visit him or afford him any comfort.

In fine, after about six months' suffering in this manner, with invincible patience, and gloriously triumphing over chains, dungeons, and torments, during which he often repeated these words, 'Lord Jesu, O! I am not worthy that I should suffer these things for Thee! much less am I worthy of those rewards which thou hast promised to give to such as confess thee:' he was brought to his trial, and condemned for denying the Queen's supremacy; and was executed according to sentence, being cut down while he was yet alive, dismembered, bowelled, and quartered. He suffered at Tyburn, February 7, 1578, at the age of fourteen.

¶ E. H. Burton and J. H. Pollen, *Lives of the English Martyrs, vol. 1, 1583–1588* (Longman, 1914), pp. 78–9

Maxims of English Catholic Martyrs, 1583–1588

[Before he came to the hurdle, one of the underkeepers said to him: 'O Mr Towsham, if I were in the like danger as you are, and might avoid it as easily as you may by going to church, surely I would soon yield to that.']

The happy priest answered: 'I pray thee be contented, good friend; within this hour I shall conquer the world, the flesh and the devil.'

[He was so laid on the hurdle that one of his legs draggled on the ground

as he was drawn, and being urged by a schismastic woman to draw it up, he replied,] 'No, all is too little for Christ's sake' (Venerable Stephen Rowsham, martyred York, 23rd March 1587).

[As Sir William Fleetwood, the Recorder of London, in a white hot rage, was about to hit him:] 'Use your right, for I will gladly suffer anything for the Catholic faith' (Venerable George Haydock, Tyburn, 12th February 1584).

'He was a man of extraordinary Christian simplicity and sincerity, in a word, a true Israelite in whom there is no guile' [Dr Champney speaking about the three years' imprisonment of the Venerable John Robinson, martyred at Ipswich, 1st October 1588].

[On being sentenced to execution] 'What is all this? Is it any more than one death?' (Venerable Richard White, martyred at Wrexham, 15th October 1584).

'I have received this night greater consolation than I deserved' (said on the morning of his martyrdom by Venerable Robert Sutton, at Stafford, 27th July 1587).

(Referring to prison:] '. . . our school of patience . . .' (Venerable John Body, martyred at Andover, 2nd November 1583)

[Sheriff Fawcet wanted her to confess that she died because of treason.] 'No, no, Mr Sheriff, I die for the love of my Lord Jesu.'
[On receiving her death sentence] 'God be thanked, all that he shall send me shall be welcome; I am not worthy of so good a death as this.' (Venerable Margaret Clitherow, martyred at York, 26th March 1586)

[On being sentenced to death on a Thursday, expecting it to be carried out, as was usual, on the Saturday, Mr Taylor said on Friday, having said Mass and his office:] 'How happy should I be, if on this day, on which Christ died for me, I might encounter death for him.'
[Scarcely had he said this than the officer unexpectedly came and took him to his execution.] (The Venerable Hugh Taylor, York, 26th November 1585)

¶ E. H. Burton and J. H. Pollen, *Lives of the English Martyrs, vol. 1, 1583–1588* (Longman, 1914), pp. 44, 46, 196, 165, 138, 198, 286, 307, 504

Edmund Campion

Blessed Edmund Campion was born in London; he was first taught in Christ's Hospital, and later at Oxford, in St John's College, where, after he had passed with great applause though the University by the persuasions of some of his friends he suffering himself to be made a deacon after the new fashion. He went to the new seminary at Douay, then chose to become a member of the Society of Jesus, and was, in Rome, admitted in 1573. In 1580, the day after midsummer he happily landed at Dover, being by God's great goodness delivered out of the searchers' and officers' hands, who detained him upon suspicion for some hours.

After he had laboured, often preaching three times a day, in God's harvest near thirteen months, being betrayed by one George Eliot, after long search he fell into the persecutors' hands on 17th July 1581. In his way to London, besides the tying of his legs under his horse, and the binding his arms behind him, the Council appointed a paper to be set upon his hat with large capital letters, CAMPION, THE SEDITIOUS JESUIT; and gave orders so to parade him through the streets at the most crowded part of the day. He was divers times racked to force out of him, by torments, whose houses he had frequented, by whom he was relieved, whom he had reconciled, when, which way, and for what purpose and by what commission, he came into the realm; how, where, and by whom he printed and dispersed his books and such like.

At his first racking, they went no further with him; but afterwards, when they saw he would not give way in religion, which was the thing they most desired, they forged matter of treason against him, and framed their demands accordingly; about which he was so cruelly torn and rent upon the torture, the two last times, that he thought they meant to make him away in that manner. Before he went to the rack, he used to fall down at the rack-house door, upon both knees, to commend himself to God's mercy; and upon the rack he called continually upon God, repeating often the holy name of Jesus. He most charitably forgave his tormentors. His keeper asking him the next day, how he felt his hands and feet, he answered, 'Not ill, because not at all.'

The poor jury did that which they understood was looked for at their hands, and pronounced Father Campion to be 'Guilty'. Mr

Popham, the Attorney-General, sentenced him to be hanged, drawn, and quartered, as in cases of high treason. On 1st December Campion was taken to Tyburn on a hurdle, from which he cried to the crowds, 'God save you all, God bless you, and make you all good Catholics'. Father Campion was brought into the cart, where, after some little pause, he began to speak upon that text of St Paul, 'We are made a spectacle to the world' (1 Cor. 4:9), but was interrupted by Sir Francis Knowles and the Sheriffs urging him to confess his treason. To whom he answered, 'For the treason which has been laid to my charge and I am come here to suffer for; I desire you all to bear witness with me, that thereof I am altogether innocent.'

Whereupon answer was made to him by one of the Council, that he might not deny what had been proved by sufficient evidence. 'Well, my lord,' said he, 'I am a Catholic man, and a priest; in that faith have I lived, and in that faith do I intend to die: and if you esteem my religion treason, then am I guilty; as for any other treason I never committed, God is my judge: but you have now what you desire.'

And the cart being drawn away, he meekly and sweetly yielded his soul unto his Saviour, protesting that he died a perfect Catholic. His mild death, and former sincere protestations of his innocency, moved the people to such compassion and tears, that the adversaries 'were glad to excuse the matter.'

He suffered at Tyburn, 1st December 1581, being forty-two years of age.

¶ *The English Martyrs Under Henry VIII and Elizabeth, 1535–1583* (Catholic Truth Society, 1901), pp. 80–8

Illustrations of persecution of Catholics

Six striking engravings, made from copper plates in the first edition of the Italian translation of William Allen's book *Campion and his Companions*, show how Catholics were arrested, mocked, led off to prison, examined, tortured, drawn and executed. These engravings give the earliest representations of the sufferings of the [Catholic] English martyrs, and as Allen's book was the seed, as it were, of the subsequent martyrologies, so these pictures became the models for later artists. The following captions to the pictures give a rare insight into the tortures of Catholic martyrs.

1. APPREHENSION

The priest, in secular disguise, is recognised in the street by a spy or priest-catcher, and on the cry being raised 'a traitor! a traitor!' the men and boys take up stones to throw at him. He is arrested, bound, and led away to prison amidst the jeers of the people.

2. THE ROAD TO PRISON

The priest has been taken at Mass, and is led away to prison through the streets in his sacred vestments, accompanied as fellow prisoners by the devout people who have heard his Mass. Other priests are brought in on horseback from the country, men with torches leading the way at night. One of the priests, who is riding with his feet tied together, has on his hat, 'Edmund Campion, the seditious Jesuit.'

3. EXAMINATION WITH TORMENT

A man is being whipped at the cart's tail, and on his return from this punishment an official heats an iron with which his ears are to be pierced and he is to be branded as a rogue. Two ministers are looking on.

4. THE RACK

When a man was examined on the rack, cords were tied on his wrists and ankles, and by means of windlasses these were tightened as the examiners directed. Other prisoners were sometimes brought to witness the torture or to hear the groans of the victims, to induce them to say what was required of them.

5. TO TYBURN

The hurdle is dragged through the streets at a horse's heels, the sheriff and other officials accompanying it, and the poor 'traitor' is worried with controversy when he would prepare himself for death. The gallows, the cart, the fire and cauldron are all in readiness for his arrival.

6. EXECUTION

There have been three victims. One is just cut down, one is stripped and his bowels are thrown into the fire, the third is already cut up, his head is on the pole and parts of him are in the cauldron of boiling pitch preparatory to being hung over the city gates.

¶ J. H. Pollen, *Father Edmund Campion and his companions* (Burns and Oates, 1908), pp. 120–5

Mary Queen of Scots

Mary Queen of Scots was beheaded in Elizabeth I's reign, as a Roman Catholic threat to the English throne, on 8th February 1587.

Mary conducted her own defence, but it was clear from the start of her trial that the Star Chamber would only reach one verdict. Mary was declared a dangerous instrument for the restoration of the Roman Church. Mary wrote the following letter to Elizabeth:

> Madame, for the sake of that Jesus to whose name all powers bow, I require you to ordain that when my enemies have slaked their black thirst for my innocent blood, you will permit my poor desolated servants altogether to carry away my corpse, to bury it in holy ground with the other queens of France. As they tell me that you will in nothing force my conscience nor my religion, and have even conceded me a priest, refuse me not this my last request, that you will permit free sepulchre to this body when the soul is departed, which, when united, cold never obtain liberty to live in repose, such as you would procure for yourself; against which repose – before God I speak – I never aimed a blow: but God will let you see the truth of all after my death.
>
> ... To conclude, I pray God, the just Judge, of his mercy that he will enlighten you with his Holy Spirit, and that he will give you his grace to die in the perfect charity I am disposed to do, and to pardon all those who have caused, or who have co-operated in, my death. Such will be my last prayer.

On 7th February 1587, the Earls of Kent and Shrewsbury arrived at Fotheringay with a warrant for Mary's execution. That night Jan Kennedy read to her from her Book of Hours. In the morning her ladies dressed her in a magnificent black satin gown with long sleeves, over a petticoat of crimson satin, a long white veil and shoes made of Spanish leather.

Guards and a crowd of spectators filled the great hall. The scaffold, the chair, and the block were draped in black. The Queen, in matching black, sat while the warrant was read and the Dean of Peterborough preached an interminable sermon. Mary interrupted him. They argued about the teaching of their respective churches, and ended up denouncing the other in their prayers. Mary's black gown was removed to leave a figure standing in crimson on the scaffold.

Mary knelt clumsily, as she was stiff from lack of exercise and illness. She held the block with her hands until one of the executioners took them into his own hands. The other executioner took aim, struck and missed. His third blow severed Mary's head. The Dean of Peterborough was heard to say, 'So perish all the Queen's enemies.'

John Amias and Robert Dalby

'Martyrdom is an honour, and Carmelites do not seek honours'
(Bernanos).

John Amias, born in Yorkshire, was alumnus of Douay College, where he was priested in 1581 and sent on the English mission with Mr Edmund Sykes. In 1588 Robert Dalby, who was born in Durham, and who had also been an alumnus and priest at Douay College, was sent on the English mission. Both Amias and Dalby fell into the hands of the Protestant persecutors, and were condemned to die the death of traitors, on account of their priestly character. Dr Champney (in his MS History, ad annum Elizab. 31), gives the following account of them:

> This year, on 15th March, John Amias and Robert Dalby suffered at York, as in cases of high treason, for no other cause but they were priests, ordained by the authority of the See of Rome, and had returned to England, and exercised their priestly functions for the benefit of the souls of their neighbours. I was myself an eye-witness of the glorious combat of these holy men, being at that time a young man, 20 years old, and I returned home confirmed, by the sight of their constancy and meekness, in the Catholic faith, which by God's grace I then followed; for they visibly appeared to be like lambs led to the slaughter.
>
> They were drawn about a mile out of the city to the place of execution, where, being arrived and taken off the hurdle, they prostrated themselves upon their faces to the ground, and then employed some time in prayer, till Mr Amias, being called by the sheriff, rose up, and, with a serene countenance, walked to the gallows and kissed it. Then kissing the ladder, went up. The hangman, after fitting the rope to his neck, bade him ascend a step or two, affirming that thus he would suffer the less. He then turned to the people, and declared that the cause of his death was not treason, but religion. But here he was interrupted and not allowed to go on. Therefore composing himself for death, with his eyes and hands lifted up to heaven, forgiving all who had anyways procured his death, and praying for his

persecutors, he recommended his soul to God, and being flung off the ladder, he quietly expired; for he was suffered to hang so long, till he seemed to be quite dead. Then he was cut down, dismembered and disembowelled, his head cut off and the trunk of his body quartered.

All this while, his companion, Mr Dalby, was most intent in prayer; who, being called upon, immediately followed the footsteps of him that had gone before him, and obtained the like victory.

¶ *Martyrs Omitted by Foxe, compiled by a member of the English Church* (1870), pp. 86–8

Roman Catholics persecuted

In Hallam's *Constitutional History of England,* we are told that 'the rack seldom stood idle for all the latter part of Queen Elizabeth's reign'. The Roman Catholic martyrs under her amounted to 204 according to Milner. Many other died of hardships in prison; many, deprived of their property, were banished, mutilated, condemned to be burnt, and reprieved. Dr Bridgewater names over 1,200 who suffered in this way before 1588, that is, before the greatest heat of the persecution. He lists:

3 archbishops	49 doctors of divinity
1 abbot	18 doctors of the law
4 whole convents of religious	15 masters of colleges
13 deans	1 queen
14 archdeacons	18 peers
60 prebendaries	26 knights
530 priests	326 gentlemen
	60 peeresses and gentlewomen

Many of these died in prison, several under sentence of death.

In Stowe's *Chronicles,* we find that 4,000 peasants were massacred for not accepting Protestantism, under Lord John Russell, in Devonshire.

Hume says that 645 monasteries
90 colleges
2374 chantries and free chapels
110 hospitals
were ruined under Henry VIII.

¶ *Martyrs Omitted by Foxe, compiled by a member of the English Church* (1870), pp. 1–2

Richard Barry

Let us now turn to one of the blackest pages in our English history, and give a few examples of Puritan intolerance in Ireland. With the wholesale butcheries, such as that at Drogheda, where Roman Catholics were slain without an offer of mercy, through apostatising from their faith, a butchery lasting in that town for five days, the blood of fellow-Christians – man, woman, and child – running in the streets like rivers; – with these we need not to trouble the reader. It is only of martyrdoms wherein death was willingly submitted to for conscience's sake, that we shall treat; for his and for our own edification.

At Cashel, when all resistance of the people to their barbarous invaders had ceased, the priests, together with very aged men and women (some stated to have been in their hundredth year), took refuge at the foot of the altar in the cathedral; among whom was Father Theobald Stapleton, who, crucifix in hand, and in his sacred vestments, was cut to pieces; and when all the rest had fallen in the same way, Richard Barry, of the order of St Dominic, alone survived.

Struck by his noble and sanctified appearance, the captain said to him, 'Your life is your own, provided you fling off that habit. But if you cling to such a banner, verily you peril life itself.'

To this Barry replied, 'My habit is an emblem of the passion of the Redeemer, and more dear to me than life.'

'Think more wisely,' rejoined the captain. 'Indulge not this blind passion for martyrdom; for, if you comply not with my orders, death awaits you.'

'But if so,' replied the devoted man, 'your cruelties will be to me a blessing, and death itself a great gain.'

Infuriated, they bound the holy man to a stone chair, kindled a slow fire under his feet and legs, and, 'after two hours of torture, his eyes flashed their last upon that heaven which he was about to enter.'

¶ *Martyrs Omitted by Foxe, compiled by a member of the English Church* (1870), pp. 181–2

A True Confession of Faith of the Brownists

Robert Browne formed a 'gathered church' in Norwich in 1580 and published three books in 1582, one entitled, A Treatise upon the 23 of Matthewe, both for an order of studying and handling the Scriptures, and also avoyding the Popish disorders, and ungodly communion of all false Christians, and especially of wicked Preachers and hirelings. *By 1583 a royal proclamation ordered the destruction of all of Browne's books. Browne's followers became known as the 'Brownists'.*

An extract from A True Confession of Faith of the Browneists *(1596) states:*

'We have been miserably entreated by the Prelates and cheef of the Clergie: some of us cast into most vile and noisome prisons and dungeons, laden with irons, and there, without all pitie, deteyned many years, as the cities of London, Norwich, Gloucester, Bury, and many other places of the land can testify. Yet here the malice of Satan stayed not it self, but raised up against us more grievous persecution, even unto the violent death of some, and lamentable exile of us all.

'So that through their barbarous crueltie 24 souls have perished in their prisons, with in the Citie of London only (besides other places of the land).

'Margin: In Newgate Mr Crane a man about 60 years of age; Richard Jacson, Thomas Stevens, William Howton, Thomas Drewet, John Gwalter, Roger Ryppon, Robert Awoburne, Scipio Bellot, Robert Bowle, John Barnes being sick unto death, was carried forth and departed this life shortly after. Mother Maner of 60 years, Mother Roe of 60 years, Anna Tailour, Judeth Myller, Margaret Farrer beeing sick unto death was carried forth, and ended her life within a day or two after. John Purdy in brydwel, Mr Denford in the Gatehouse about 60 years of age. Father Debnham in the white-lyon about 70 years, George Bryty in Counter wood street, Henry Thomson in the clink, John Chandler in the Count. Poultry, being sick unto death was carried forth, and died within few days. Walter Lane in the Fleet, Thomas Hewet in Counter Woodstreet.'

¶ Albert Peel, *The Noble Army of Congregational Martyrs* (Independent Press, 1948), pp. 42–4

English Martyrs, 1535–1583

Decree [of the Congregation of Sacred Rites] confirming the honour given to the blessed martyrs John Cardinal Fisher, Thomas More, and others, put to death in England for the faith from the year 1535 to 1583.

England, once called the Island of Saints and the Dowry of the Virgin Mother of God, as even from the first ages of the Church it had been renowned for the sufferings of many Martyrs, so also, when it was torn by the fearful schism of the sixteenth century from the obedience and communion of the Roman See, was not without the testimony of those who, for the dignity of this See, and for the truth of the orthodox Faith, did not hesitate to lay down their lives by the shedding of their blood.

In this noble band of Martyrs nothing whatever is wanting to its completeness or its honour: neither the grandeur of the Roman purple, nor the venerable dignity of Bishops, nor the fortitude of the Clergy both secular and regular, nor the invincible firmness of the weaker sex. Eminent amongst them is John Fisher, Bishop of Rochester and Cardinal of the Holy Roman Church, whom Paul III speaks of in his Letters as 'conspicuous for sanctity, celebrated for learning, venerable by age, an honour and an ornament to the kingdom, and to the Clergy of the whole world.'

With him must be named the layman Thomas More, Chancellor of England, whom the same Pontiff deservedly extols, as 'excelling in sacred learning, and courageous in the defence of truth.' The most authoritative ecclesiastical historians, therefore, are unanimously of opinion that they all shed their blood for the defence, restoration, and preservation of the Catholic Faith.

Names of martyrs of the Church of England, both of ancient and of more recent times, have been engraved at Rome on copper-plate with the title: *Sufferings of the Holy Martyrs who, in ancient and more recent times of persecution, have been put to death in England for Christ, and for professing the truth of the Catholic Faith.*

Those who suffered death under King Henry VIII:
John Fisher, Bishop of Rochester, Cardinal of the Holy Roman Church
Thomas More, Chancellor of England
Margaret Pole, Countess of Salisbury, mother of Cardinal Pole
Richard Reynolds, of the Order of St Bridget
John Haile, Priest
Eighteen Carthusians, namely:

John Houghton	Robert Laurence

Augustine Webster
Humphrey Middelmore
Sebastian Newdigate
John Rochester
James Walworth
William Greenwood
John Davy
Robert Salt

William Exnew
Walter Pierson
Thomas Green
Thomas Scryven
Thomas Redyng
Thomas Johnson
Richard Bere
William Horne

John Forest, Priest of the Order of St Francis
John Stone, of the Order of St Augustine
Four Secular Priests:

Thomas Abel
Edward Powel

Richard Fetherson
John Larke

German Gardiner, a layman.

Those who suffered under Elizabeth:
Priests:

Cuthbert Mayne
John Nelson
Everard Hanse
Rodolph Sherwin
John Payne
Thomas Ford
John Shert
Robert Johnson
William Fylby

Luke Kirby
Laurence Richardson
William Lacy
Richard Kirdman
James Hudson, or Tompson
William Hart
Richard Thirkeld
Thomas Woodhouse
—— Plumtree.

Also three Priests of the Society of Jesus:
Edmund Campion
Alexander Briant
Thomas Cottam.
Laymen:
John Storey, Doctor of Laws
John Felton
Thomas Sherwood

The present Decree was issued on this 29th day of December, sacred to the Martyr Thomas Archbishop of Canterbury, whose faith and constancy these Blessed Martyrs so strenuously imitated.

D. Cardinal Bartolini, *Prefect of the Congregation of Sacred Rites*
Laurence Salvati, *Secretary*

¶ *The English Martyrs under Henry VIII and Elizabeth* (Catholic Truth Society, 1901), pp. i–iv

John Ogilvie
Scotland, 1614

In these more enlightened and less intolerant days [1877] it is not easy
even to imagine the wretched sort of life which was the lot of those
amongst the Scotch who at the beginning of the seventeenth century
still clung to the faith of their fathers. Still less easy is it to picture all
the hardships and perils to which Scotch missionary priests were
exposed. The Catholic religion had been declared no longer the religion of Scotland, as the great monument to John Knox in the
Necropolis of Glasgow triumphantly, but rather suggestively, informs
the Protestant passer-by. The cruellest laws had been passed against
the Catholics, and their faith was continually made the subject of the
foulest misrepresentations and the bitterest ridicule.

According to popular ideas, carefully nourished by the instructions
of the preachers, all Catholics were idolaters, traitors, parricides,
everything that is bad. The Pope's jurisdiction had been abolished
from Scotland in 1560 and a further Act of Parliament declared that
to say Mass, or even to hear Mass, was a criminal offence. The first
time this law was broken it was punished with the confiscation of
goods, the second time by banishment, and the third time by death.
As Dr Gordon wrote in his *Scotichronicon*, 'It appears hardly credible
that the wanton barbarities which Father Ogilvie had to endure could
have been directed and sanctioned by the constituted authorities.
They are scarcely to be paralleled by the refined cruelty of the persecutions of Christians during the first three centuries of the church, or of
the Indian savages and cannibals.'

It was towards the end of 1613 that Father Ogilvie succeeded with
Father Moffet in getting back into Scotland. He would of course have
come disguised, to avoid being captured by the Presbyterians, who
were ever watching for anyone having the least appearance of being a
Catholic priest. He devoted himself with unflagging energy and with a
zeal truly apostolic as he sought out the faithful, exhorting them to be
courageous and administering to them the holy sacraments. However,
Father Ogilvie was captured in October 1614. Within six months of
his arrest he was condemned to death, and within three hours from
his condemnation had won, at the early age of thirty-four, a martyr's
crown.

During his trial Father Ogilvie said:

If I should be exiled for any evil deed committed, I should certainly take care not to come back, but if I were exiled for this cause which I sustain, I should not fail to retrace my steps to the country. And would that every hair of my head might convert a thousand to the orthodox faith, and you, Archbishop, in the first place. I do not consider that consciences are bound by these iniquitous statutes of yours enacted without law and without authority.

The judges soon pronounced on him sentence of death, which was of this kind, viz., that he should be conducted to a gibbet erected for him in the public street, and having been there hanged, his head should be cut off, and the four quartered parts of his body should be left exposed to sight, in four different public places.

After the repated commands of the sheriff to throw him off the ladder, the executioner at last reluctantly, and with great compassion, cast him down from the step. When this was done, there arose a tumult and murmur, every sex and age regretting his unjust death, and expressing their detestation of the cruelty of the ministers and esepcially the archbishop.

¶ C. J. Karslake, *An Account of the Imprisonment and Martyrdom of Father John Ogilvie* (Burns and Oates, 1877), pp. 40–9

Pursuivants and the harrying of Catholics

During the reigns of James I and Charles I priest-hunters or pursuivants often forced magistrates to enforce laws against priests, and even have them executed. Many of the pursuivants were 'the riff-raff of the population' who stood to personally benefit from their operations.

King James' laws, adding to those of Queen Elizabeth's are most severe and cunningly planned to bring about the ruin of the Catholics. Lest they should prove a dead letter, informers are encouraged by the prospect of ample rewards. The most inveterate enemies of our religion among the ministers and the laity have been appointed inquisitors and judges, who, to win the approval of the King and Parliament, set no limits to their vexations and extortions. In this they are fully supported by their underlings, known as pursuivants, who for the most part are men of damaged reputation, thieves, suspected or rather known coiners, or those guilty of other felonies. These miscreants ply their trade not only in London, but have the country parcelled out among them, with full licence to act as if in an enemy's territory.

They visit at any hour of the night that suits them the dwellings of Catholics, and those of Protestants also, if there exists the slightest suspicion of their containing Catholic inmates, taking the precaution to surround them with musketeers or soldiers, to prevent any one escaping. If not admitted at once, they break down the doors, then, as it may suit their pleasure, confine the members of the household to their rooms, while they go over the house, prying into every corner, chest and cupboard. If the keys are not forthcoming, they force the locks; expostulation or resistance, they answer with abuse or blows; if they find any money they seize it without hope of recovery, under the pretext that it is stored up for the support of priests and Jesuits, or for the seminaries, Colleges or Religious Houses beyond the seas. As for books, sacred vessels, vestments, especially such as are marked with a cross, and other church stuff, they profane and confiscate them, and by dint of threats compel the owners to satisfy their insatiable greed. It is needless to mention the demolition of walls, the tearing up of floors and pavement in order to discover some lurking priest or Jesuit. Decency forbids us to particularise their treatment of gentle and virtuous women, in order to discover books, rosaries, Agnus Deis and the like. Lest they should be called to account for their misdeeds, they bring the master of the house before a Justice of the Peace, who tenders the oath of allegiance, thus forcing him to choose between apostasy and utter ruin.

The tragic fate of a certain priest, who, though not a Jesuit, should yet be mentioned in this annual report, shows how dangerous it is to await the arrival of the pursuivants and to flee by night. A few weeks since, the mansion of a noble lady was surrounded in the dead of night in consequence of information given by a false brother, of a priest being there. As they began their search, the priest jumped out of bed, and without waiting to dress, snatched up his coat, and sought to escape by the roof of the house, but his foot slipped and he fell headlong. It is thought that he was slain by the posses of armed men posted round the house, for his death was caused by a wound in the head, not by the fracture of his limbs, and not only did the marks on the ground show that he alighted on his feet, but he was heard by some people to cry out, 'Where are you dragging me to? What are you going to do to me? Do you want to murder me?' The heretics, taking up the corpse, buried it at a cross-road, driving a stake through the stomach, the usual way in this country of burying suicides, as they reported him to be.

¶ 'Annual Letters of the English Mission, 1614.' Henry Foley, *Records of the English Province of the Society of Jesus* (1877), vol. 6, part ii, p. 1061

A layman's exhortation to Catholic priests

And you, religious fathers and reverend priests, to whom is committed the care of this devastated vineyard, and who are unto us in our distress the sole dispensers of the divine sacrament, venture still, I beseech you, as hereto you have done, the loss of your lives, to distribute unto us this divine food and to break unto us this celestial bread. For in your hands only it is, in this time of dearth, to preserve the lives of your brethren, lest they perish by famine. And we again, my Catholic brethren, let us boldly adventure our lives to give them harbour and entertainment. Imitating herein our noble patron and proto-martyr of England, blessed St Alban, who presented himself, yea gave his own life, to preserve the life of his priest Amphibalus.

Even so, when either foolish heretics or foolish friends shall condemn you of folly for losing your goods or exposing your lives for to harbour priests, consider with yourselves that you harbour him who bringeth unto you the body and blood of Jesus Christ, and that if you shed your blood to receive him who consecrateth in your house the blood of Christ, what else do you do but render blood for blood, and spend your blood for the blood of Christ. You, therefore, the right honourable and worshipful of the English nation, which have brought this holy sacrifice at a hundred marks, and such as were poorer with the utter deprivation of all the poor little they had in the world, and further, such as have not had so much money, have laid to pawn their very carcasses into sundry prisons, goals and loathsome dungeons, and with what great and unspeakable reward will our Saviour one day repay and requite your charity! In a word, all the sufferances, all the ignominies, all the injuries, all the damages and all the detriments which you shall endure for the defence of this sacrifice, will minister matter to all ensuring posterity of your most noble and heroical acts, which, though you die, will ever live to future memory, resound to your own immortal glory and to the everlasting renown of our English nation.

¶ John Heigham, *A Devout Exposition of the Holy Mass* (1614), Preface

Edmund Arrowsmith
1628

*Between the accession of James I and the death of Cromwell, 39
priests, two Jesuit brothers and 6 laymen were executed under the
penal statutes. Only Edmund Arrowsmith, a priest, and a labourer
Richard Herst were martyred in Charles I's reign.*

*Arrowsmith, ordained at Arras in 1612, having studied at Douai,
was sent on the English mission in 1613, became a member of the
Society of Jesus in 1623, before being arrested and executed at Lan-
caster in 1628.*

Various were the affections of the persons who assisted at this tragedy
and beheld B. Edmund Arrowsmith's exit. Many Protestants, moved
by his fortitude and patience, wished their souls with his, who then
died. Some judged it very laudable to be constant to their religion, but
thought it too great a stretch of obligation to die for that cause. Some,
touched with compassion, esteemed it barbarous to use a person thus
for his religion. Mr Leigh [who had shouted at the martyr during his
trial and called on him to recant just before his execution] and some
of his malicious temper seemed the only people pleased with this
inhumanity.

The behaviour of the sanguinary judge [Sir Henry Yelverton]
increased the martyr's glory, and in that respect, must be allowed a
place in the Acts of the martyr. Pleased with the success of his illegal
and barbarous proceedings, he had anticipated the day of execution
to see with satisfaction the death of Fr Arrowsmith, whom he condemned without regard even to the known laws of civilised nations.
He was ashamed to appear at the place of execution, perhaps to
indulge his cruel temper more, in seeing the butchery at a distance
through a prospective glass, without any constraint from the spectators who would justly be surprised at this extraordinary procedure
in an administrator of justice. Thus he sated his eyes with blood, having first taken an oath not to sit down to table till Arrowsmith was
dead.

Dinner was ordered up in a kind of triumph when his oath was dis-
charged; here he seemed religious, to be more cruel. After dinner
some venison came in, a present to the judge; while he admired the

venison, Fr. Arrowsmith's quarters were brought in, that he might enjoy the bloody act of which he was the author. To glut himself with horror he barbarously handled the quarters of the deceased, laid them by the venison and was not ashamed inhumanly to compare them together.

¶ *The Life of Edmund Arrowsmith*

Peter O'Higgins
Dublin, 1641

Peter O'Higgins, of the order of St Dominic, was led to the scaffold in the courtyard of Dublin Castle in 1641, a pious and an eloquent man. He was arrested and brought before the lords-justices on a charge of endeavouring to seduce Protestants from their religion. Failing to sustain any capital charge against him, he was informed by those in authority that, if he abandoned his faith, he should have many and great privileges, but that all depended on his embracing Protestantism.

It was on the morning fixed for his death that this message was sent to him. In reply, O'Higgins desired to have this proposal under the signature of the justices, and that it should be handed to him when in sight of the gibbet. Hearing this, the justices sent the written document for pardon on the before-named conditions, together with the warrant for his execution.

O'Higgins had just ascended the first step of the ladder leading to the gibbet, when the executioner placed the paper in his hand. He bowed courteously on receiving it. There was a loud demonstration of exultation on the part of the mob at the supposed apostasy of the martyr from his faith. Standing yet on the scaffold, he exhibited the document he had received, and commented warmly on the avowed iniquity of his judges.

Addressing the members of his own faith among the crowd, he said: 'My brethren, God has so willed that I should fall into the hands of our relentless persecutors; they have not been able, however, to convict me of any crime against the laws of the realm. But my religion is an abomination in their sight; and I am here today to protest, in the sight of God and man, that I am condemned for my faith. For some time I was in doubt as to the charge on which they would ground my condemnation; but, thanks to heaven, it is no longer so; and I am about to die for my attachment to the Catholic faith. See you here the condition on which I might save my life? Apostasy is all they require; but, before high heaven, I spurn their offers, and with my last breath will glorify God for the honour he had done me, in allowing me thus to suffer for his name.'

He then cast the conditional reprieve into the crowd, and bade the executioner perform his office; the bystanders hearing him give thanks to God with his last breath.

¶ *Martyrs Omitted by Foxe, compiled by a member of the English Church* (1870), pp. 184–5

Hugh Green
1642

Hugh Green, 1584–1642, born in London, was trained at Douai, where he was ordained in 1612. He then worked for the next thirty years on the English mission, before being executed at Dorchester.

On Friday 19th August, the Reverend Hugh Green, alias Ferdinand Browne, of London, an alumnus of this College, bravely suffered at Dorchester an illustrious martyrdom or, rather, an unheard-of butchery on account of his priesthood. For when his belly was cut open by the executioner and his abdomen placed on his breast, he gazed at it, and with his left hand touched his bowels, while with his right hand he fortified himself with the sign of our redemption. And while the executioner was tearing out his liver and, disturbing his entrails, was searching for his heart, he distinctly pronounced several times the saving name of Jesus. His forehead was bathed with sweat, and blood and water flowed from his eyes and nose. And when on account of the gushing streams of blood his tongue could no longer pronounce the saving name of Jesus, his lips moved, and the frequent groans which he uttered from his inmost heart were proof of the most bitter pain and torture which, with his eyes lifted to heaven, he bore with an unconquered soul for half an hour and more. He suffered in the fifty-seventh year of his age, the cause of his death being that he was a Roman priest.

¶ Douai Diary, 1642, in *Douay College Diaries*, ed. E. H. Burton and T. L. Williams (Catholic Record Society, 1911)

Brabant and the Gospellers

To speak nothing of the infinite dissensions, hurliburlies, massacres, murders, wars, treasons which have been caused in the Christian world by these new Gospellers and their gospel, for they are patent to the eye, and France, Germany, England, Scotland, the Low Countries and wheresoever these Gospellers come, do find it by woeful experience too true. To omit thousands of examples which are well known to every man, I will only mention that unheard-of villainous cruelty of their exercised not many years since upon the poor citizens of Tuelmont, a village in Brabant, where what cruelty soever hath been committed by any tyrant, what rape or beastliness by any savage or brutish men, what sacrilege soever by Jew, Turk or infidel what these also committed by the followers of these new Gospellers. To lock up hospitals and burn both lame, maimed and sick alive was nothing, to pluck young infants from their mothers' breasts and by the legs fling them up in the air and catch them on their dagger's point was common: to kill young and old, little and great, of all sexes and ages was their sport. They had no horror or scruple to ravish chaste matrons and violate sacred virgins publicly in the churches and chapels, and after they had by the multiplicity of those obscene acts killed them, afterwards brutishly to abuse their bodies. Yea, which makes me even tremble to think of it, they dreaded not in the most vile manner which could be invented to abuse Christ our Lord in the Blessed Sacrament, and all this not by the private soldier alone or upon the sudden, or in the height of fury, but in the cold blood, after three days consult, by approbation of all their officers.

¶ Peter Wright, executed at Tyburn 1651

Charles I

'The chief arms left me were those only which the ancient Christians were wont to use against their persecutors, prayers and tears. These may serve a good man's turn, if not to conquer as a soldier yet to suffer as a martyr' (Charles I, Eikon Basilike).

Charles, dressed in black, refused to plead when put on trial, rather preferring to question the right a few members of the House of Commons had to try at all. After adjourning three times the court then decided that Charles would not be allowed to speak and they said they found him guilty of treason against the people and that he was condemned to death.

Soldiers lined the streets Charles walked through on his way to the scaffold. No one was supposed to hear his last words. Nevertheless two newspaper reporters managed to take down the following words from the martyr-king which were subsequently published in the London newspapers.

> The people's liberty and freedom consist in having government, in having those laws by which their lives and their goods may be most their own. It is not their having a share in the government. If I would have given way to an arbitrary way, to have all laws changed by the power of the sword, I needed not to have come here; and therefore I tell you that I am the martyr of the people.' At this point he said words to Bishop Jexon which subsequently become very famous, 'I go from a corruptible to an incorruptible crown, where no disturbance can be.'

Persecution in the valleys of Piedmont in the seventeenth century

Pope Clement VIII sent missionaries into the valleys of Piedmont, to induce the Protestants to renounce their religion. One of the first people who attracted the attention of the Papists was Mr Sebastian

Basan, a zealous Protestant, who was seized by the missionaries, imprisoned, tortured for fifteen months, and then burnt alive.

Before the persecution began, the missionaries used kidnappers to steal the Protestants' children, so that they could be brought up Roman Catholics. Later, they took these children away by force, and killed any parents who objected.

This was followed by a most cruel ordeal, which was sanctioned by Duke Andrew Gastaldo on 25th January 1655. This order set out that the head of every family, with the members of that family, of the reformed religion, living in Lucerne, St Giovanni, Bibiana, Campiglione, St Secondo, Lucernetta, La Torre, Fenile and Bricherassio, should, within three days, leave. If they refused to do this they would be killed and their goods and property confiscated, unless they became Roman Catholics.

The suddenness of the order affected everyone. Notwithstanding this the Papists drove them from their homes and many people perished on the mountains through the severity of the winter or from lack of food. Those who remained behind were murdered by the Popish inhabitants or shot by the troops. These cruelties are described in a letter from a Protestant who managed to escape:

> The army, having got footing, became very numerous by the addition of a multitude of the neighbouring Popish inhabitants, who, finding that we were the destined prey of the plunderers, fell upon us with impetuous fury. As well as the Duke of Savoy's troops, and the Roman Catholic inhabitants, there were several regiments of French auxiliaries, some companies belonging to the Irish brigades, and several bands formed from outlaws, smugglers, and prisoners, who had been promised pardon and liberty in this world; and absolution in the next, for assisting to exterminate the Protestants from Piedmont.
>
> This armed multitude being encouraged by the Roman Catholic bishops and monks fell upon the Protestants in a most furious manner. All now was horror and despair: blood stained the floors of the houses, dead bodies bestrewed the streets, and groans and cried shocked the ears of humanity from every quarter. In one village they vented their cruelty on 150 women and children after the men had fled, beheading the women, and dashing out the brains of the children.

It was with reference to this persecution that Milton wrote the following well-known sonnet:

Avenge, O Lord, thy slaughtered saints, whose bones
  Lie scattered on the Alpine mountains cold;
  Even them who kept thy truth so pure of old;
When all our fathers worshipped stocks and stones,
Forget not; in thy book record their groans,
  Who were thy sheep, and in thine ancient fold,
  Slain by the bloody Piedmontese, that rolled
Mother with infant down the rocks. Their moans
The vales redoubled to the hills, and they
  To heaven. Their martyr'd blood and ashes sow
O'er all the Italian fields, where still doth sway
  The triple tyrant: that from these may grow
A hundredfold, who, having learned thy way
  Early, may fly the Babylonian woe.

¶ John Foxe, *The Book of Martyrs,* revised with notes and an appendix by
W. Bramley-Moore (London, 1869), pp 207–11

Rawlins White

Among the more humble people who suffered martyrdom was Rawlins
White, a fisherman, from Cardiff. He was brought before the Bishop
of Llandaff and the bishop declared that he had been sent for because
of his heretical opinions and because through his instruction he had
led many people into error. In conclusion, he exhorted him to consider how own state, and offered him favour if he recanted.

When the bishop had finished, Rawlins boldly replied, 'My lord, I
thank God I am a Christian man, and I hold no opinions contrary to
the Word of God; and if I do, I desire to be reformed out of the Word
of God, as a Christian ought to be.'

The bishop then told him plainly that he must proceed against him
according to law, and condemn him as a heretic.

'Proceed in your law, in God's name,' said the fearless Rawlins;
'but for a heretic you shall never condemn me while the world stands.'

'But,' said the bishop to his company, 'before we proceed any
further with him, let us pray to God that he would send some spark
of grace upon him, and it may so chance that God, through our
prayers, will here turn his heart.' Accordingly, having prayed, the

bishop said, 'Now, Rawlins, wilt thou revoke thy opinions or not?'

The man of truth replied, 'Surely, my lord, Rawlins you left me, Rawlins you find me, and, by God's grace, Rawlins I will continue.'

The bishop then had the definitive sentence read. Rawlins was then dismissed and taken to Cardiff, where he was put into the prison of the town, called Cockmarel, a very dark and loathsome dungeon.

The day being at hand whereon the servant of God should crown his faith by martyrdom, he spent the night before in solemn preparation.

On perceiving that his time was near, he sent to his wife, and desired her by the messenger that she should make ready and send him his wedding garment, meaning his shirt in which he should be burned. This request, or rather commandment, his wife performed with grief of heart, and sent it to him early in the morning.

The hour of his execution having come, the martyr was brought out of prison, having on his body the long shirt, which he called his wedding garment, and an old russet-coat which he was wont to wear. Besides this, he had upon his legs an old pair of leather buskins. And being thus equipped, he was accompanied, or rather guarded, with a great number of bills and weapons, which sight when he beheld, 'Alas!' said he, 'what meaneth all this? By God's grace, I will not run away: with all my heart and mind I give God most hearty thanks that he hath made me worthy to abide all this for his holy name's sake.'

He now came to a place where his poor wife and children stood weeping and making great lamentation, the sudden sight of whom so pierced his heart, that the tears trickled down his face. But soon afterwards, as though he were ashamed of this infirmity of his flesh, he began to be, as it were, angry with himself; insomuch that, striking his chest with his hand, he said, 'Ah, flesh, hinderest thou me so? Well, I tell thee, do what thou canst, thou shalt not, by God's grace, have the victory.'

But this time he approached the stake that had been set up, and was surrounded with some wood for the fire, which, when he beheld, he went forward boldly; but in going towards the stake, he fell down upon his knees, and kissed the ground; and, in rising, a little earth stuck to his nose, when he said, 'Earth unto earth, and dust unto dust; thou art my mother, and unto thee I shall return.'

Then he went cheerfully, and set his back close to the stake. A smith then came with a great chain of iron, whom when he saw, he cast up his hand, and, with a loud voice, gave God great thanks.

When the smith had fastened him to the stake, the officers began to lay on more wood, with a little straw and reeds, wherein the good old man was no less occupied than the rest; for as far as he could reach his hands, he would pluck the straw and reeds, and lay it about him in places most convenient for his speedy dispatch.

When all things were ready, directly over against the stake in the face of Rawlins White, there was a stand erected, which a priest mounted and addressed the people, who were numerous, because it was market day. When Rawlins perceived him, and considered why he came, he, reaching a little straw unto himself, made two little stays, and set them under his elbows. The priest proceeded with the sermon, and began to inveigh against Rawlins' opinions, in which harangue he cited the place of Scripture whereby the idolatrous mass is commonly defended. When Rawlins perceived that he went about not only to preach and teach the people false doctrine, but also to confirm it by Scripture, he suddenly started up, and beckoned his hands to the people, saying twice, 'Come hither, good people, and hear not a false prophet preaching.' Then said he unto the preacher, 'Ah, thou wicked hypocrite! Dost thou presume to prove thy false doctrine by Scripture?'

Upon this, fearing the effects of his truth upon the people, some that stood by cried out, 'Put fire! Put fire!' which being done, the straw and reeds cast up a great and sudden flame. While the martyr was being consumed, which was a somewhat long process, he cried with a loud voice, 'O Lord, receive my spirit!' until he could not open his mouth. At last, the extremity of the fire was so vehement against his legs, that they were wasted before the rest of his body was hurt, which made his body fall over the chain into the fire sooner than it would have done. So perished a fisherman, one of the noble army of martyrs, whose brightest ornaments are some of the rough fishermen who mended their nets, in old time, on the shore of Gennesaret.

¶ John Foxe, *The Book of Martyrs,* revised with notes and an appendix by W. Bramley-Moore (London, 1869), pp. 482–7

Christopher Waid

'Show some good upon me, O Lord, that they which hate me may see it, and be ashamed: because thou, Lord, hast helped me, and comforted me' (Ps. 86:17).

Christopher Waid, a linen-weaver, was condemned for heresy, by Maurice, Bishop of Rochester, and sentenced to be burnt at Dartford, which was his native town. The usual spot for executions was a place called the Brimth, a gravel pit, about a quarter of a mile out of the town; and it was decided that Waid should suffer there. Accordingly, on the morning appointed for his death, a cart was sent early from Dartford with the stake, a load of faggots and tall wood, and a good supply of reeds, that all might be in readiness for the arrival of the martyr. About ten o'clock Christopher Waid and one Margaret Polley (a widow who had been previously condemned for heresy) arrived, both riding pinioned, and accompanied by the sheriff, with a large retinue, and many other gentlemen.

When Mrs Polley saw in the distance the large crowd assembled round the gravel pit where they were to suffer, she said, cheerfully, to Waid, 'You may rejoice to see such a company gathered to celebrate your marriage this day.'

The procession passed the place, and proceeded down the town, where Mrs Polley was left until the sheriff returned from Waid's execution. Christopher had his clothes taken off in an inn, where he put on a long white shirt, which was sent for him by his wife, and being again pinioned, he proceeded on foot to the place of execution. When he reached the stake, he put his arms round it and kissed it, he then put his back against it, and stood in a pitch barrel, brought for that purpose; a smith brought a hoop of iron, and fastening two staples under his arms, made him fast to the stake. When he was settled, he lifted up his eyes and hands to heaven, and repeated the last verse of the 86th Psalm: 'Show some good upon me, O Lord, that they which hate me may see it, and be ashamed: because thou, Lord, hast helped me, and comforted me.' A pulpit had been erected on a little hillock near the stake, which a friar entered with a book in his hand. Immediately Waid espied him, he called earnestly to the people to take heed of the doctrine of the whore of Babylon, and to embrace the gospel as preached in King Edward's time. While he was thus speaking, the sheriff interrupted him, saying, 'Be quiet, Waid, and die patiently.'

'I am quiet,' said he, 'I thank God, Mr Sheriff, and so trust to die.' During this time the friar stood still, making as though he was going to speak, but whether astonished at Waid's earnestness, or thinking it hopeless to make the people listen to him, he suddenly came down, and went away to the town. The reeds were then piled about Waid, who arranged them himself, so as to leave an opening for his face, that his voice might be heard. His enemies, perceiving that, kept throwing faggots at his face, but as long as he could he pushed them aside again, though his face was much hurt by the end of one which struck him. When the fire was applied he showed no signs of fear or impatience, but often cried out, 'Lord Jesus, receive my soul.' At length his voice could no longer be heard, but even after he was dead his hands remained clasped over his head, as if in the act of prayer; and it pleased God to show him this token for good, vindicating his own character as a hearer and an answerer of prayer, to the encouragement of the martyr, and to the confusion and shame of the enemy, which is the due promotion of fools.

¶ John Foxe, *The Book of Martyrs*, revised with notes and an appendix by W. Bramley-Moore (London, 1869), pp. 543–4

Persecution of the Quakers
New England, 1661

The persecution of the Quakers in New England, by the Puritans and Independents, who had themselves fled from home to enjoy religious liberty, formed a dreadful scene, the very recital of which is revolting to humanity. Some they caused to have their ears cut off; and, among many other cruelties, which would fill a volume, they ordered three Quaker women to be stripped to the waist, and flogged through eleven towns, a distance of eighty miles, in all the severity of the frost and snow. But, as if this was not enough, they actually hanged three men and one woman for Christ's sake, who all acquitted themselves, at their awful exit, with that firmness and submission which a

Christian martyr is enabled to sustain at such an hour of nature's extremity, giving full proof of their sincerity and trust in the goodness and support of him, who had called them to make a public profession of his name before a wicked and perverse generation. Their names were William Robinson, Marmaduke Stevenson, William Leddra, and Mary Dyer.

On the day appointed for the execution of these innocent victims, they were led to the gallows by military officers, accompanied by a band of about 200 armed men, besides many horsemen – a measure which plainly indicated that some fear of popular indignation was feared; and, that no appeal might be made to the feelings of the crowd, a drummer was appointed to march in front of the condemned people, to beat the drum, especially when any of them attempted to speak.

Glorious signs of heavenly joy and gladness were visible in the countenances of these holy martyrs, who walked hand in hand to the place where they were to suffer. 'This is to me an hour of greatest joy,' exclaimed Mary Dyer; adding that no eye could see, no ear could hear, no tongue could utter, no heart could understand, the sweet refreshings of the Spirit of the Lord which she then felt.

Coming to the ladder, and having taken leave of each other with tender affection, they yielded up their lives into the hands of their enemies. Robinson's last words were, 'I suffer for Christ, in whom I live, and for whom I die.' Stevenson's last words were, 'This day shall we be at rest with the Lord.' William Leddra's last words were, 'I commit my righteous cause unto thee, O God.' As he took his last breath he said, 'Lord Jesus, receive my spirit!' When Mary Dyer climbed the ladder, some of the crowd told her that she would be reprieved if only she would do as they said. But this magnanimous sufferer did not shrink from her doom, knowing well for whom and in whom she was about to die. She was content to lay down her life, as she said, 'In obedience to the will of the Lord, I abide faithful unto death.'

¶ George Fox, *Journal* (London, 1852), vol. i, pp. 389–90

Quakers in prison in England and Wales

'Remember those in prison as if you were their fellow-prisoners'
(Heb. 13:3 NIV).

Now there being very many Friends in prison in the nation, Richard
Hubbertorn and I drew up a paper concerning them, and got it
delivered to the king, that he might understand how we were dealt
with by his officers.

About this time, 1661, persecution was very hot, and from esti-
mates deduced from documents of the period, it is probably that, in
1661 or 1662, there were no less than 4,500 Friends in prison, in
England and Wales, at one time, for meeting to worship God, refusing
to swear etc. And in such prisons too! Little is known about the
savage persecution they underwent and their firmness and patience in
their suffering.

In 1662, 20 died in different prisons in London and 7 more after
they were freed, as a result of their ill-treatment. In 1664, 25 died, and
in 1665 52 died. The number of Quakers who died in this way in the
whole kingdom, amounted 339.

The interruption of family ties, the breaking up of households, the
loss to many of all means of support, were hard and cruel sufferings
for conscience' sake, but they were grievously aggravated at this time
by the damp and filthy condition of the prisons, holes, and dungeons
in which the sufferers were confined, as well as by their very crowded
condition. And to all these circumstances of trial, must be added those
of personal abuse, fines, distraints, and, it may be strictly be said, of
wholesale robberies they endured. Some died of the beatings which
they received in the breaking up of their meetings, and many from the
filthy and close state of the prisons, in some of which they were so
closely packed that they had to take it by turns to stand up, while
others sat or lay down. There were also often overrun with lice and
other vermin.

Oliver Atherton

Among those who were in prison were four Friends for tithes, who
had been sent at the suit of the Countess of Derby, and had laid there
for nearly two and a half years. One of these, Oliver Atherton, a man
of weakly constitution, was, through his long and hard imprisonment

in the cold, raw, unwholesome place, brought so low and weak in his body, that there appeared no hope of his life, unless he might be removed. So a letter was written on his behalf to the Countess of Derby, and sent by his son Godfrey Atherton, wherein were laid before her 'the reasons why he and the rest could not pay tithes; because if they did, they should deny Christ come in the flesh, who by his coming had put an end to tithes, and to the priesthood to which they had been given, and to the commandment by which they had been paid under the law. His weak condition of the body was also laid before her, and the apparent likelihood of his death if she continued to hold him there; that she might be moved to pity and compassion, and also warned not to draw the guilt of innocent blood upon herself.

When his son went to her with his father's letter, a servant of her's abused him, plucked off his cap, and threw it away, and put him out of the gate. Nevertheless the letter was delivered into her own hand, but she shut out all pity and tenderness, and continued him in prison till death. When his son returned to his father in prison, and told him, as he lay on his dying bed, that the Countess denied his liberty, he only said, 'She hath been the cause of shedding much blood, but this will be the heaviest blood that ever she spilt.' Soon after this he died. Friends having his body delivered to them to bury, as they carried it from the prison to Ormskirk, the parish wherein he had lived, they struck up papers upon the crosses at Garstang, Preston, and other towns, through which they passed, with this inscription: 'This is Oliver Atherton, of Ormskirk parish, persecuted to death by the Countess of Derby for good conscience' sake towards God and Christ, because he could not give her tithes.' It set out in detail the reasons for him refusing to pay tithes, the length of his imprisonment, the hardships he had undergone, her hard-heartedness towards him, and the manner of his death.

¶ George Fox, *Journal* (London, 1852), vol. i, p. 399; vol. ii, pp. 16, 22

James Renwick

Reverend James Renwick, minister of the Gospel, was martyred on 17th February 1688 in the Grassmarket of Edinburgh.

Before he went out of the Tolbooth, he was at dinner with his mother, sisters, and some Christian friends, when the drum beat the first warning of his execution; which so soon as he heard, he leapt up in a ravishment of heavenly joy, saying, 'Let us be glad and rejoice, for the marriage of the Lamb is come;' and I can say, in some measure, 'The bride, the Lamb's wife, hath made himself ready.' And, till dinner was over, he enlarged upon the parallel of a marriage, and invited all of them come to the wedding, meaning his execution. When he was come to the scaffold, the drums being beat all the while, none of the distant spectators could hear anything that he said; only some very few, that were close by him, did hear it; whereof one has collected the following account. He delivered himself to this effect:

> Spectators, I must tell you I am come here this day to lay down my life for adhering to the truths of Christ, for which I am neither afraid nor ashamed to suffer; nay, I bless the Lord that ever he counted my worthy, or enabled me to suffer anything for him; and I desire to praise his grace that he hath not only kept me free from the gross pollutions of the time, but also from many ordinary pollutions of children; and such as I have been stained with, he hath washen from them in his own blood. I am this day to lay down my life for these three things:
>
> 1. For disowning the usurpations of the tyranny of James Duke of York.
>
> 2. For preaching that it was unlawful to pay the cess expressly exacted for bearing down the Gospel.
>
> 3. For preaching that it was lawful for people to carry arms for defending themselves in their meetings for receiving the persecuted Gospel ordinances.
>
> I think a testimony for these is worth many lives, and if I had ten thousand I would think it little enough to lay them all down for the same.
>
> Dear friends, spectators, I must tell you that I die a Presbyterian Protestant.
>
> I own the Word of God as the rule of Faith and manners; I own the Confession of Faith, Larger and Shorter Catechisms, Sum of Saving Knowledge, Directory for Worship, etc.; Covenants, National and Solemn League; Acts of General Assemblies – and all the faithful contendings that have been for

the work of reformation.

I leave my testimony approving the preaching of the Gospel in the fields, and the defending the same by arms.

I adjoin my testimony to all that hath been sealed by blood, shed either on scaffolds, fields, or seas, for the cause of Christ.

I leave my testimony against Popery, Prelacy, Erastianism, etc.; against all profanity, and everything contrary to sound doctrine; particularly against all usurpations made upon Christ's right, who is the Prince of the kings of the earth, who alone must bear the glory of ruling his own kingdom, the church; and, in particular, against the absolute power usurped by this usurper, that belongs to no mortal, but is the incommunicable prerogative of Jehovah, and against this toleration flowing from that absolute power.

Upon this, he was bid have done. He answered, 'I have near done.' Then he said:

Ye that are the people of God, do not weary in maintaining the testimony of the day, in your stations and places; and whatever ye do, make sure an interest in Christ, for there is a storm coming that shall try your foundation. Scotland must be rid of Scotland before the delivery come. And you that are strangers to God, break off from your sins by repentance, else I will be a witness against you in the day of the Lord.

Here they caused him desist. Upon the scaffold he sung a part of Psalm 103, from the beginning and read chapter 19 of the Revelation. In prayer he said:

Lord, I die in the faith that thou wilt not leave Scotland, but that thou wilt make the blood of thy witnesses the seed of thy church, and return again, and be glorious in our land. And now, Lord, I am ready – 'the bride, the Lamb's wife, hath made herself ready.'

The napkin then being tied about his face, he said to his friend attending him:

Farewell. Be diligent in duty. Make your peace with God, through Christ. There is a great trial coming. As to the remnant I leave, I have committed them to God. Tell them from me not to weary, nor be discouraged in maintaining the testimony. Let them not quit nor forego one of these despised truths. Keep your ground, and the Lord will provide you teachers and ministers, and when he comes, he will make these despised truths glorious upon the earth.

Then he turned over the ladder, with these words in his mouth: 'Lord, into they hands I commit my spirit, for thou has redeemed me, Lord God of truth.' And having thus finished his course, served his generation, and witnessed a good confession for his Lord and Master, before many witnesses, by the will of God, ye yielded up his spirit into the hands of God who gave it. He was the last that sealed the testimony of this suffering period in a public way upon a scaffold.

¶ John H. Thomason (ed.), *A Cloud of Witnesses* (Edinburgh, 1781), pp. 489–91

On a monument in Greyfriars churchyard, Edinburgh

Upon the head of the tomb there is the effigy of an open Bible, drawn with these Scripture citations:

'And when he had opened the first seal, I saw under the altar the souls of them that had been slain for the Word of God, and for the testimony which they held. And they cried with a loud voice, saying, How long, O Lord, holy and true, dost thou not judge and avenge our blood on them that dwell on the earth? And white robes were given unto every one of them, and it was said unto them, that they should rest yet for a little season, until their fellow-servants also, and their brethren, that should be killed as they were, should be fulfilled' (Rev. 6:9–11).

'These are they which have come out of great tribulation, and have washed their robes, and made them white in the blood of the Lamb' (Rev. 7:4).

Halt, passenger, take heed what thou dost see:
This tomb doth shew for what some men did die.
Here lies interred the dust of those who stood
'Gainst perjury, resisting unto blood;
Adhering to the Covenants and Laws,
Establishing the same, which was the cause
Their lives were sacrificed unto the lust
Of prelatists abjured. Though here their dust
Lies mixt with murderers', and other crew,
Whom justice justly did to death pursue;
But as for this, in them no cause was found
Worthy of death; but only they were found
Constant and steadfast, zealous, witnessing
For the prerogatives of Christ their King.
Which truths were sealed by famous Guthrie's head,
And all along to Master Renwick's blood,
They did endure the wrath of enemies,
Reproaches, torments, deaths, and injuries.
But yet they're these two from such troubles came,
And now triumph in glory with the Lamb.

¶ John H. Thomson (ed.), *A Cloud of Witnesses* (Edinburgh, 1781), pp. 563–4

INDEX

MARTYRS FROM THE
17TH – 20TH CENTURIES

CHINA

Martyrs in the eighteenth century in China

In 1732, the emperor by an edict banished all missionaries. Peter Sanz went to Macao, but returned to Fokieu, in 1738, and founded several new churches for his numerous converts. The viceroy, provoked at this, arrested him in the middle of his flock, together with four Dominican friars, who laboured with him. They were beaten with clubs, buffeted on the face with gauntlets made of several pieces of leather, and at length condemned to lose their heads. The bishop was beheaded on the same day, May 26, 1747.

These four fellow-martyrs of the Order of St Dominic were, Francis Serranus, fifty-two years old, who had laboured nineteen years in the Chinese mission, and became bishop of Tipasa: Joachim Roio, fifty-six years old, who had preached in that empire thirty-three years: John Alcomber, forty-two years old, who had spent eighteen years in that mission: and Francis Diaz, thirty-three years old, of which he had employed nine in the same vineyard.

The martyrs of Tonquin, 1744

In Tonquin, a kingdom south-west of China, in which the king and mandarins follow the Chinese religion, though various sects of idolatry and superstition reign among the people, a persecution was raised against the Christians in 1713. In this storm one hundred and fifty churches were demolished, many converts were beaten with a hammer on their knees, and tortured various other ways, and two Spanish missionary priests from the order of St Dominic, suffered martyrdom for the faith, Francis Gil de Federick, and Matthew Alfonso Leziniana.

F. Gil arrived there in 1735, and found more than 20,000 Christians in the west of the kingdom. This vineyard he began assiduously to cultivate; but was arrested in 1737 and condemned to die the following year. The Tonquinese usually execute condemned people only in the last moon of the year. The confessor was often pressed to save his life, by saying that he came into Tonquin as a merchant; but this would have been a lie, and he would not suffer any other to give in such an answer for him. F. Matthew had preached for ten years in Tonquin and after he was arrested and refused to trample on a crucifix, was condemned to die in 1743 and in May, 1741, was taken into the prison where F. Gil was kept.

The idolaters were so astonished to see their ardour to die, and the sorrow of the latter upon an offer of his life, that they cried out: 'Others desire to live, but these men to die.' They were both beheaded together on January 22, 1744.

¶ Alban Butler, *The Lives of the Saints* (Dublin, 1833), vol. I, p. 204

The Boxers

It is now estimated that over 30,000 Chinese Christians, 30,000 Catholics and 2,000 Protestants, were killed by the Boxers, as they stormed through China, chanting their imperial command, 'Exterminate the Christian religion! Death to the foreign devils!' Never had so many Protestant missionaries been killed in the field in one year. In 1900, 135 missionaries and 53 missionary children were killed in China, of whom 79 were linked to the China Inland Mission (CIM).

Thirteen missionaries from the American Board, which sponsored and supported Congregationalists from America to be missionaries China, were killed in the Boxer uprising of 1900 in North China. The following letter from Mrs Atwater, also published in *The Times* on 15th October 1900, bears partial testimony to the thousands of Chinese Christians were massacred in 1900.

> Boxers were sweeping through the city, massacring the native Christians and burning them alive in their homes ... As the patrol was passing a Taoist temple on the way, a noted Boxer meeting-place, cries were heard within. The temple was forcibly entered. Native Christians were found there, their hands tied behind their backs, awaiting execution and torture;

some had already been put to death, and their bodies were still warm and bleeding. All were shockingly mutilated. Their fiendish murderers were at their incantations burning incense before their gods, offering Christians in sacrifice to their angered deities.

The following letter from Mrs Atwater which she wrote home, before she was herself martyred on her own mission station at Fenchow on 15th August, 1900 is dated 3rd August 1900:

I have tried to gather courage to write to you once more. How am I to write all the horrible details of these days? I would rather spare you. The dear ones at Shouyang, seven in all, including our lovely girls, were taken prisoners and brought to T'aiyuan in irons, and there by the Governor's orders beheaded, together with the T'aiyuan friends, thirty-three souls. The following day the Roman Catholic priests and nuns from T'aiyuan were also beheaded, ten souls yesterday. Three weeks after these had perished, our Mission at Taku was attacked, and our six friends there were beheaded. We are now waiting our call home. We have tried to get away to the hills, but the plans do not work. Our things are being stolen right and left, for the people know that we are condemned. Why our lives have been spared we cannot tell. The Proclamation says that whoever kills us will be doing the Governor a great service. Our Magistrate has kept peace so far, but if these men come from Taku, there is not much hope, and there seems none any way we turn. The foreign soldiers are in Pao-ting-fu, and it is said that peace is made. This would save us in any civilised land, no matter what people may say. The Governor seems to be in no haste to finish his bloody work, for which there is little doubt he was sent to Shansi.

Dear one, I long for a sight of your dear faces, but I fear we shall not meet on earth. I have loved you all so much, and I know you will not forget the one who lies in China. There never were sisters and brothers like mine. I am preparing for the end very quietly and calmly. The Lord is wonderfully near, and he will not fail me. I was very restless and excited while there seemed a chance of life, but God has taken away that feeling, and now I just pray for grace to meet the terrible end bravely. The pain will soon be over, and oh the sweetness of the welcome above.

My little baby will go with me. I think God will give it to me in Heaven, and my dear mother will be so glad to see us. I cannot imagine the Saviour's welcome. Oh, that will compensate for all these days of suspense. Dear ones, live near to God and cling less closely to earth. There is no other way by which we can receive that peace from God which passeth all understanding. I would like to send a special message to each of you, but it tries me too much. I must keep calm and still these hours. I do not regret coming to China, but I am sorry I have done so little. My married life, two precious years, has been so full of happiness. We will die together, my dear husband and I.

I used to dread separation. If we escape now it will be a miracle. I send my love to you all, and the dear friends who remember me.

> Your loving sister,
> Lizzie

¶ CIM Magazine, 1901

Blind Chang

Chang Men was one example of the many thousands of Chinese Christians who died during the Boxer uprising of 1900. Chang became blind in his thirties and his character was then accurately summed up by his nickname 'Wu so pu wei te', meaning, 'one without a particle of good in him'. He neighbours believed that he had been struck blind as a judgment on his evil way of life, He threw his wife and daughter out of his home, gambled, stole and became a womaniser.

When Chang learnt that blind people were being cured at a mission hospital he went there. As a result he received both physical and spiritual sight. He longed to be baptised as a Christian and was told that if he went home and told his village about Jesus Christ, a missionary would visit him and then baptise him. When James Webster visited Chang five months later he discovered that God had been greatly blessing Chang as a faithful evangelist. Webster was inundated with over four hundred people wanting to become Christians.

Later Chang lost his eyesight again, after a Chinese doctor operated on him, trying to improve his partial sight. However, this did not deter Chang, who became well-known as the itinerant blind Christian evangelist, able to quote nearly all of the New Testament by heart, as well as many complete chapters from the Old Testament. The Boxer rebels came across blind Chang in Tsengkow, in Manchuria. The Boxers captured fifty Christians there but were told that for every one they killed a further ten would appear, and that they needed to deal with the ring leader of the Christians, blind Chang. The Boxers said that they would free their fifty Christian prisoners if one of them would tell them where blind Chang was. No one betrayed blind

Chang, but one of the fifty managed to escape and went and told blind Chang what was happening.

Blind Chang went to the Boxers at once. But he refused to worship the god of war in the temple. Chang was forced into an open cart and paraded through the town to a cemetery outside the city. As he went through the crowds blind Chang sang a song he had learned in the Christian hospital:

> Jesus loves me, He who died
> Heaven's gate to open wide;
> He will wash away my sin,
> Let His little child come in.
>
> Jesus loves me, He will stay,
> Close beside me all the way;
> If I love Him when I die,
> He will take me home on high.

The last words blind Chang uttered, as the Boxer's sword gleamed in the sun on its way to cutting off Chang's head, were, 'Heavenly Father, receive my spirit.'

¶ CIM Magazine, 1901

The pocket text-book of a missionary martyr

China, 1900

A pathetic little memento of our martyred sister, Miss Georgiana Hurn, has recently reached us from China. It is a copy of Bagster's *Daily Light* – a well-worn little volume, redolent with the odour of the loess soil and the damp, dark mountain caves of Shan-si. Many of the leaves are soiled and loose – the result of frequent handling. It is deeply interesting to turn over the pages of this little text-book and to read the notes which our sister wrote, in the margin, from day to day during their flight.

July 10th

Heard that the Boxers had begun to practise. Things looked dark. See Nov. 8th eve; also July 11th.

Daily Light texts:

(Nov 8th: 'The children of Israel pitched before them like two little flocks of kids; but the Syrians filled the country' (1 Kgs. 20:27); July 11: 'I am with thee to save thee' (Jer. 15:20).

July 21st

Left Sih-chan to escape to a village, Saturday.

[Evening] Stayed in a village

July 22nd

[Morning] Went on to Pao-tsi's home.

('Forasmuch . . . as Christ hath suffered for us in the flesh, arm yourselves likewise with the same mind' 1 Pet. 4:1.)

[Evening] Love of God manifested in a special way. Want came in to escort us to further hiding in the hills.

Daily Light texts:

'Keep yourselves in the love of God' (Jude 21).

'As the Father hath loved me, so have I loved you' (John 15:9).

July 23

[Morning] Left early for a deserted place in the hills.

[Evening] Very tired after a rush over the hills. Had a trying night with mosquitoes.

Daily Light texts:

'Brethren pray for us' (1 Thess. 5:25).

'The effectual fervent prayer of a righteous man availeth much' (Jas. 5:16).

July 24th

[Morning] Stayed in the same [hiding place] Yao-uen-tsi, li-hai. Mosquitoes very troublesome. God's word very comforting.

Daily Light texts:

'Patient in tribulation' (Rom. 12:12).

[Evening] Slept in the same place as last night.

Daily Light texts:

'He staggered not at the promise of God through unbelief' (Rom. 4:20).

'Is anything too hard for the Lord?' (Gen. 18:14)

July 25th

[Morning] Towards afternoon went to another place.

[Evening] Slept in the open-air by the rocks. 1900.

Daily Light texts:
'In my Father's house are many mansions: if it were not so, I would have told you. I go to prepare a place for you' (John 14:2).
'Thou wilt show me the path of life' (Ps. 16:11).

July 26th
Went further into the hills to a most secluded spot.
Daily Light texts:
'We walk by faith, not by sight' (2 Cor. 5:7).

This was the last entry.

¶ *China's Millions* (China Inland Mission, 1901), p. 82

A martyr-year
1900

The year 1900 – the last year of the century – has been a sadly memorable one in the history of our thirty-four and a half years' work in China. It has been the Martyr-year of our beloved mission. No fewer than 52 adults and 16 children have, during its latter half, laid down their lives for Christ's sake. Nor does this number – great as it is – we fear, include all who have been put to death. At the time of writing little hope is entertained of the survival of our six beloved workers with four children who were stationed at Ta-tong, Shan-si. In this province alone, of the ninety-one missionaries who were happily at work there in June last, forty-one are known to have suffered martyrdom.

Other missions have suffered in like manner, though not to the same extent.

The Baptist Missionary Society has lost thirteen Missionaries
The Sheo-yang Mission, eleven
The Society for the Propagation of the Gospel, three
The British and Foreign Bible Society, two
Other missions, including American, forty-six

Making the total of Protestant Missionary Martyrs one hundred and thirty-three.

One of the saddest and most touching features of these sad days has been the death of so many little children, most of whom have suffered with their parents, while others have succumbed to the privations and hardships during the long and perilous journey to the coast.

The church in China, slowly built up through years of toil and struggle, has been in some districts well-nigh wiped out; hundreds of native converts have been cruelly killed, and others relentlessly persecuted because of their fidelity to Christ and his gospel.

¶ *China's Millions* (China Inland Mission, 1901), Editorial Notes

---

A Boxer Placard

From a government Blue-book, No 3 (1900) – translation of a placard posted in West City, Peking:

In a certain street in Peking some worshippers of the I-ho ch'uan (Boxers) at midnight suddenly saw a spirit descend in their midst. The spirit was silent for a long time, and all the congregation fell upon their knees and prayed. Then a terrible voice was heard saying:

I am none other than the Great Yu Ti (God of the unseen world) come down in person. Well knowing that ye are all of devout mind, I have just now descended to make known to you that these are times of trouble in the world, and that it is impossible to set aside the decrees of fate. Disturbances are to be dreaded from the foreign devils; everywhere they are starting Missions, erecting telegraphs, and building railway. They do not believe in the sacred doctrine, and they speak evil of the gods. Their sins are numberless as the hairs of the head.

So soon as the practice of the I-ho ch'uan has been brought to perfection then shall the devils meet their doom. The will of heaven is that the telegraph wires be first cut, then the railways torn up, and then shall the foreign devils be decapitated. In that day shall the hour of their calamities come. The time for rain to fall is yet afar off, and all on account of the devils.

I hereby make known these commands to all your righteous folk, that ye may strive with one accord to exterminate all foreign devils, and so turn aside the wrath of heaven. This shall be accounted unto you for well doing; and on the day when it is done the wind and rain shall be according to your desire.

Therefore I expressly command you make this known in every place.

This I saw with my own eyes, and therefore I make bold to take my pen and write what happened. They who believe it shall have merit; they who do not believe it shall have guilt. The wrath of the spirit was because of the destruction of the Temple of Yu Ti. He sees that the men of the I-ho ch'uan are devout worshippers, and pray to him.

If my tidings are false, may I be destroyed by the five thunderbolts. 4th moon, 1st day (29th April 1900)

¶ M. Broomhall, *Martyred Missionaries of China Inland Mission* (China Inland Mission, 1901), pp. 304–5

Ten Swedish Holiness Union missionaries

In Memoriam – 'Martyrs of Jesus'
The blood of Christ's faithful witnesses in China 'speaketh better' than anything else for the extreme need of Chian's evangelisation. Among a painfully large number of martyrs, there was a group of ten who had to lay down their lives for their brethren, when they – so far as we know – were gathered together in conference in the city of Soh-p'ing Fu. They all belonged to the Swedish Holiness Union, and were associated with the China Inland Mission.

Soh-p'ing Fu tragedy
Mr Mills, at Tien-tsin, has been able to gather the following particulars of the massacre at Soh-p'ing, from a native evangelist, who has been in the employ of the Holiness Union friends for some eight years. The trouble first arose because of the excessive drought. In Hwen-yuen Chau prayers and processions for rain were unceasing. The foreigners were reported to sweep away the approaching clouds with yellow paper broom. Also it was said that the meetings held were for the purpose of praying to God that it should not rain. On 19th June there was a great annual fair at Hwen-yen Chau, and on that day the mob came battering at the doors of the Mission house. They eventually broke in, and the foreigners fled to the Ya-men, where they were effectually protected and treated with great kindness.

The Mandarin said, however, that it would be impossible to protect them if rain did not fall, and advised their going on to Ying-chau. He gave them Tls. 300, probably as compensation for loss of property, and they went under escort to Ying-chau. There they found Mr G. E. Karlberg. He did not at first think it well to go on to the approaching conference at Soh-p'ing Fu, as he feared the rowdy element at Ying-chau would take the opportunity of his absence to loot and destroy the Mission House. About that time the Boxers appeared in the city, and began to post up threatening placards. Matters became worse, and the Magistrate, who was very friendly to the missionaries, advised their leaving for a time, and they went on to Soh-p'ing Fu.

Two days later the mob attacked the mission premises, but the Magistrate succeeded in preventing their doing much damage, and ordered the native evangelist who was left in charge to pack six or seven boxes, which were afterwards put in the Ya-men for security. The evangelist himself then started for Soh-p'ing Fu. He arrived at Tso-yuin in time to see the Mission House there in flames. Some church members were in the Ya-men, being protected by the Mandarin, who was supplying them with food.

On arrival at Soh-p'ing Fu he found thirteen foreigners and one child: of the Holiness Union, S. A. and Mrs Persson, O. A. L. Larsson, Miss J. Lundell, Miss J. Engvall, E. Pettersson, G. E. Karlberg, N. Carleson, Miss M. Hedlund and Miss A. Johansson; and of the Christian and Missionary Alliance – Mr and Mrs C. Blomberg and child, and a man whose name he did not know. There were also many native Christians gathered for the annual conference which is held yearly at the same time as one in the Mother Church in Sweden, namely, 24th June.

Everything was still quiet but Boxer placards were being widely posted up and there was much excitement. After full discussion, the missionaries decided that as danger similar to that experienced in their other stations seemed increasingly imminent, they had better all go to Kalgan if they could get an escort from the Mandarin. This was agreed to by him, but before they could get away the mob gathered and burst into the house. The missionaries all escaped to the Hsien Ya-men by back ways. Their house was looted and burned. After the work of destruction the mob went to the Ya-men and demanded that the foreigners be given up to them that they might kill them. This the Hsien Magistrate refused to do, but to pacify the mob he declared that he had orders to send them to Peking to be killed there, and to give colour to his words he had manacles made by the blacksmith and five of the men of the party were handcuffed. The mob seemed happy and dispersed. About 10 pm that same evening the evangelist was taken out of the Ya-men by Manchu soldiers and Boxers and beaten and left for dead.

Before daylight, however, he recovered, and two men finding him helped him to escape from the city. When he was about forty li from the city he was told that on the same night all the foreigners had been killed by Manchu soldiers and Boxers, and that their heads had been put up on the city wall. The church members and servants suffered in like manner at the hands of these same ruffians. This was on the 3rd day of the 6th moon, i.e. 29th June.

On the previous day at Ying-chau, the Mandarin had tried to save the Christians, and had given them carts to take them to Soh-p'ing Fu. The Boxers, however, turned them back into the mission premises with the carts and carters, and they were all burned together. Among those who suffered at Ying-chau were the evangelist's mother and little daughter.

At Hwen-yuen Chau he heard that none of the native Christians had suffered martyrdom, but that they had lost everything they had. At Tsoyuin it was reported that all the Christians had been taken to Ta-t'ung Fu, and there, with one hundred others, natives and foreigners, Protestants and Catholics, had been put to death. While he was being detained at Fu-ping, it was commonly reported that all the foreigners at Kwei-hua-ch'eng had been killed, and so fierce were the Boxers against everything foreign, that even vendors of matches were said to have been killed, and no one was allowed to wear anything of foreign made material.

¶ *China's Millions* (China Inland Mission, 1901), pp. 4–6

Hattie Jane Rice and Mary Elizabeth Huston

Hattie Rice and Mary Huston were two of six Canadian workers killed in China in 1900. Miss Huston was directed to proceed to the station of

Lu-Ch'eng where she became associated with Miss H. J. Rice. This arrangement proved to be a most suitable and happy one, and a friendship was formed between Miss Huston and Miss Rice which ripened more and more, and became ever increasingly helpful to each. Through varying changes of station life, these two sisters went on in their service, but always in the joy of the Lord. The work at Lu-ch'eng was strengthened in 1898, by the location there of Mr and Mrs E. Cooper, two devoted servants of God.

Then there fell suddenly upon them the heavy stroke of persecution, and in the terrible heat of summer, when the workers would vain have sought something of quiet and rest, Miss Huston and her companions were forced to flee southward, with the hope of escaping into Ho-nan and Hu-peh, and thus into the treaty port of Han-kow. However, a Boxer band was met before they escaped out of Shan-si, between the cities of Kao-p'ing Hsien and Tseh-chau Fu, and the sudden and unexpected attack of these poor, misguided men, resulted in the separation of Miss Huston and Miss Rice from the rest of the party.

Miss Rice, previous to this, had become so exhausted by the sufferings which she had passed through, that she declared to her missionary companions that she could go no further; and now both she and Miss Huston told their persecutors that they were quite prepared to die, but that they could not proceed. At this their enemies became so enraged that they fell upon the two missionaries, striking them down in the public highway, and beating them with the intention of killing them on the spot. Happily, Miss Rice did not suffer long, for as her heart was weak she soon succumbed to the treatment which she was receiving. Thus, the spirit which had longed for so many years to be wholly surrendered to Christ and to obtain God's best, was granted its highest desire in being made a member of that glorious martyr-band which serves above. With her it was 'very far better'; but poor China in that hour lost a friend whose prayers and service had meant for its salvation not less than infinite good.

Miss Huston was beaten at the roadside until almost no life was left in her body. The members of the party who had been driven on, and who thus had not been able to do anything for the two young ladies left behind, finally reached the city of Tseh-Chow Fu, where they begged the official to send a cart back for the two missionaries, and to bring them on their way, so that they all might be united once more and thus proceed on their journey to Hankow. The official promised to fulfil this request, and kept his word as far as he was able to. Ten days after this his bearers arrived, bringing Miss Huston in a litter, who then reported that Miss Rice was dead. Miss Huston herself was in a terrible physical condition. She informed her friends that she had not lost consciousness while being beaten; that she had known when Miss Rice passed away, and that after her tormentors left her, she had lain all night alongside the body of her friend, not leaving her until the morning had come, when she crept away to a place of shelter to die; she had been found there by the official, and had thus been brought on to join her companions in travel. Miss Huston, in spite of her serious and pitiable condition, lived on for nearly a month, often in great pain, but still managed to testify to the peace which guarded her heart. The body, however, had been too severely strained, and just two days before reaching Han-kow, the gentle spirit took its flight heavenwards and homeward.

¶ *China's Millions* (China Inland Mission, 1901), pp. 15–16

South Central Shan-si

The report of this district unhappily is awful. Of the missionaries of the China Inland Mission labouring here thirty-one have been called upon to suffer the loss of their lives, while nineteen have escaped to Han-kow.

Concerning the Ho-tsin friends, there follows information received from Miss Ullff regarding Mr and Mrs McConnell and child, Mr and Mrs J. Young, with Misses Burton and King, and a native servant.

During the 5th Chinese moon (28th May 28 – 26th June) Mr and Mrs McConnell, accompanied by Misses Burton and King, left Ho-tsin to spend the summer among the hills, at a place called San-heo, about 20 li from Ki-chan. About the 16th of the 7th moon (12th July), Mr McConnell and family decided they had better leave the hills, and so they prepared to return to Ho-tsin, and cross over into the Shen-si border. It is presumed that they were joined by Mr and Mrs John Young.

Anticipating trouble they did not enter Ho-tsin, but passed on their way toward the Yellow River. They had only gone a short distance when a band of mounted soldiers overtook them, and led Mr McConnell to understand that they had been sent as escort from the Yamen. They advised that instead of taking the main road to Yu-men-k'eo, a quieter road, and a nearer, should be taken to a place called Ts'ing-kia-uan, where a ferry-boat would be provided. Mr McConnell, knowing that the Yu-men-k'eo people occasionally were turbulent, acceded to the suggestion. Arriving at Ts'ing-kia-uan, the soldiers said they had not come to protect them, but to murder them, except they desisted from worshipping God and preaching against idolatry.

Mr McConnell was then dragged from his mule and dispatched with a sword, his wife and child, it is said, meeting with a similar fate. Mr McConnell's little boy Kenneth was heard to say, 'Papa puh chuen shah siao Kennie' (Papa does not allow you to kill little Kennie). Miss King besought the murderers, Boxers hired by three military graduates, to desist, saying, 'We have come to do you good'; and seeing that the men were relentless, she embraced Miss Burton, and, clasped in one another's arms, they were put to death. At the same time a man and his wife (believed to be Mr and Mrs Young) were seen to clasp one another, as they were put to death in a similar way. The native servant, K'eh-t'ien-hsuen, declining to recant, also met with a violent death. Thus perished in all eight people, seven foreigners and one native.

¶ M. Broomhall, *Martyred Missionaries of China Inland Mission* (China Inland Mission, 1901), pp. 30–31

Extracts from martyrs' last letters

Miss Edith Searell (Martyred 30th June 1900)
'You speak in your letter of the possibility of one place being safer than another; I think, dear Eva, from the human standpoint all are equally unsafe, from the point of view of those whose lives are hid with Christ in God all are equally safe! His children shall have a place of refuge, and that place is the secret place of the Most High.

'"A mighty fortress is our God", and in him we are safe for time and for eternity. Shall we murmur if we have less of time than we expected?

'"The less of time, the more of heaven."

'"The briefer life, earlier immortality."'

Mr George McConnel (Martyred 16th July 1900)

This text was mentioned in his last letter: 'I trusted in thee, O Lord: I said, Thou art my God. My times are in thy hand: deliver me from the hand of mine enemies, and from them that persecute me' (Ps. 31:14–15).

Mrs Young, letter dated 5th July (Martyred 16th July 1900)

'I feel I must write you a few words at this time. We are so quiet here that we can scarcely realise the trouble you are having down on the plain. But I know that the God of Peace will keep your hearts and minds. The winds may blow, and the waves may roll high; if we keep our eyes off them to the Lord we shall be all right. May God bless and keep you all.'

Mrs Kay (Martyred 30th August 1900)

'Mr Kay will not leave here till he is driven out. The natives are so good and have declared that they will stand by us till death, if needs be. We have had many friends from the street to comfort us and to tell us not to be afraid. It is from outsiders we fear. Our trust is in God. I want to give you my home address in case we should be taken home to glory. If anything should happen to us, God will make a way for our children at Chefoo. I have a desire in my heart towards them – that is to be spared for their sake – but His will be done.'

Miss Francis Edith Nathan (Martyred August or September 1900)

'If "the very hairs of our head are all numbered", then no man can touch us unless our Father willeth. From earthly powers we shall get very little help, if the Empress Dowager is secretly using these men to rid China of the foreigners. Yet we know the Lord removeth kings. May He indeed keep our hearts in peace, His own perfect peace.'

Mr W. G. Peat (Martyred August or September 1900)

'The 15th of the Chinese month is mentioned here as the date of our destruction. But we are in God's hands, and can say, "I will fear no evil, for thou art with me."'

Mr David Barratt (Martyred summer 1900)

'Our blood may be as a true cement (for the foundation), and God's kingdom will increase over this land. Extermination is but exaltation. God guide and bless us! "Fear not them which kill," He says, "are ye not of much more value than many sparrows". "Peace, perfect peace," to you, brother, and all at Luch'eng. "We may meet in the glory in a few hours or days." Let us be true till death. "Be thou faithful unto death, and I will give thee a crown of life."'

¶ M. Broomhall, *Martyred Missionaries of China Inland Mission* (CIM, 1901), pp. 29ff.

CIM's Diary of Events, 1900

1899
Dec 31
Murder of Rev S. P. Brooks of the SPG (Society for the Propagation of the Gospel).

1900
Jan 17
Sir Claude Macdonald sends a protest to the Tsung-li-yamen saying, 'The whole of the present difficulty can be traced to the late Governor of Shan-tong, Yh-hsien, who secretly encouraged the seditious society known as "The Boxers".'

May 14
Elder Si of Hung-tung, Shan-si, stabbed by Boxers.

May 17
Sir Claude Macdonald reports Boxers destroyed three villages and killed sixty-one Roman Catholic converts near Pao-ting-fu.

May 18
Sir Claude reports Boxers destroyed LMS (London Missionary Society) chapel at King-ts'un, and killed preacher forty miles S.W. of Peking.

May 23
Boxers plunder Pastor Hsi's home (Shan-si).

May 29
Railway between Peking and T'ien-tsin torn up.

June 1
Mr Robinson murdered and Mr Norman carried off.

June 2
Mr Norman murdered.

June 7
Imperial decree issued justifying action of the Boxers.

June 8
Massacre of native Christians at Tung-chau.

June 13
Boxers enter Peking. Hundreds of converts killed.

June 27
Mrs Coombs killed.

June 29
Massacre of thirteen Swedish missionaries at Soh-p'ing, Shan-si.

June 30
Miss Whitchurch and Miss Searell murdered at Hiao-i.

July 1
Massacre at south side of Pao-ting-fu, including Mr and Mrs Bagnall and child, and Mr William Cooper.

July 2
Imperial edict ordering expulsion of all foreigners and persecution of Christians.

July 9
Massacre at T'ai-yuan-fu, including Mrs W. Millar Wilson, Miss Stevens, and Miss Clarke.

July 13
Miss Rice murdered.

July 16
Murder of the Ho-tsin party, including Mr and Mrs Young, Miss King, and Miss Burton.

July 21
Murder of Mr and Mrs Thompson and Miss Desmond, inside K'u-chau city, Chehkiang.

July 22
Murder of Mr and Mrs Ward and Miss Thirgood, outside K-u-chau.

July 24
Murder of Miss Sherwood and Miss Manchester in K'u-chau city.

August 15
Murder of Fen-chau party, including Mr and Mrs Lundgren and Miss Eldred.

August 30
Mr and Mrs Kay and child put to death, and Mr and Mrs Peat and party put to death.

¶ M. Broomhall, *Martyred Missionaries of China Inland Mission* (China Inland Mission, 1901), pp. 299–301

The Province of Cheh-kiang

Prior to the foundation of the CIM in 1866, Mr Hudson Taylor had in 1857 commenced work in this province. The work then started has been greatly blessed by God. According to the last statistics the China Inland Mission had as many as 3,710 communicants in Cheh-kiang alone.

Recently there has been a time of severe persecution in many of the stations, and not a few native Christians have suffered the loss of all things, and others sealed their testimony by death. The sad outbreak which has occasioned the death of eight members of the Mission and three children, had nothing, as far as we can see, to do with the Boxer movement. It was a local rebellion.

The following are the names of those martyred: stationed at K'u-chaufu, Mr and Mrs D. B. Thompson, and their two boys, Edwin and Sidney, Miss J. Desmond, Miss Edith Sherwood, and Miss Etta Manchester; stationed at Ch'angshan, Mr and Mrs G. F. Ward and infant, Herbert, and Miss E. A. Thirgood.

On 21st July, the day after Mr Thompson wrote, 'God, our Father, take care of us, or take us,' God took them to himself for ever.

A large and unmanageable crowd gathered at the Mission premises, and commenced to loot and destroy everything, and Mr Thompson was badly bruised on the head. The evangelist Ch'en-t'ien-fu escaped through the back door, and sought aid from the Tao-t'ai (intendant of circuit), who practically refused to interfere.

When the evangelist returned to the Mission-house the ladies were sent to the Tao-t'ai's Yamen, but only to find the district (Hsien) magistrate being beheaded in the court of Yamen itself. They at once returned to the already destroyed Mission premises. About noon they again went to the Taot'ai's Yamen, and as a report had gained currency that the rebels were attacking the city, all the crowd had gone to the city wall, so they found the Yamen quiet.

In the afternoon the people returned. When they found the foreigners there, they first seized Mr Thompson, took him outside the front door, and put him to death. They then returned and murdered Mrs Thompson, her two children, and Miss Desmond. The native evangelist says they were killed at once and had no prolonged suffering.

The ladies' house where Miss Sherwood and Miss Manchester resided had been rioted at the same time as the Thompsons', but the ladies were hidden by neighbours until the 24th. The natives then refused to afford them any further shelter. Being discovered they were taken to the city temple, where they were speedily put to death.

Mr Thompson had been expecting Mr and Mrs Ward and Miss Thirgood to arrive from Ch'ang-shan, where the danger was greater. The ladies started to travel by boat, and reached the jetty at K'u-chau. Here they were killed on the afternoon of 22nd July. Mr Ward, with his servant Li-yuen, travelled overland, and were also killed on the morning of the same day about five miles from K'u-chau.

¶ M. Broomhall, *Martyred Missionaries of China Inland Mission* (CIM, 1901), pp. 182–5

John and Betty Stam

The martyrdom of John and Betty Stam took place in China while they were missionaries with the China Inland Mission, CIM (now the Overseas Missionary Fellowship, OMF), in 1934.

An army of two thousand Communists, soon increased to six thousand, was now in possession of the district, and the people, already suffering from semi-famine conditions, had to see their meagre supplies disappear as before hungry locusts. But that was a minor misery. For when The Reds abandoned Tsingteh the next morning, they left many dead behind them and carried away many captives. Their next destination was Miaosheo, the little town twelve miles across the mountains; and how John and Betty must have dreaded what that would mean for their dear friends there.

Over the familiar road John walked, a prisoner, carrying his precious little one, not yet three months old. Betty was on horseback part of the way, and they both smiled at the few people who saw them as they passed. That little Helen was there at all seems to have been the first miracle in her deliverance, for her life was to have been taken even before they left Tsingteh. Part of the torture of her parents, it is stated, was that their captors discussed before them whether or not they should kill the infant out of hand, to save trouble. But someone said, 'Why kill her? She'll die anyway.'

So the captors left the child; that remark had saved her life and John and Betty had their treasure with them as they travelled wearily over the mountains to Miaosheo.

Arrived in the town, how they must have longed to go to the home of their friends the Wangs! But, of course, terror reigned supreme. All who could had fled, before the looting of the place began. Betty and John were hurried into the postmaster's shop and left there under guard, thankful to be out of sight of all that was taking place.

'Where are you going?' asked the postmaster, when he recognised the prisoners.

'We do not know where they are going,' John answered simply, 'but we are going to heaven.'

The postmaster offered them fruit to eat. Betty took some – she had the baby to nurse – but John made the most of the opportunity for writing again to Shanghai. This note he entrusted to the postmaster to forward.

Miaosheo, An.
December 7, 1934

China Inland Mission.

Dear Brethren,

We are in the hands of the Communists here, being taken from Tsingteh when they passed through yesterday. I tried to persuade them to let my wife and baby go back from Tsingteh with a letter to you, but they wouldn't let her, and so we both made the trip to Miaosheo today, my wife travelling part of the way on a horse.

They want $20,000 before they will free us, which we have told them we are sure will not be paid. Famine relief money and our personal money and effects are all in their hands.

God give you wisdom in what you do and give us grace and fortitude. He is able.

Yours in Him,

John C. Stam

Not a word of self-pity or of fear. Not a sign of faltering. He who had sent them was with them. They were strong in the quiet strength of Him who said: 'For this cause came I unto this hour. Father, glorify thy name.'

> Afraid? Of What?
> To feel the spirit's glad release?
> To pass from pain to perfect peace,
> The strife and strain of life to cease?
> Afraid? Of What?
>
> Afraid? Of What?
> Afraid to see the Saviour's face,
> To hear His welcome, and to trace
> The glory gleam from wounds of grace?
> Afraid? Of What?
>
> Afraid? Of What?
> A flash, a crash, a pierced heart;
> Darkness, light, O heaven's art!
> Afraid? Of What?
>
> Afraid? Of What?
> To do by death what life could not –
> Baptise with blood a stony plot,
> Till souls shall blossom from the spot?
> Afraid? Of What?

'Baptise with blood a stony plot, till souls shall blossom from the spot' – oh, how John and Betty longed, whether by life or by death, to win precious souls to Christ for South Anhwei!

Little remains to be told, for, thank God, their sufferings were not prolonged. When the Communists again turned their attention to them, they were taken to a house belonging to some wealthy man who had fled. There they were put in a room in an inner courtyard, closely guarded by soldiers, and though Betty seems to have been left free to care for the baby, John was tightly bound with ropes to a post of the heavy bed. How long must have seemed the hours of that cold, winter night, when he was not able to move or even change his position!

> I'm standing, Lord:
> There is a mist that blinds my sight.
> Steep jagged rocks, front, left and right,
> Lower, dim, gigantic, in the night.
>   Where is the way?
>
> I'm standing, Lord: –
> Since thou hast spoken, Lord, I see
> Thou hast beset – these rocks are Thee!
> And since thy love encloses me,
>   I stand and sing.

No one knows what passed between John and Betty, or what fears assailed those young hearts [they were still only 27 and 28 years of age]. Silence veils the hours sacred to him alone who, for love of us, hung long hours in darkness upon a cross. Certain it is that he who is never nearer than when we need him most sustained his children in that hour of trial. Betty was not overwhelmed, but was enabled to plan with all a mother's tenderness for the infant they might have to leave behind, alone and orphaned, amid such perils. Could that little life survive? And if it did, what then? But had they not given her to God in that so recent dedication service? Would not he care for his own?

Never was that little one more precious than when they looked their last on her baby sweetness, as they were roughly summoned the next morning and led out to die. Yet there was no weakening. Those who witnessed the tragedy marvelled, as they testify, at the calmness with which John and Betty faced the worst their misguided enemies could do. Theirs was the moral, spiritual triumph, in that hour when the very forces of hell seemed to be let loose. Painfully bound with ropes, their hands behind them, they passed down the street where he was known to many, while the Reds shouted their ridicule and called the people to come and see the execution.

Like their Master, they were led up a little hill outside the town.

There, in the clump of pine trees, the Communists harangued the unwilling onlookers, too terror-stricken to utter protest – But no, one man broke the ranks! The doctor of the place and a Christian, he expressed the feelings of many when he fell on his knees and pleaded for the life of his friends. Angrily repulsed by the Reds, he still persisted, until he was dragged away as a prisoner, to suffer death when it appeared that he too was a follower of Christ.

John had turned to the leader of the band, asking mercy for this man, when he was sharply ordered to kneel – and the look of joy on his face, afterwards, told of the unseen Presence with them as his spirit was released. Betty was seen to quiver, but only for a moment. Bound as she was, she fell on her knees beside him. A quick command, the flash of a sword which mercifully she did not see – and they were reunited.

'Absent from the body . . . present with the Lord.'

'Thanks be to God, which giveth us the victory through our Lord Jesus Christ.'

'They shall walk with me in white; for they are worthy.'

[The baby Helen was miraculously rescued by Evangelist Lo, and became known as the 'miracle baby'.]

¶ Mrs Howard Taylor, *The Triumph of John and Betty Stam* (China Inland Mission, 1935), pp. 103–8

NORTH AMERICA

Martin Luther King
1968

'The most perfect peace we can attain in this miserable life, consists in meek and patient suffering. He who has learned to suffer will certainly possess the greatest share of peace. He is the conqueror of himself, the lord of the world, the friend of Christ, and the heir of heaven' (The Imitation of Christ, ascribed to Thomas a Kempis).

Champion of civil rights for American blacks, Martin Luther King explained his non-violent approach to smashing injustice in these words: 'Our aim must be never to defeat or humiliate the white man, but to win his friendship and understanding. We must come to see that the end we seek is a society at peace with itself, a society that can live with its conscience. That will be a day not of the white man, not of the black man. That will be the day of man as man.' In December 1964 he received the Nobel Peace Prize Award, presented by King Olav of Norway, in recognition of his tireless campaign against oppression and prejudice.

Negro dustmen had been on strike in Memphis for a week and Martin Luther King went there to orchestrate a massive non-violent protest. Dr King was being put under great pressure from some other negro leaders like Stokely Carmichael over his avowedly non-violent approach to gaining simple justice for American blacks. Dr King spoke at a pre-march rally on 3rd April in which he make clear exactly what he supported in this unequal struggle. He also referred to the numerous threats of violence that he had received, some threatening his life. He said quite openly that he had been warned not to go to Memphis if he wanted to stay alive. Dr King ended his speech, his last recorded public address, with these words:

And then I got into Memphis and some began to talk about the threats of what would happen to me from some of our sick white brothers. But I don't know what will happen now. We've got some difficult days ahead. But it really doesn't matter with me now. Because I've been to the mountain-top and I don't mind. Like anybody, I would like to live a long life, longevity has its place, but I'm not concerned about that now. I just want to do God's will, and he's allowed me to go up to the mountain. And I've looked over and I've seen the Promised Land. I may not get there with you, but I want you to know tonight that we as a people will get to the Promised Land. So I'm happy tonight. I'm not fearing any man. Mine eyes have seen the glory of the coming of the Lord.

Dr King was taking a short break the following morning on the balcony of the Lorraine Motel where he was engaged in a conference. As he turned to return to his room the assassin's bullet rang out, making a direct, deadly hit on Dr King's face. In vain the dying, 39-year-old Dr King was rushed by ambulance to St Joseph's hospital where he never regained consciousness.

On hearing the news American President Johnson said to the nation on the television, 'I ask every citizen to reject the blind violence that has struck Dr King.' On Dr King's tombstone are inscribed the same words that he spoke on the famous march on Washington, in August 1963:

> FREE AT LAST,
> FREE AT LAST,
> THANK GOD ALMIGHTY
> I'M FREE AT LAST.

THE FAR EAST

Thailand

Roy Orpin

'Except a corn of wheat fall into the ground and die, it abideth alone: but if it die, it bringeth forth much fruit' (John 12:24).

Many Christians became missionaries through reading the stories of Christians who became Christian martyrs as they served Christ in foreign countries. Roy Orpin, from New Zealand, had been inspired by reading the stories of John and Betty Stam, and of the five missionaries killed by the Auca Indians in Ecuador. After being accepted by the Overseas Missionary Fellowship, Roy was sent to Thailand, where he married his fiancée, a young English girl whom he had met in Auckland while they were both studying at the New Zealand Bible Training Institute.

The newly married couple tried to make their home in a small village in Namkhet in Thailand, among a tribal people known as the Meos. Within a year of their being there, violence erupted around them ominously. Three Thai opium dealers had been killed, even though they begged for their lives. Roy left his pregnant wife in their village as he travelled around surrounding villages. One night he came home having stumbled across the bodies of two more murdered Thais.

Roy, and his wife Gillian, had moved to another village, Bitter Bamboo, in order to teach some new Christians there. Then, as the day for their baby's birth came close, Gillian moved into a mission hospital. Roy had decided to follow Gillian. On the day before he was to join Gillian Roy set out to visit one of the surrounding villages. On his return he was attacked by three men who held him up at gunpoint, demanding that Roy should give them all he had. Roy gave him what little he had, but this hardly satisfied them and they proceeded to shoot him. Roy was able to struggle on with his fatal wound and was taken to a government hospital. Gillian was at Roy's side for four days, as his life slowly ebbed away, until the twenty-six-year-old missionary finally died of kidney failure. During these days Roy asked Gillian to recite one of his favourite choruses:

> Jesus! I am resting, resting
> In the joy of what Thou art;
> I am finding out the greatness
> Of Thy loving heart.

Not many days after Roy's funeral Murray Roy was born. Gillian returned to work among the Meo tribespeople when they had just begun to sow their grain seeds. Along with two other single women missionaries, Gillian saw a spiritual harvest when twelve families from the Meo people decided to turn to Christ and burn their pagan charms. This happened just as they were harvesting their crops. 'Except a corn of wheat fall into the ground and die, it abideth alone: but if it die, it bringeth forth much fruit' (John 12:24).

Japan

Martyrs of 1597

Francis Xavier arrived in Japan in 1549, baptised great numbers, and whole provinces received the faith. The great kings of Arima, Bungo, and Omura, sent a solemn embassy of obedience to Pope Gregory XIII in 1582: and in 1587 there were in Japan over 200,000 Christians, and among these several kings, princes and bonzas, but in 1588, Cambacundono, the haughty emperor, having usurped the honours of a deity, commanded all the Jesuits to leave his dominions within six months: however, many remained there disguised.

In 1592, the persecution was renewed, and several Japanese converts received the crown of martyrdom. The emperor Tagcosama, one of the proudest and most vicious of men, was worked up into a rage and jealously by a suspicion suggested by certain European merchants desirous of the monopoly of this trade, that the view of the missionaries in preaching the Christian faith was to facilitate the conquest of their country by the Portuguese or Spaniards. Three Jesuits and six Franciscans were crucified on a hill near Nangasaqui in 1597. The latter were partly Spaniards and partly Indians, and had at their head F. Peter Baptist, commissary of his Order, who was born in Avila, in Spain. As to the Jesuits, one was Paul Michi, a noble Japanese and an eminent preacher, at that time thirty-three years old. The other two, John Gotto and James Kisai, were admitted into the Society in prison a little before they suffered.

Several Japanese suffered with them. The martyrs were twenty-six in number, and among them were three boys, two aged fifteen and one aged twelve. Each showed great joy and constancy in their sufferings. Of these martyrs, twenty-four had been brought to Meaco, where only part of their left ears was cut off, by a mitigation of the sentence which had commanded the amputation of their noses and both ears. They were conducted through many towns and public places, their cheeks stained with blood, for a terror to others. When the twenty-six soldiers of Christ arrived at their place of execution near Nangasaqui, they were fastened to crosses by cords and chains, about their arms and legs, and an iron collar about their necks, were raised into the air, the foot of each cross falling into a hole prepared for it in the ground. The crosses were planted in a row, about four feet apart, and each martyr had an executioner near him with a spear ready to pierce his side; for such is the Japanese manner of crucifixion. As soon as all the crosses were planted, the executioners lifted up their lances, and at a signal given, all pierced the martyrs almost in the same instant; upon which they expired and went to receive the reward of the sufferings.

¶ Alban Butler, *The Lives of the Saints* (Dublin, 1833), vol. I, p. 201

Martyrs of 1602–22

In 1599, one hundred Jesuit missionaries converted 40,000 Japanese people, and in 1600 over 30,000 Japanese were converted and fifty churches were built. But bloody persecution resulted in many Japanese converts being beheaded, crucified or burned.

In 1614, new cruelties were exercised to overcome their constancy, as by bruising their feet between certain pieces of wood, cutting off or squeezing their limbs one after another, applying red-hot irons or slow fires, flaying off the skin of the fingers, putting burning coals to their hands, tearing off the flesh with pincers, or thrusting reeds into all parts of their bodies, and turning them about to tear their flesh, till they should say they would forsake their faith: all which, innumerable persons, even children, bore with invincible constancy till death.

In 1616, Xogun succeeding his father Cubosama in the empire, surpassed him in cruelty. The most illustrious of these religious heroes was F. Charles Spinola. He was of a noble Genoese family, and entered the Society of Nola, whilst his uncle cardinal Spinola was bishop of that city. Out of zeal and a desire of martyrdom, he begged to be sent on the Japanese mission. He arrived there in 1602; laboured many years in that mission, gained many to Christ, by his mildness, and lived in great austerity, for his usual food was only a little rice and herbs. He suffered four years a most cruel imprisonment, during which, in burning fevers, he was not able to obtain from his keepers one drop of cold water apart from his meals: yet he wrote from his dungeon:

> Father, how sweet and delightful is it to suffer for Jesus Christ! I have learned this better by experience than I am able to express, especially since we are in these dungeons where we fast continually. The strength of my body fails me, but my joy increases as I see death draw nearer. O what a happiness for me, if next Easter I shall sing the heavenly Alleluia in the company of the blessed!

In a long letter to his cousin Maximilian, Charles Spinola wrote:

Letter from Omura, a Japanese prison, 1622

O, if you had tasted the delights with which God fills the souls of those who serve him, and suffer for him, how would you condemn all that the world can promise! I now begin to be a disciple of Jesus Christ, since for his love I am in prison, where I suffer much. But I assure you, that when I am fainting with hunger, God hath fortified me by his sweet consolations, so that I have looked upon myself as well recompensed for his service. And though I were yet to pass many years in prison, the time would appear short, through the extreme desire which I feel of suffering for him, who even here so well repays our labours. Besides other sickness, I have been afflicted with a continual fever a hundred days without any remedies or proper nourishment. All this time my heart was so full of joy, that it seemed to me too narrow to contain it. I have never felt any equal to it, and I thought myself at the gates of paradise.

His joy was excessive at the news that he was condemned to be burnt alive, and he never ceased to thank God for so great a mercy, of which he owned himself unworthy. He was conducted from his last prison at Omura to Nangasaqui, where fifty martyrs suffering together on a hill within sight of that city, nine Jesuits, four Franciscans, and six Dominicans, the rest beheaded. The twenty-five stakes were fixed all in a row, and the martyrs were tied to them. Fire was set to the end of the pile of wood twenty-five feet from the martyrs, and gradually approached them, two hours before it reached them. F. Spinola stood unmoved, with his eyes lifted up towards heaven, till the cords which tied him being burnt, he fell into the flames, and was consumed on 2nd September 1622, being fifty-eight years old. Many others, especially Jesuits, suffered variously, being either burnt at slow fires, crucified, beheaded, or thrown into a burning mountain, or hung with their heads downwards in pits, which cruel torment usually put an end to their lives in three or four days.

¶ Alban Butler, *The Lives of the Saints* (Dublin, 1833), vol. I, pp. 201–2

20,000 massacred, 1662

Some Portuguese missionaries were the first to introduce Christianity into Japan. They landed on the island in 1552, and their efforts were more successful than they dared to anticipate. Their labours continued to be successful until 1616, when they were accused of being implicated in a conspiracy to overthrow the government and dethrone the emperor. For a few years they remained unmolested, though the greatest jealousy existed against them at the court; but in 1662 a dreadful persecution broke out against both the foreign and native Christians. It is asserted that between 1662 and 1666 no less than 20,000 Christians were massacred. The churches were shut and any profession of Christianity was punished with death. At length the Christians moved to the town of Siniabara, on the island of Ximio, where they determined to defend themselves to the last. The Japanese army followed them and besieged the town. The Christians, although much inferior in discipline, equipment and resources, defended themselves with the greatest bravery, and resisted all attacks for three months. Then, as their provisions were so scarce they became weak and had to surrender. Every age and sex were then ruthlessly murdered by the conquerors, and Christianity, after its brief existence, was completely extirpated from the dominions of the Tycoon.

¶ John Foxe, *The Book of Martyrs,* revised with notes and an appendix by W. Bramley-Moore (London, 1869), pp. 170–1

Martyrs of 1660–73

After the downfall of the insurgents of Shimabara in 1638 the Catholics in Japan were completely isolated from the Mother Church, while the government, both central and feudal, persecuted them severely and persistently. In 1640 the central Shogunate government organised a Commission for Inquisition, and the Chief Commissioner was endowed with the power to control the several feudal states in regard to their measures of inquisition and persecution. In most cases the arrested were first examined by the local authorities, then

Fate of 220 people of Matsudaira Yamato-no-kami

We classify under four heads: those who were executed; those who died in prison; those who remained in prison, supposedly, somewhere; those released on investigation or on promising to give up their faith.

VILLAGE COMMUNITY	EXECUTED	DIED IN PRISON	STILL IN PRISON	RELEASED	TOTAL
Katsuragi	27	24	9	32	92
Monden	18	12	10	19	59
Kami-Mitsunaga		2	1	1	4
Shimo-Mitsunaga	6	9	8	4	27
Mera			1	3	4
Magaya	3		3	1	7
Kobu-gari		2			2
Senzai	2		2	2	6
Otozu		2		3	5
Yamazu		2			2
Takajo-mura		3		1	4
Harumura		1			1
Takajo-machi	1		1		2
Tsumori		2	2	1	5
TOTALS	57	59	37	67	220

In the province of Bungo, which included the feudal territory of Matsudaira, between 1660–73 at least 472 people were persecuted, 77 being executed and 103 died in prison.

- The oldest among the executed was Ichisuke, 73 years old when arrested and 74 when executed.
- The oldest among those who died in prison was Kichizaemon, 74 when arrested and 75 when he died.
- The youngest executed was Fuji, aged 14 when arrested and 16 when executed.
- The youngest who died in prison were Tsuru, 12 when arrested and 16 when she died, and Shio, 14 when arrested and 20 when she died.

Some previously unrecorded Japanese martyrdoms of the Catholic Church, in the second half of the seventeenth century are set out in a study of newly disclosed documents from the prefectural library of Nagasaki. Masaharu Anesaki writes a chapter about this topic in the book *Scritti di Storia E Paleografia*, vol. III (Rome: Biblioteca Apostolica Vaticana, 1924), pp. 343–57.

detained in their local prisons to induce the converts to apostatise – to 'turn over' (*korobu*), as it weas termed. Those who withstood were sent to Nagasaki, where further measures were taken to cause them to 'turn over'; when they were obstinate enough to defy persuasion or threats or temptations, they were sentenced to death. In many cases the prisoners died in prison within less than a year, but some lasted imprisonment for up to sixteen years.

Manchurian martyrs

The Japanese took over the southern part of Manchuria in 1905. They discovered that thousands of the people of Manchuria had turned to Christ. The Japanese believed that their emperor was an incarnation of the Sun Goddess and should be worshipped as a god. However, the new Christians in Manchuria refused to honour the emperor in this way. The Japanese soldiers indulged in wholesale massacres of Christians as they burnt the homes of Christian villagers. When they arrived in a Christian village they started by setting fire to huge sacks of straw and barley. As the men left their homes they were shot, and any who did not die outright were covered with burning straw or bayonetted. Then the houses were set alight, often with women and children left inside. Up to 150 Christians were killed in one village in this way.

SOUTH AMERICA

Bolivia

The Ayore Indians

In the jungle between Brazil and Paraguay live Bolivian Indians, whose land has been ravaged for many decades. Five missionaries from the New Tribes Mission became the first martyrs to be killed by these Indians. The concept behind the founding of the New Tribes Mission in 1942 by Paul Fleming and Cecil Dye was simple: to take the gospel to new tribes who had never been visited by Christians before. In 1944 Paul Fleming, Cecil Dye, together with three others, Bob Dye, Dave Bacon and George Hosbach arrived in Bolivia to reach the Ayores, who were known to the Bolivians as 'the tribe that was impossible to tame.' The five men, three of whom were married, left their wives and the Flemings' three children at their base camp in the jungle at Santo Corazon, and went further into the jungle seeking the Ayores. Before they left on 10th November 1944, they told two men colleagues to search for them if they had not returned within a month. After a month nothing had been heard from them, so Clyde Collins, Wally Wright and four Bolivians went in search of the missionaries. They managed to track their trail until they saw a group of Ayores who immediately scattered on seeing them. Soon after this they came across some personal belongings of the missionaries: a sock belonging to Cecil, a machete of George's and a cracked camera lens. They decided to return from their search when Wally was shot and wounded by an arrow.

A bigger search party, consisting only of Bolivians, was then sent out. Although they reached an Ayore plantation and found some more personal belongings of the missionaries, they did not discover their bodies. When the second search party returned an army commander was keen to send in some troops and teach the Ayores a lesson, but the three wives prevented this by stressing that they wanted to reach the Ayores for Christ and not exact revenge. A year later some missionaries, including Jean Dye, moved further into the territory of the Ayores. Three years later, in 1948, a group of naked Ayores came to the mission station in the jungle with no warning. The missionaries tried to show them friendship and gave them gifts before they disappeared back into the jungle. Six weeks later these Indians came back and slept the night with the missionaries. The next day they told the missionaries how a different clan from them had met and killed five white men and thrown their bodies into the river. However, next year, Jean Dye was told by a member of the Ayore tribe, Degui, that his warriors and killed five men and buried them. Further details about the killing of the five missionaries emerged from another Ayore friend of Degui. They were killed with spears and machetes and clubs.

A number of friends of the killers came to Christ and expressed their sorrow to the wives of the three dead missionaries. One of the ringleaders responsible for the death of the missionaries, Upoide, came to the mission station, and as soon as he realised that the wives of the missionaries had forgiven him, became a Christian himself. Since then a permanent mission station in the jungle for the Ayores has been established and no further killings have taken place.

Ecuador

Jim Elliot
1956

'He is no fool who gives what he cannot keep to gain what he cannot lose' (Jim Elliot, written aged 22).

Soon after Jim Elliot graduated from Wheaton College, Wheaton,

Illinois, USA, in 1949, he had premonitions that he would die young in God's service. He became convinced that God was calling him to pioneer missionary work in Ecuador. He spent most of 1952 in Quito, Ecuador, learning Spanish and orientating to a new culture. Jim then went to Shandia, and helped to build up a jungle mission station, where he also had to learn a new language so he could speak with the Quichua Indians.

Since his college days Jim had been fascinated by a remote Stone Age tribe who lived in Ecuador, known as the Aucas. Jim knew that they had a deserved reputation for killing anyone, Indian or white, who dared to intrude into their land. Nevertheless, Jim felt it right to pray especially for these Aucas. While he worked with his recently married wife Elisabeth among the Quichua Indians Jim's thoughts often turned to how he might be able to contact the Aucas.

Then, in September 1955 a pilot with the Mission Aviation Fellowship, Nate Saint, spotted from the air a small Auca settlement, while he was flying with Ed McCully. They quickly reported their discovery to Jim Elliot. The three of them, Ed, Nate and Jim then spent the next three months making weekly flights over the Aucas, dropping gifts of ribbons and cloth on every occasion. Soon the Aucas would leave their oval-shaped, leaf-thatched houses and dugout canoes and wait for the weekly visit from the air. They even started to reciprocate gifts and managed to pop into the rope-suspended bucket a lovely feather crown. Another Auca had made a model of their plane and raised it on a pole outside his house. When the plane circled overhead the men surprised the Aucas at first, by shouting in their own language, 'We like you.' 'We are your friends.' 'We are your friends.'

At the beginning of 1956 the four men, together with Pete Fleming and Roger Youderian from the Gospel Missionary Union, who had now joined their team, thought it right to try and meet up with the Aucas. Nate had found a suitable flat beach on the Curray River where he could land his Piper Family Cruiser. Then, on January 3, Nate landed Jim, Ed, Roger and Pete in a number of shuttle flights, on the beach. There they built a tree house and looked forward to meeting the Aucas from the neighbouring jungle. The plane then flew over the Aucas and they could hardly believe their ears when they were heard the words in their own language: 'We are on the Curray.' 'Come and see us.' To the delight of the missionaries three young Aucas, two men and one woman, visited them. The visit seemed to be a total success. They gave them hamburgers and lemonade, and one of the Aucas, named 'George' by the missionaries, even went for a ride in the plane. However, three days later, Nate saw ten Aucas leaving their Indian village heading for their airstrip. Nate returned to the other four with this news. Together they all sang:

> We rest on Thee, our Shield and our Defender,
> We go not forth alone against the foe.
> Strong in Thy strength, safe in thy keeping tender,
> We rest on Thee, and in Thy name we go.
>
> Yea, in Thy name, O Captain of Salvation,
> In Thy blest name, all other names above,
> Jesus our Righteousness, our sure Foundation,
> Our Prince of Glory, and our King of Love.
>
> We go in faith, our own great weakness feeling,
> And needing more each day Thy grace to know,
> Yet from our hearts a song of triumph pealing,
> We rest on Thee, and in Thy name we go.
>
> We rest on Thee, our Shield and our Defender,
> Thine is the battle, Thine shall be the praise
> When passing through the gates of pearly splendour,
> Victors, we rest with Thee through endless days.

The five missionaries did not use the guns they had, but were speared to death by the primitive wooden spears of these ten Aucas. Their plane was destroyed.

Update on the Auca Indians

Waorani New Testament

When the first translators came to Ecuador and were introduced to the President as people interested in minority groups, they were warned to avoid the notorious Waorani (Auca) Indians. When the President's plane had flown over Waorani territory, they had thrown spears at it. But he was surpised by the bold reply, 'When God opens the door, it will be safe to go.'

Five young men were killed at the hands of the Waorani when they made their first approach. But after much prayer and persistence their confidence was gained, translation began, and a number of them became Christians.

When the President heard that Waoranis (of all people) had become Christians he arranged to visit some of them. His plane landed in a clearing in the jungle, where a group of Waorani men were standing quietly waiting for him. When they were presented to the President they were wide-eyed with astonishment, because he was completely bald! One of them stepped forward with his arm stretched out in front of him. Not knowing quite qhat was coming, the President backed away, but the man just wanted to rub the top of the President's head!

The President for his part, amazed at the change in the Waorani people, turned to the translator and said, 'Do you really think these people can understand theology?'

'Ask them,' came the wise reply.

So the President addressed one of them, 'What do you know about Jesus?' Immediately the man's eyes lit up and for a good thirty minutes he preached the gospel to the President of the Republic.

Back in the capital, the President summoned his cabinet to meet the translator. 'I was a believer, but I have wandered away from the Truth,' he said. Turning to his cabinet ministers, he asked them, one by one, 'What about you?' After much embarrassment, the President resumed, 'This man will tell you about the power that is transforming the people in our jungle.'

Last month, thirteen people were baptised and the Waorani New Testament was presented to the people. Two of the pastors present were involved in the deaths of the missionaries thirty-six years before. One Waorani leader said in his speech, 'We no longer want to live like those who killed each other and outsiders. We want to live by what God says. Ever since I was a small boy I have heard that we were going to get this book; now we have it.'

¶ Wycliffe Bible Translators, press release (June 1992)

Columbia

Señor Juan P. Coy

Pat and Helen Symes wrote in World Wide, *March and April 1958, the magazine of Worldwide Evangelization Crusade, about news of persecution and the laying down of another life for the cause of the Gospel in Columbia.*

After being in jail for two weeks, Pedro Moreno was released without having signed, as had been demanded by the mayor, a statement that he would not return to that region to preach the Gospel. Early next morning, after his release, Pedro, together with others of the believers in Saboya, received word that Senor Juan P. Coy, who had been in jail with Pedro for one day, had been severely wounded in three places. Pedro and the wounded man's brother-in-law went to the home of Senor Coy and found him in agony. He had been shot in the morning when he went out to attend to the cattle. They were able to ask him a few questions, and then took him to Chiquinquira to the doctor, but while they were entering the town he died.

When Pedro returned to Saboya where he had been threatened in the street by the priest who told the people to stone him. Three policemen refused him protection, but finally two stood by him. In company with a brother of the dead man, we were able to obtain an interview with the Minister of Justice and he sent a special investigator to the scene of the happening. We have been able to write, speak to, and pray with these people, and the words of consolation given to them were from Colossians 1:24, 'Who now rejoice in my suffering for you, and fill up that which is behind of the afflictions of Christ in my flesh for his body's sake, which is the Church.' These people are not really the imprisoned, the wounded, and the killed of the enemies of the Gospel, but sufferers with Jesus, and they are filling up his sufferings on behalf of the Church in that region, and we expect to see it work mightily for the building up of the Church and the salvation of still more unbelievers.

San Salvador

Archbishop Romero

SHOT AS HE SAID MASS, 1980

'If they succeed in killing me, I pardon and bless those who do the deed' (Archbishop Romero).

'Martyrdom is considered by the church to be an eminent grace and the supreme proof of charity' (Vatican II).

When Romero became Archbishop of San Salvador in 1977 few expected that he would become an internationally known champion of the oppressive regime that killed people and priests alike. Romero preferred to champion the status quo and the establishment and viewed some of the more revolutionary theological ideas with deep suspicion. This all changed when a close friend of Romero's, Rutilio Grande, was assassinated. Grande worked with some young Jesuits among 30,000 peasants in the parish of Aguilares. The peasants were ruthlessly exploited, often having no land of their own, and were forced to work for tiny wages during the cane harvest. In the eyes of those in power Grande's 'crime' was his suggestion that the peasants should become 'delegates of the Word'. When they organised themselves into small communities and read the Bible together for the first time they discovered that God hated injustice, was on the side of the poor, and that a labourer is worthy of his hire. Romero learned about the details of Grande's assassination. As Grande walked through a sugar cane field, with a 15-year-old teenager and an old man a rain of bullets rained on them and killed them in the open field.

Romero's change of attitude to those in ecclesiastical and government authority underwent a sea change. Commenting on this some writers have called this his 'conversion'. Although Archbishop Romero was even-handed in his condemnation of evil government practices, and violent guerrilla attacks, he became identified as the voice of the poor. Six weeks before he was killed, on 2nd February 1980 he told a conference of Latin American bishops about the rampant injustice and inhumane treatment of poor people in his country. He told them that defending the poor now brought about something new in their church – persecution. He went on to enumerate some of the atrocities of the past three years: 6 priests killed as martyrs, 50 priests attacked; many others tortured and expelled. Hundreds and even thousands of peasants, delegates of the Word, catechists, assassinated or tortured. Romero emphasised how the ordinary poor Christian people bore thebrunt of these persecutions.

On the night before he was assassinated, Romero pleaded with the army, in a radio broadcast, 'Stop the oppression.' He did not mince his words, he even ordered them in God's name to stop the killings.

On 24th March 1980, Archbishop Romero was celebrating mass in a hospital in San Salvador. The reading from the gospel during the service had been, 'Jesus replied: "The hour has come for the Son of Man to be glorified. I tell you the truth, unless a grain of wheat falls to the ground and dies, it remains only a single seed. But if it dies, it produces many seeds. the man who loves his life will lose it, while the man who hates his life in this world will keep it for eternal life' (John 12:23–25 NIV). Romero took these words as the text of his sermon. He pointed out how his own work was bound to bring risks to his own personal safety, but that anyone who is killed in Christ's service is just like the grain of wheat. It dies. But the reality is that it only appears to die. He continued: 'If they kill me I shall rise again in the Salvadorean people. As a pastor, I am obliged by divine decree to give my life for those I love – for all Salvadoreans, even for those who may be about to kill me. From this moment I offer my blood to God for the redemption and resurrection of El Salvador.'

Soon after saying these words, Romero was gunned down on the steps of the altar. The bullets had hit him in the stomach. He was rushed into the emergency area of the hospital, but died within minutes.

AFRICA

Uganda

Catholic and Protestant martyrs

'Nothing is more acceptable to God, and more beneficial to the soul, than to suffer for the sake of Christ' (The Imitation of Christ, *ascribed to Thomas à Kempis*).

Cardinal Lavigerie set about the evangelisation of equatorial Africa by sending, in 1878, ten French White Fathers, into the interior of Africa, as far as the great lakes. Five of these missionaries established a base at Rubaga in Buganda [Uganda], where a number of slaves, children and pages from king Mwanga's court turned to the Christian faith.

However, the ambitions of European colonialisation arrived in Africa at the same time as these missionaries. Mwanga decided to oppose them both. A local prophecy predicted that an invader from the east would 'devour' Buganda. Unfortunately Mwanga identified the travelling Anglican Bishop Hannington as this invader and had him killed [see entry on James Hannington].

The leader of the African Christians in Rubaga, a man called Joseph Mukasa, was also the king's chief page, and acted as the king's counsellor. King Mwanga became most upset when Joseph managed to spirit away the catechumens whenever he wanted to indulge in his homosexual activities with them. The king then thought of Joseph as a rival king to him. When the king had a fever Joseph had given him a pill to swallow, but the king's fever grew worse. When the king recovered he accused Joseph of attempting to poison him and ordered the executioner to burn Joseph. The executioner, out of love for

The twenty-six martyrs of Uganda

The sixteen Catholic martyrs were young men or youths:

Luke Banabakintu	aged 34
Bruno Serunkuma	aged 30
James Buzabaliawo	aged 29
Charles Lwanga	in his early 20s
Adolph Mukasa Ludigo	in his early 20s
Anatole Kiriggwajjo	in his early 20s
Mukasa Kiriwawanvu	in his early 20s
Achilles Kiwanuka	aged 18
Ambrose Kibuka	aged 18
Gyavira	aged 17
Mugagga	aged 17
Mbaga Tuzinde	aged 17
Denis Kamyuka	aged 13–15
Simeon Sebutta	aged 13–15
Charles Werabe	aged 13–15
Kisito	aged 13–15

The ten Anglican martyrs were also young men or youths:

Kiwanuka	a young page
Mukasa	a young page
Lwanga	a young page
Dani Nnakabanda	a young page
Mubi	a young page
Noah Walukagga	the king's chief smith
Kifamunyanya	
Frederick Kizza	
Alexander Kadoko	brother of Bruno Serunkuma
Albert Munyagabyanyo	

Joseph, beheaded him, before burning his body. Joseph's last words to the executioner were, 'Tell Mwanga that I forgive him for killing me for no good reason.' Thus, Joseph became the first Catholic martyr in Uganda, being martyred on 15th November 1885.

The number of pages at king Mwanga's court who embraced Christianity greatly upset the king. They were nicknamed 'the praying ones' and were accused of being unpatriotic because they refused to take part in some of the ancestral customs and to indulge in any of the king's homosexual practices.

In May 1886, Mwanga had over forty Christians put to death. On 27th May 'the praying ones' were tied up and thrown into little huts, at Namugongo, while Mwanga's men collected wood for their execution. The older Christians encouraged the younger Christians, saying, 'Do not be afraid. Our Christian friends are with the Lord. We shall soon join them.' Among the Christian prisoners were Abudala, a Muslim, and Aliwali, who did not pray. Two of the Anglicans told their guards about Abudala and Aliwali and they were set free.

On the evening of 2nd June the sixteen Christians heard the tam tam and death chants and realised what would follow in the morning. The Anglicans and Catholics encouraged each other and their one hundred executioners, with their faces painted red and black, dressed in animal skins and head-dresses, were amazed that the Christian martyrs approached death as if it was a festival. The sixteen martyrs, bound hand and foot, were wrapped up in reeds, placed on top of a great mound of wood. Then more wood was placed on top of them and set alight so that the whole spectacle looked like a giant hut on fire.

James Hannington

'I am about to die for the Baganda and have purchased the road to them with my life' (Bishop Hannington's last words).

The Church Missionary Society decided, in 1884, that the mission churches of Eastern Equatorial Africa should be placed in the hands of a bishop. The one they chose, James Hannington, said at his farewell meeting that he intended to became 'a very troublesome bishop'. Hannington arrived in Freretown, the diocesan headquarters, in January 1885, where he discovered that 12 clergy and 11 lay workers looked after all the CMS stations. Hannington consecrated the first African CMS deacons in East Africa as he passionately believed that educated Africans should not be relegated to menial work. When he met violent African chiefs who looked to him for guns Hannington persuaded them to receive a Christian teaching instead.

Hannington longed to travel to Uganda, a journey which had caused him to have a breakdown three years earlier on his previous visit to Africa. As he pondered his plans, he found himself reading words from Psalm 146, 'The Lord preserveth the strangers'. He took this to be a message from God and gathered together his 200 porters for his 600 mile journey. After Hannington tried to complete the last part of the journey with a party of 50 men, he himself was attacked and captured by twenty men from the Mwanga tribe. That night Hannington recorded in his dairy that he 'sang "Safe in the Arms of Jesus" and then laughed at the very agony of my situation'. Hannington was kept in an airless hut for eight days and then taken out to an open space where he was surrounded by his own men. Hannington thought that they were going to be allowed to proceed. But they were attacked and killed by the Mwanga tribe, and only four people escaped with their lives, and they were only spared so that they could explain how Hannington's luggage could be opened. According to one of these four men, Hannington's last words were, 'I am about to die for the Baganda and have purchased the road to them with my life.'

Archbishop Luwum
1977

'I am the Archbishop. I must stay.' (Archbishop Luwum, replying to the suggestion that he should escape from Amin.)

Archbishop Luwum's assassination was the spur that made the Dean and Chapter of Canterbury Cathedral set aside a special chapel in Canterbury Cathedral to commemorate twentieth-century Christian martyrs.

Idi Amin and his reign of terror in Uganda came to a head in February 1977 when he ordered the massacre of thousands of supporters, both soldiers and civilians, of the former president Milton Obote. However it was Amin's murder of the Archbishop of Uganda, Janani Luwum, along with two other Christians, former cabinet ministers, that hit the headlines around the world and prompted *Time* magazine to call Amin 'The Wild Beast of Africa'.

Luwum did not hesitate to publicly point out the evils of Amin's régime. Amin retaliated. Eight of his soldiers burst into the Archbishop's home at 1.30 on Saturday morning, while the Archbishop and his wife were in bed. They ransacked his house, on the pretext of looking for hidden guns. As one soldier pressed a gun into the archbishop's stomach he told the soldiers that the only armament he had was the Bible. He also told them that he prayed for the President, and prayed that he would learn to rule Uganda without destroying it.

The Anglican bishops sent a very strongly worded letter to Amin stating:

> We are deeply disturbed. In the history of our country such an incident in the Church has never before occurred. This is a climax of what has been constantly happening to our Christians. We have buried many who have died as a result of being shot and there are many more whose bodies have not yet been found; yet their disappearance is connected with the activities of some members of the Security Forces.

Archbishop Luwum delivered the letter to President Amin personally on 12th February. Amin gave the archbishop a cup of tea but accused him of plotting to overthrow him and informed him that a secret supply of arms had been found near his house. On 16th February Amin angrily summoned Luwum and six of his bishops. After a two-hour wait in the blazing sun Luwum was subjected to a mock 'trial' in front of 3,000 soldiers. With a cache of arms on display in front of him the archbishop was accused of striking a deal with Obote. The Vice-President, who was orchestrating the trial, called out: 'These men are traitors. What should be done with them?'

The obedient soldiers, baying for blood, shouted back, 'Kill them. Kill them.' Amin said that the archbishop with the two former cabinet ministers would be taken away and given military trials. When Archbishop Luwum left Bishop Festo Kivengere for the last time he told him something that he had not previously shared with him. Three days before a girl had come to the archbishop and told him about a conversation she had overheard in which she heard that the archbishop was on the security forces' death list. She had advised the archbishop to escape but he told her kindly, 'I cannot. I am the Archbishop. I must stay.'

Amin called them in for questioning. Later Bishop Festo Kivengere saw a Mercedes Benz race past him with the two government ministers, Erinayo Oryema and Oboth Ofumbi, and the archbishop inside. The following morning Radio Uganda announced that the three of them had been killed in a car accident.' Nobody believed the official version of of the archbishop's death as it became known on 17th February.

The true story of Luwum's death started in a torture room where the archbishop was taken with the two Christian cabinet ministers. There, they found four other men who were condemned prisoners. Luwum put his hands on each man's head as he prayed for them. From this room the archbishop and cabinet ministers were forced into a Land Rover and taken to a secret location outside the capital.

Amin appeared later and demanded that the archbishop should sign a confession about his involvement in a plot to overthrow him. The archbishop constantly refused and was eventually stripped of his clothes and made to lie on the floor. Amin then ordered two soldiers to whip the archbishop mercilessly. Luwum did not sign the confession, but prayed for his torturers. Amin, in a fit of rage, hit out at the archbishop and forced the soldier to carry out perverted sexual acts with the archbishop before he shot the archbishop through the heart twice with his own revolver.

Madagascar

Persecutions in the 19th century

Agents of the London Missionary Society reached Madagascar in 1818, and received a most cordial welcome from this enlightened monarch. They reduced its language to writing, arranged its grammar, and translated the Holy Scriptures. In the space of ten years 15,000 natives could read, and a large number write, while multitudes were converted to Christianity. But in 1828 a reaction set in led by the monarch's wife. The schools were closed, the old regime reinstated, and the idol keepers once more held their pernicious sway over the heathen.

In 1835 it was enacted that no Malagasy should profess Christianity, and the missionaries are the foreign artisans were ejected from the island. On their departure, many who were suspected of being Christians had to pass through the ordeal of drinking the tanjena, or poison water, and the following year several others were punished by fine, imprisonment, and perpetual slavery.

The first Christian martyr suffered in 1837 and during the last twenty-six years more than a hundred martyrs have been added to the Church triumphant.

The missionaries were expelled in 1836, but they left behind them the oracles of God. The history of Christianity in this island is remarkable as the secretly circulated Word of God maintained spiritual life in the island. After the exile of the teachers various persecutions broke out. The converts wandered about in the deserts and caves of the earth, until, in 1842, sixteen of them were arrested while trying to escape from the island, and nine of them were put to death in the capital. But, as of old times, the wrath of man fulfilled the purposes of God, and general attention was thus drawn to the subject of the Christian religion. In 1846 the Crown Prince renounced heathenism, and was baptised, and proved himself a faithful protector. His conversion greatly angered the queen mother, who regarded him as the victim of witchcraft, and vented her wrath in the violent persecution of 1849, when more than 2,000 people were mulcted in some form or other, and many put to death. We subjoin some details, extracted from the work of the Rev. William Ellis, who visited Madagascar in 1853, 1854, and 1856:

The authorities in Madagascar, who sought, by torture and death, to extinguish the Christian faith, by whatever motives they may have been actuated, only imitated the Diocletians of the early ages, and the Alvas, the Medicis, and the Marys of more recent times, and with corresponding results in the invincible constancy of those who fell, and the subsequent fruits of the imperishable seed which was scattered in the martyrs' blood. The following verbatim statements refer to the severe persecution in 1849:

'On 14th March 1849 the officer before whom the Christians were examined, said, "Do you pray to the sun, or the moon, or the earth?"

'R—— answered, "I do not pray to these, for the hand of God made them."

' "Do you pray to the twelve mountains that are sacred?"

'R—— answered, "I do not pray to them, for they are mountains."

' "Do you pray to the idols that render sacred the kings?"

'R——: "I do not pray to them, for the hand of man made them."

' "Do you pray to the ancestors of the sovereigns?"

'R——: "Kings and rulers are given by God that we should serve and obey them, and render them homage. Nevertheless, they are only men like ourselves. When we pray, we pray to God alone."

' "You make distinct and observe the Sabbath-day."

'R——: "This is the day of the great God; for in six days the Lord made all his works. But God rested on the seventh, and he caused it to be holy; and I rest or keep sacred that day."

'And in similar manner answered all the Christians. Before dawn on the following day the people assembled at A——y. Then they took the eighteen brethren that chose God and bound them hand and foot, and tied each of them to a pole, wrapped in mats, and placed them with the other prisoners. When the officers, and troops, and judges arrived, they read over the names of each class of prisoner, and then placed them by themselves, and stationed around them soldiers with muskets and spears; and the sentences were then delivered, consigning some to fine and confiscation, others to slavery, others to prison and chains, some to flogging, and eighteen to death – four to be burnt, and fourteen to be hurled from the rocky precipice, and afterwards burnt to ashes.

'And the eighteen appointed to die, as they sat on the ground, surrounded by the soldiers, sang this hymn:

> When I shall die, and leave my friends
> When they shall weep for me,
> When departed has my life,
> Then I shall be happy.

After this hymn they sang the hymn that ended, "When I shall behold him rejoicing in the heavens."

'And when the sentences were all pronounced, and the officer was about to return to the chief authorities, the four sentenced to be burned requested him to ask that they might be killed first, and then burned; but they were burned alive. When the officer was gone, they took those eighteen away to put them to death. The fourteen they tied by their hands and their feet to long poles, and carried on men's shoulders. And these brethren prayed and spoke to the people as they were being carried along. And some who beheld them said that their faces were like the faces of angels. And when they came to the top of Nampaminarina, they cast them down, and their bodies were afterwards dragged to the other end of the capital, to be burned with the bodies of those who were burned alive.

'And as they took the four that were burned alive to the place of execution, these Christians sang the 90th hymn, beginning, "When our hearts are troubled," each verse ending with "Then remember us". Thus they sang on the road. And when they came to Faravohitra, there they burned them, fixed between split bars. And there was a rainbow in the heavens at the time, close to the place of burning. Then they sang the hymn:

> There is a blessed land,
> Making most happy;
> Never shall the rest depart,
> Nor cause of trouble come.

'That was the hymn they sang after they were in the fire. Then they prayed, saying, "O Lord, receive our spirits, for thy love to us has caused this to come to us; and lay not this sin to their charge." Thus they prayed as long as they had any life. Then they died; but softly, gently: indeed, gently was the going forth of their life. And astonished were all the people around that beheld the burning of them there."'

¶ John Foxe, *The Book of Martyrs,* revised with notes and an appendix by W. Bramley-Moore (London, 1869), pp. 694–8

Swaziland

Swazi Tidings

The latest news from Swaziland is that all stations appear to be in good order, with one exception of Mount Hermon, where Mr and Mrs Wehmeyer have been working. The native Christians have been persecuted, and in some case have had to lay down their lives: some have given way under the very severe test, but the majority remained true to God . . .

On 3rd April the messenger arrived at Ezulwini (Miss Harris and Miss Thomson's Station).

He found Jan, the evangelist, in good health and the place generally in good condition, but alas, the few Christians had sadly gone back. They were very weak in the faith, and we, in our highly favoured circumstances, little know what fearful testing and persecution they might have had to go through by remaining faithful to their Lord.

As an instance of this, we hear that one native Christian living not far from Ezulwini Station was murdered, and Jan, our evangelist, was afraid for his own life at the hands of those bloodthirsty Swazis, sent forth to do such awful work.

We are very sorry to hear from our friend Mr Dawson, of the Alliance Mission, Swaziland, that his house has been broken into, and everything wantonly destroyed. This was the work of the heathen Swazis. A lady worker in the same mission, named Miss Moe, who remained in the country during the war, has wonderfully proved God's faithful care. A letter was received from her recently saying that she had been imprisoned in Pietretief, a small town in the Transvaal, for two months, but was then allowed to return to her station in Swaziland, where God has greatly used her. She gives the sad details of the murder of a Christian native who lived near Ezulwini. The wild, heathen Swazis came upon him to kill him. He besought them to take his cattle, and spare his wife and himself. This they refused to do, and he then prayed to God. As the 'Amen' came from his lips, they stabbed him to death.

How sad, and yet what a glorious home-going! 'The noble army of martyrs praise thee,' and this one has entered the presence of the King, having been 'faithful unto death'. His wife escaped to the hills.

And so it has gone on – month after month – this terrible 'killing off'. The orders given to the murderers were that they were to kill off every one, old and young, so that there should be on one left to tell the white people when they returned.

This ends our report, and gives the condition of things up to 12th May. We pray that ere long God will open up the way for our return to work among them again.

¶ George F. Gale, Durban, Natal, 22nd August 1900, in *The South African Pioneer* (October 1900), published by Africa Evangelical Fellowship

Liberia

Tom and June Jackson

The report in the *Liberian Daily Observer* was brief and to the point.

> An American national and his British wife have been reported killed during fighting between government troops and rebel forces in Nimba County. The two reported killed have been identified as missionary Thomas K. Jackson and his wife June M. Jackson. Mr and Mrs Jackson were killed in fighting near Bahn City last Saturday, 24th March. The two were members of Liberia Inland Church.

Tom Jackson left Canada for Liberia on 21st February 1941. On the same boat was another WEC candidate, Billie Price, unknown to him at that time. However, in 1943 they were married and assigned to Bahn where they began a life-long ministry to the Gio people. Tom was a brilliant linguist and translator and their loving and happy home was used in outreach and fellowship.

For a few years Tom took up two pastorates in the States because of deterioration in Billie's health. In 1978 Billie was called home and Tom returned to his other beloved land, Liberia.

There, in 1980, he married British Weccer June Hobley, also a gifted translator. Between them they spoke fluently Bassa, Gio and Mano and completed the translation of the New Testament in each of these languages. At the time of their death they were working on Old Testament books.

The Jacksons were in Monrovia on business when hostilities began with the invasion of Nimba Country on 24th December. In spite of dangers they decided to return to Bahn on 10th January.

'We had sought the Lord and he had given us peace,' Tom wrote in his last newsletter dated 14th January. 'It was so right for us to come as we have been able to help and reassure our people.'

Tom and June now rejoice together in glory.

¶ *Worldwide* (July/August 1990), published by Worldwide Evangelization Crusade

Congo

Winnie Davis
1967

Clutching her Bible, she staggered at the head of the rebel column.

It was their vain attempt to escape the Congolese troops. After the skirmish Winnie Davis (51) was beyond the reach of further suffering. General Ngalo had killed her – and fled. It was 17th May 1967.

Winnie was born in Coedpoeth, Denbighshire, and educated at Penygelli. She became secretary to a dental surgeon, and later trained as a nurse, gaining her SRN, SRFN, and CMB. From 1941, she was for two years a student of the Emmanuel Bible College, Birkenhead, and on 25th July 1946 sailed for Congo with Worldwide Evangelization Crusade. Posted early to Nebobongo, she reopened the maternity centre closed by the home-call of Mrs Edith Moules. In 1961, after an evacuation of missionaries from Congo, she accepted the invitation of the Church at Opienge to return. The believers were aware of the danger and promised to guard her. On 17th July 1964 Mr Arthur Scott left Opienge and was the last Crusader to see her alive.

The Simba rebellion took her into captivity a few weeks later. At irregular intervals we heard she was alive, and nationwide prayer was focused for her release.

Thirty-four months of captivity
The last European in the hands of the Congo Rebels was Reverend Father Alphonse Strijbosh, a Dutch Roman Catholic missionary, freed by the Congolese Army on 27th May 1967.

Report on the death of a Protestant missionary by a Dutch Roman Catholic missionary

Alphonse Strijbosh gave the only details we shall ever be likely to know about Winnie's captivity and death. At the airport in Kinshasa, Congo, where he was in transit to Brussels, he reported:

Miss Davis had served as a midwife in the Rebel Camp. The General Gaston Ngalo had ten wives. The other rebels had their wives also with them. For my part, I baptised thirteen infants. Miss Davis was taken captive with me at the commencement of hostilities in 1964. Although she was never maltreated, her health failed. She suffered from having to accompany the rebels when they were 'on the run' from 1965–67. This was very hard for her, but she held services for the rebels to the end.

Jungle camp
We lodged at first in the jungle at Batama, some 100 miles north of Opienge, at the camp of the late Minister of Defence of the Congo rebels, Dominique Babu, also of Peking and Moscow. He was a convinced communist.

The morale of Miss Davis was high and General Ngalo himself promised her in the jungle to release her. Twice, on 15th May this year, he was aware by radio of the efforts of the British Ambassador in Kinshasa to bring about a surrender. He did not seem hostile to the idea. But he was not going to let the National Army take Miss Davis by force of arms. In any case, it is to the English that I owe the fact that I am still alive today. As soon as the General knew the Army was in the area, the rebel group fled at his orders. We marched three days without food, save for a little elephant meat at the end of the march.

At dawn on the fourth day, a fresh start was made by the column with Miss Davis at its head. I was at the end with an old rebel porter. It is to him I owe my deliverance. I could not keep up any longer. I had crossed two rivers and was lost in a maze of buffalo and elephant paths. Suddenly I saw Miss Davis.

Resting?
At first I thought she was resting, being exhausted by the long marches through the jungle. Then I saw two knife wounds in her face and throat, and blood coming from her mouth. I realised she was dead. It must have been fifteen minutes since she was killed. They had stolen her watch, but it was about 10 a.m. I was smitten with consternation. I rearranged my haversack and said to myself, 'My turn is to come.' Suddenly I saw three soldiers on the path. I thought they were Simbas and again said to myself,

'This is the end.' But they were regular Congolese Army soldiers, and I was saved.

Miss Davis' body was to be transported to Kisangani and interred in the communal grave of those massacred on the Congo River in 1964.

Winnie's last message to us in the WEC was at the June Month-end conference in 1961, a month prior to her sailing. Her text was Philippians 1:20: 'It is my eager expectation and hope that I shall not be at all ashamed, but with full courage, now as always, Christ will be honoured in my body, whether by life or by death' (RSV). This triumphant entry into His Presence is surely the fulfilment of the Spirit's word that day.

¶ Len Moules, in *Worldwide*, July–August 1967, published by Worldwide Evangelization Crusade

Senegal

Pierre Senghor
1959

Alastair and Helen Kennedy writing from France say that they have had this sad but triumphant latter from Andy and Betty Macindoe, Senegal, with the news of the martyrdom of a young Diola. Pierre found the Lord just before they left Ziguinchor, and gave his fine testimony in the church there just a few days before they came away.

Our beloved brother, Pierre, was called into the presence of the Lord on Sunday 19th July, at around 10.45 a.m. On Saturday he was here with us, left his work just after 7 p.m., said he'd see us tomorrow and spent part of the evening with Amathe laughing and chatting. On Sunday morning about breakfast time a youngster called up to tell us that Pierre was ill and could not get up. We thought that his rheumatism was worse or that he had fever or something. When we had finished breakfast Andy and I (Betty) went down in the car to his home. I took a few medicines with me thinking to be of some help. But when we got there we were shocked to find Pierre already unconscious, his face swollen, his eyes dilated, saliva coming out of his mouth, his breathing then stertorous and his pulse exceedingly rapid. We were alarmed and called for the chief of his compound, a Moslem and told him we'd have to get medical help at once.

Then we rushed off to hospital not knowing what we'd find or whom we'd find there to help on a Sunday morning. By the time we arrived in the hospital Pierre's pulse had weakened, and his breathing was almost imperceptible. The Chief (doctor) came and ordered injections which they gave as soon as Pierre had been moved into the ward. But within a few minutes he had passed away to be with the Lord.

When I talked with the chief of the compound I asked him if Pierre had eaten his supper. He said he had taken a good meal, but in the night he had vomited a lot, had cried a lot and then gone unconscious and that he had not rallied. When they took him off his mattress at the hospital I noticed that his saliva was blood-stained. When I looked at him in the house I had very grave suspicions, and as soon as we were in the car I said to Andy what I thought – poisoning – and he had the same thought. As soon as Amathe heard he voiced the same opinion, and so did Dominique. We have no proof, but what can say? After all, he is with the Lord now, having courageously, faithfully and zealously fought the good fight which for him lasted only seven hot months. A few weeks ago Pierre visited his own village of Kadyinor for the first time since his conversion, and although he was there at the time of a big fetish feast, and although he stayed in the compound of the fetish-chief, he did not hide his light. But he held meetings right there in the village, and had times of witnessing especially to the young men.

We cannot understand, we do not try to, all the ways of the Lord. If wicked men have devised this young man's death, then may the Lord turn this sad and tragic event to his glory. If he has become our first Christian martyr in the Casamance, then may the 'blood of the martyr be the seed of the Church.'

¶ *Worldwide*, September–October 1959, front page, published by Worldwide Evangelization Crusade

INDIAN SUBCONTINENT

Kashmir

Ron Davies
1947

Congratulations, Ron. You lived a Crusader's life and died a Crusader's death. Ron Davies always warmed my heart. He had this abandonment of a Crusader. He lived out the words of the pilgrim song, 'I'll fling the world away to go crusading.' I can imagine the warmth of the meeting with his Lord on that day of sudden promotion in Kashmir.

Before the war he loved his work among the Kashmiris in north India. He was fond of wearing native dress, which sometimes got him into difficult situations, but certainly gave him his heart's desire of getting into the hearts of the people. With the war [in India] ended Ron went back to England on leave before demobilisation, and he had only one thought – back to Kashmir with the Gospel in the shortest possible time. We found him just the same lovable Ron, but with this difference, responsibility had made him more capable himself of taking responsibility. so he went back this time as leader of the WEC Northern Kashmir field, a territory which also relieves the work around Haripur in N.W.F. He went with five workers, four women and a man.

Then came his earthly end, like a bolt from the blue – from the rifle of one of those whom he loved and went to save. He died as we would expect Ron to die – saving others physically and spiritually. He went to rescue the three lady workers in danger from the Pathan invasion. He was seeing them off to safety, but stayed himself behind, we understand, as there was not transport for all. Then the wild tribes-men came – and silence.

He has gone gloriously from the battle line – all one for Christ and souls. Congratulations, Ron. By God's grace we will fill up the gaps and carry on with the holy war of preaching the Gospel to all Kashmir.

¶ Norman Grubb, quoted in *World Conquest,* March–April 1948, pub-lished by the Worldwide Evangelization Crusade

RUSSIA AND EASTERN EUROPE

Ukraine

Yakim Bely and Iosyf Tyshkevich
1873

In the early 1870s Christians in the Ukraine were persecuted by the Russian establishment, as well as by the some conservative members of the Orthodox Church. A Mennonite pastor, Johann Wieler, braved the authorities by holding a communion service in Russian in Rohrbach. Some Ukrainian Christians who had only recently been baptised attended this service. After the service the local police arrested Johann Wieler. His place was taken by Mykhaolo Ratushny, but six months after Wieler's arrest eleven more Christians were arrested and imprisoned in Tarashcha. In the spring of 1873 eight of these prisoners were taken to Kiev prison, tortured and put on trial. The first two Ukrainian evangelical martyrs, Yakim Bely and Iosyf Tyshkevich, died during their imprisonment at Kiev.

Soviet Union

The martyrdom of thousands upon thousands of Christians in Russia in the twentieth century is reminiscent of Nero's persecution of the Christians in Rome. When the communists came to power in 1917 they launched a wholesale attack on the Orthodox churches. Stalin became Party Secretary in 1922, and Premier in 1929.

8,100 martyrs

In 1922, when valuables which belonged to the Orthodox churches were confiscated, over eight thousand clergy were either tortured to death or shot. 2,691 'white' clergy, 1,962 monks and 3,447 lay-sisters and monks suffered in this way. The number of Christians martyred varied greatly from region to region: in Moscow there were 36 martyrs, but in the Barnaul region 441, in OdessaKherson 191, in the Stavropol region 139, and in the Poltava there were 124 martyrs.

General Registers of martyrs, 1917–22

[These extracts record the death of 416 of these martyrs]

The following table sets out a general register, from 1918 to 1922, of some of the Russian laymen and clergy who were martyred by the Communists.

1917
- Archpresbyter John Kochurov from Tsarskoe Selo became the first clergyman to be martyred.

1918–22
- One clergyman from the Kherson region was crucified.
- Three priests were crucified in the Kherson region.
- Archimandrite Matthew, who was rector of the Perm Ecclesiastical Academy, was cut into pieces by swords.
- Rev. Koturov, fleeing from Cherdin, was caught by the Communists. In the sub-zero temperatures they forced him to undress and poured cold water over him until he became an icy statue.
- During 1918–19, seventy clergymen were martyred from the Kharkov region.
- In Kuban province, at Krasnodar, six priests were killed; and in the Stavropol diocese one elder, three psalm-readers, four deacons and fifty-two priests were killed.
- Father Michael, aged twenty-eight, had just finished conducting the Divine Liturgy when he was seized by communists in front of his congregation. They wept as the was taken away, but they just heard him say, 'Do not weep for me, but weep for yourselves and your children.' His dead body was lifted up on the bayonets of soldiers of the Red Army. He left a widow and two children behind.

- A priest, a deacon and a psalm-reader. In the village of Bezopasny, Leonid Soloviev, a priest, aged 27, Vladimir Ostrikov, a deacon, aged 45, and a 51-year-old psalm-reader, Alexander Fleginsky were martyred, even though no charges were ever brought against them. The communists forced them to go to an area where diseased cattle had been buried, then made them dig their own grave, before mutilating with swords and burying them while they were still alive.
- An old man, more than eighty years old, the Rev. Zolotovsky, was taken by some Red soldiers, dressed in women's clothes and ordered to dance in front of them. He refused and so was summarily hanged.
- Nikolai Milutkin, a clergyman from Novo-Nikolsky, was brought before the local CHEKA who beat him with the butts of their guns and wounded his head, removing half his scalp, and one of his legs with two strokes of a sword. Then they released him, before arresting him again two hours later, shooting him at point blank range and mutilating his dead body. They then stripped the body and dumped it in the river Don hoping it would float downstream to Novocherkask and serve as an example to the people there, where they intended to go next week.

1918
- Archpresbyter John Vostorgov, rector of St Basil's Cathedral, Moscow
- Archpresbyter Alexander Veraskin, from Chercassi, was hanged on the outside of the gates of his own home.
- Rev. Peter Diakonov, from the Nadezhdinsky factory, in the Verhouturie district, was buried alive, up to his head, and then shot.
- Archpresbyter Gregory Pospelov from Kronstadt was shot for taking a funeral service for sailors who had fought against the communists. Pospelov was shot clutching the ceremonial cross in his hands which the communists were unable to take away from him.

1919
- The communists occupied the city of Voronezh in December 1919, and shot 160 priests from the diocese of Voronezh before the end of 1919.

1920
- Rev. Nikodim Pedicoultzev, from Kamen, was hacked to death with a kitchen knife while in prison.

1921
- Seven priests, Dobrolubov, Friazinov, Nadezhdin, Lorlov, Sokolov, Vishniakov, and Zaozersky, and an Archimandrite, Telegin, were all shot in Moscow.
- In the Tobolsk region of West Siberia over ninety priests were shot in 1921.

- Serge Shein, Secretary of the Moscow all-Russian Council, was killed in Petrograd.
- Rev. John Moslovsky from a village called Verhne-Poltavky was shot dead through the window of his own house.
- Rev. Seraphim Sarichov, from Gondatievka, after taking the Paschal Liturgy was shot.
- Rev. Joakim Frolov was burnt on a haystack outside his village of Mikhailovsk. A metal cross was the only thing found in the ashes.
- Archpresbyter Serapion Chernikh, from Nikolaevsk, was conducting a service on the eve of Palm Sunday, consecrating willow branches, when he was thrown into the river Amur, and drowned, still wearing his vestments.

Martyrs from the monasteries
Between 1917 and 1922, monasteries of the Russian Orthodox church were ransacked and many monks martyred.

The Spasovsky monastery
A sailor, Dibenko, took a seventy-five-year-old Archimandrite Radion from his monastery and scalped him, before cutting his head off.

Alexandro-Svirsky monastery
A novice, Ivan, hiding himself in the monastery's loft, lived to recount the following attack on the Alexandro-Svirsky monastery and the martyrdom of five of its brothers and the Superior Eugene. When the monks refused to hand over the keys to the rooms so that their treasures could be taken they were forced to dig their own graves in the courtyard of the monastery. When this was completed they were told to line up on the edge of the graves so that they could be shot. The monks requested that they should be allowed to sing 'Christ is risen', a short Paschal hymn, as it was the third day of the Pascha. They were refused permission but started to sing anyway as the young soldiers fired their rifles.

Solovky monastery
The last igumen of the Solovky monastery, Archimandrite Benjamin, lived as a hermit in a poor peasant's hut on the outskirts of Archangel. The communists sealed its windows and doors and then set fire to the hut with Benjamin inside it.

Mary Magdalene monastery
On 27th June 1918, the Rev. Gregory Nikolsky of the Mary Magdalene monastery, was taken out through the gates of his own monastery by the communists. They forced Gregory to open his mouth, shouted, 'We will also

give you the Sacrament' and then shot him in the mouth.

Spasov Skete monastery
The Rev. Athanassy, a priest from Spasov Skete monastery, was taken out to be executed by a Red soldier. Athanassy knelt to pray, crossed himself and then stood up to bless the soldier, who then fired two shots into the pastor's head.

Poltava Krestovozdvizhensky monastery
The Rev. Mil from Poltava Krestovozdvizhensky monastery was interrogated many times. The Red soldiers found him so obstinate that they 'were forced to spend thirty-seven roubles on him' – the price of a bullet. On 4th July 1918, with two others, he was shot in the forest. When his body was examined it revealed the extent of the terrible tortures this martyr had endured during his interrogations.

Spaso-Preobrazhensky monastery
The Red soldiers decided to take over Spaso-Preobrazhensky monastery. They rounded up twenty-five monks and Prior Ambrose. They were commanded to bring in fire-wood and told that they would be burnt at the stake. When the Reds realised that the anti-Red Volunteer army was nearby, they took the priests to the local railway station. Commissar Bakai started the massacres of these martyr-monks and shot Prior Ambrose. Seventeen of the monks were killed outright as they were shot, but the eight other monks, who were not fatally injured, pretended that they were dead as they were shot in the dark, and later, were able to escape.

NKVD Martyrs
The NKVD (secret police) became feared, in the 1930s, for their midnight calls. During this time up to 22,000 evangelical Christians were picked up in the early hours of the morning by van and carted off to the Siberian prison camps, from where the majority never returned. One such arrest took place on Christmas Day 1937. Konstantin Korneichuk, pastor of Alma-Ata, asked for Yefrem Mikhailovich. When Mikhailovich heard his friend's voice he thought that he must have been released from prison. His happiness was shortlived, as he realised that something sinister was afoot. Pastor Korneichuk had endured unspeakable torture in prison, but had managed to resist revealing the names of members of his congregation until they put him in the electric chair and turned on the electricity. When Mikhailovich opened his door he was confronted with two men in uniform, members of the militia, who took Mikhailovich away, after he had been allowed to pray with his family. Subsequently he received a ten year prison sentence. That night scores of other Christians were arrested. Among those arrested, along

with Mikhailovich, who never saw their families again were five preachers, Rybak, Slepov, Serkyuk, Kvasha, and Levkovich. Korneichuk was rewarded for his betrayal by dying in a concentration camp.

Chronicle of martyrs in the Soviet Union, 1974–83

Between 1974 and 1983 Christians were still being frequently martyred in Russia and behind the Iron Curtain, in the Communist Block of countries. The full extent of these killings is hard to appreciate as so many Christians were martyred in circumstances that were hidden from the media in the West, and are only now surfacing. The following table of martyrs is in the form of a chronicle. Many of these people died in suspicious circumstances which make it almost impossible to prove that they were murdered. However, whether they were forced to commit suicide, openly murdered, or just died in suspicious circumstances, they are all treated as martyrs in this chronicle.

1. Ivan Ostapenko
Ostapenko, the presbyter of Shevehenko Evangelical-Christian Baptist congregation, had been imprisoned for four years, and then exiled for three years. He was told that he would be able to serve his exile near his home if he gave up his Christian beliefs. Ivan refused to do this. He was discovered hanging in a basement of a house on January 26th 1974.

2. Mikhailo Lutsky
The body of a uniate minister, Lutsky, was found in a wood near Lvov, in 1975, in the Drogobych district of Ukraine. While the authorities claimed that he had committed suicide there were reports that the secret police had murdered him.

3. Ivan Biblenko
Ivan Biblenko was a Baptist, and had already served a three year prison sentence from 1972–75. He went to Dnepropetrovsk on a church meeting on 13th September, 1975, from which he never returned. Eventually his family tracked him down to a hospital where it was claimed that he had died on 24th September, as a result of a road accident. After his body was examined it became clear to his family that he had died as a result of being tortured.

4. Mindaugas Tamonis

Mindaugas Tamonis, 1941–75, a Roman Catholic, was a poet from Lithuania who played an active role in the Lithuanian Catholic nationalistic movement. At 34 years old he committed suicide by throwing herself under the wheel of a moving train.

She refused to hand back a monument to the Red Army and had written to the Central Committee of the Communist Party seeking a referendum so that Christians could participate in an election where their interests would be catered for. At Vilnius psychiatric hospital Mindaugas was subjected to a 564-point questionnaire about religious beliefs and put on depressant drugs.

5. Raisa Ivanova

Raise Ivanova, 1929–77, belonged to the True Orthodox Church. She was interned in the Mordovian camp, where she refused to work. From there she was transferred to Kazan Special Psychiatric Hospital, after being pronounced mentally ill. There she endured great suffering from the 'treatment' they gave her, and in December 1977 she hanged herself.

6. Tatyana Krasnova

Tatyana Krasnova, 1903–79, a member of the True Orthodox Church, had endured one prison sentence from which she was released in 1955, three years exile and was in the eighth year of a nine year prison sentence when at, 76, she died in prison.

7. Fr Anatoli Gurgula

Anatoli Gurgula, 1906–80, remained pastor to the Ukrainian Catholics around his village of Tomshivtsy in the region of Kalush. The bodies of the 74-year-old priest and his wife were discovered on 27 February 1980 in their home where they had been burnt to death, where they were believed to have been murdered.

8. Bronius Laurinavicius

Bronius Laurinavicius was a Roman Catholic and pastor at Adutiskis. Over a period of twenty years, since 1960, he had signed petitions against the Soviet authorities interfering in the affairs of the church. He died in a road accident in Vilnius, where a lorry ran over him. Two witnesses say that he was pushed into the oncoming lorry on the orders of KGB officers.

Footnote: *Keston College, now in Oxford, has been monitoring and recording the persecution and martyrdom of Christians in communist lands. In Religion in Communist Lands vol. II, no. 1, Spring 1983, Carolyn Burch compiled a 'Chronicle' of thirty-seven people who had been martyred in communist countries.*

Chronicle of martyrs in Eastern Europe, 1974–83

A. CZECHOSLOVAKIA

Cardinal Stepan Trocta

Under Dubček's liberal government Trocta was made a cardinal in 1969. Trocta, ordained in the Roman Catholic church in 1932, and consecrated bishop of Litomerice in 1948, spent many years in prison. He had spent the war years in prison, was arrested again in 1951 and sentenced to 25 years' hard labour in 1954. In 1974 he was subjected to prolonged and brutal interrogations and he died the next day after a cerebral haemorrhage, and was immediately declared a martyr by the Czech Catholics.

Milan Gono

One of the people Cardinal Trocta ordained in secret was Milan Gono. Gono was arrested on trumped up charges in March 1979. He was given a two-year prison sentence for his unauthorised priestly activities. In July 1979 he died in prison, as a result of falling off scaffolding, according to the authorities. However, the doctor who examined the body declared that Gono had been dead before he fell. Gono's prison warder admitted that he had been interrogated as they tried to make him divulge the names of other people who had been secretly ordained, and that Gono died as a result of these severe tortures.

Father Premysl Coufal

Father Coufal was a Roman Catholic secret priest and was frequently harassed by the secret police for this reason. In January 1981 he was given an ultimatum by the secret police. He had until 23rd February to cooperate with them, which would have meant divulging names of other secret priests. On 24th February Coufal's friends found him dead in his flat. The authorities claimed that Coufal committed suicide by gassing himself. Coufal's friends found his head had been very badly wounded.

B. ALBANIA

Bishop Ernesto Coba

Coba, a Roman Catholic, had been the Apostolic Administrator of Shkodra before he was incarcerated in the Elbasan labour camp in 1974. He celebrated mass on Easter Day in 1979, but was caught in the act, and received a severe beating as a result. The elderly clergyman was beaten up so badly that he died from his injuries on the following day. The authorities claimed that he died of natural causes.

C. ROMANIA

Ioan Clipa

Ioan Clipa, a Baptist, was taken into custody by the authorities and savagely interrogated, accused of distributing Bibles in Romania. By the time the security police had finished with him Clipa was reduced to being a nervous wreck. In 1981 he was arrested for a second time, had a nervous breakdown and committed suicide.

Poland

Jerzy Popieluszko
1984

After being overrun by the Nazi in World War II Poland became a satellite state of Russia after the war. This predominantly Catholic country did not take kindly to being ruled as a Marxist-Leninist state and so made five brave, but unsuccessful, attempts between 1945 and 1989 to throw off the shackles of Russian domination. A man who came to symbolise this struggle was born in 1947 in the village of Okopy, in eastern Poland, Jerzy Popieluszko.

In 1965 Popieluszko entered the Warsaw seminary to train for the priesthood just at a time when the authorities were inflicting another purge on the Catholic Church. Even though people in training for the priesthood were officially exempt from national service Popieluszko had to endure a two-year course of atheistic political indoctrination. During this time a soldier caught Popieluszko with a rosary in his hand. Popieluszko refused to throw it on the ground as he was ordered and so was beaten up and locked in solitary confinement for a month. In 1972 Popieluszko was eventually ordained.

A popular mass movement called Solidarity was born in 1980–81 as a result of illegal strikes in Poland's naval dockyards at Gdansk, with Lech Walesa as one of its early, ardent supporters. During

August 1980 strikes spread throughout Poland. 10,000 steel workers at Huta Warszana demanded that a mass should be celebrated in their factory. Jerzy Popieluszko was the popular choice of both the archbishop and the strikers for this symbolic and brave act of faith and defiance. Jerzy Popieluszko became the first priest ever to enter that factory and from then on Popieluszko was known as the pastor of Solidarity. Popieluszko felt at one with the aspirations of the downtrodden workers.

In April 1981 Popieluszko started to hold services in which members of the congregation could take a greater part, singing hymns, clapping and reciting poetry. These services soon became monthly celebrations, held on the last Sunday of every month, as a kind of 'mass for the nation'. They ensured a focal point after Solidarity became a banned trade union in December 1981. The authorities became more and more angry with Popieluszko as he told the thousands of people who attended his popular masses, in his short sermons, 'you must speak of evil as a disease if you are to serve God.' Martial law soon followed with many ringleaders of Solidarity being arrested. Popieluszko's masses for Poland now became masses for the victims of martial law. Popieluszko became a folk hero throughout Poland but he also began to receive death threats through the post, in which he was told, 'You also will hang on a cross.'

During the first six months of 1984 Popieluszko was arrested and interrogated thirteen times, before being impeached on 12th July. On 19th October Popieluszko took part in a Worker's Mass at Bydgoszcz. Three KGB assassins were waiting for him and bundled him unceremoniously into a car at the end of the service. Popieluszko was never seen alive again. He was tortured, beaten, almost suffocated by a gag, before being thrown into a weir, with his body weighed down by two sackfuls of stones.

The 400,000 grateful Polish people who attended his funeral on 1st November 1984 all knew that Popieluszko had given his life for Solidarity. Poland soon became the first country formerly controlled by Russia to successfully reject atheistic communism.

WESTERN EUROPE

Germany

Maria Skobtsova
1945

'Live today as if you were going to die a martyr this evening' (Charles de Foucauld).

Maria Skobtsova, whose maiden name was Elizabeth (Lisa) Yurievna Pilenco, was brought up in the rarefied atmosphere of the Russian Czars. After the Revolution she went to Paris and became a latter-day Dr Barnardo, caring for everyone in need who crossed her path, especially outcasts. In 1932 she made a monastic profession in the Orthodox Church in the Church of the institute of St Sergius in Paris. But she joined no cloistered way of life. As Metropolitan Eulogus said when he gave her her name, Maria, it was 'in memory of St Mary of Egypt.' The Metropolitan told Maria, 'Like this Mary lived a life of penitence in the desert to and speak and minister in the desert of human hearts.' The world became Maria's monastery. She lived at 77 rue de Lourmel, which became a spiritual centre (Nicolas Berdyaev gave one of his lectures there), and a centre of compassion for the poor. It became the springboard for the formation of Orthodox Action, founded in 1935. The Orthodox group campaigned for the social welfare of the poor and made Maria Skobtsova their first president.

At the outbreak of World War II Maria made no secret of her hatred of Hitler and all he stood for. It was no surprise, therefore, that the SS broke up her work during a visit to her home on 8 February,

1947. Maria was arrested and ended up in the notorious Ravensbruck concentration camp, after a stint in camps at Romainvillle and Compiègne. In Ravensbruck Maria still carried on caring for all those suffering around her, in answer to her own prayer which she prayed shortly after her arrest: 'Lord, I am your messenger. Throw me like a blazing torch into the night.'

Prisoner 19263, from Block 27, gave courage, hope and encouragement to all around her, counselling her fellow prisoners in the most appalling human misery, 'Don't let your spirit's flame die.' With her swelling feet, ankles and legs, and becoming weaker and weaker, Maria became a mother to many of the women prisoners who went to her for a hug. One young girl had managed somehow to smuggle in a prayer book and Maria read alound the words of the Gospel and Epistle, adding her own short meditation afterwards.

The final days of Maria's life are shrouded in mystery. One account of her death tells how she became so weak that she was unable to walk and so was callously condemned to death by the Nazis. Himmler had sent orders that all sick people should be killed, in a vain attempt to cover up the inhuman treatment and medical experimentations that had been carried on in these camps. A second version of Maria's last days is very much in keeping with the tenor of her whole life. Maria exchanged places with a woman who was in a queue of condemned prisoners and went voluntarily to her martyrdom in order to help her companion to live. What is certain is that Maria's name is on the list of those people who were gassed to death on 31st March 1945, Easter Eve. The next day, Easter Day, the Red Cross arrived at Ravensbruck camp, a day too late for Maria.

Maximilian Kolbe
1941

Maximilian Kolbe, born Raymond Kolbe, was born in Zdunska Wola, in Poland on 8th January, 1894. He became a Franciscan at sixteen. Then he founded the Niepokalanon friars who grew to 763 in number by the outbreak of the Second World War. Maximilian set up a printing press which became the envy of all printers in Poland where the circulation of his *Knights* magazine eventually rose to a 60,000 monthly circulation. As Hitler began to overrun Poland in 1939, Maximilian Kolbe, who by then was something of a celebrity, was arrested and taken to Amtlitz concentration camp. After being freed once, he was rearrested on 17th February 1941 for helping Jews escape from the Germans. On 28th May 1941, after a journey by cattle truck with 300 other prisoners, Maximilian arrived at the dreaded death camp at Auschwitz.

In Auschwitz Kolbe continued to inspire and encourage other prisoners, and heard confessions, said masses and preached, even though each of these activities was punishable by death. One morning sirens droned their frightening sound, announcing the escape of another prisoner of war. Everyone knew what that meant. Ten prisoners would die as a reprisal, but they were made to die in a terrible way. They were placed in airless concrete bunkers. In that underground position they were then left to slowly die of thirst and hunger.

The day after the escape the camp's Deputy Commandant, Karl Fritsch, had an important visiting guest to take with him along the pathetic lines of prisoners – Gestapo chief Gerhardt Palitsch. Colonel Fritsch said tersely, 'The escaped prisoner has not been found. Ten of you will die.' They pointed to different men, who were thus selected for this painfully slow form of execution. The ninth man they selected could not bear the thought. 'I don't want to die. I'm young. I can work for you. I have a wife. I have young children. I shall never see them again.'

At that moment a smaller man, wearing wire rimmed glasses, came forward, without asking anyone's permission. The Franciscan stood to attention in front of the Deputy Commandant. 'What do you want, Polish pig?' screamed the Deputy Commandant.

The little man replied, 'I would like to die in the place of this man. I am a Catholic priest, whereas he has a wife and family.' They allowed prisoner 16670 to be a substitute for Francis Gajowniczek. The ten condemned men went through agonies before they died, although the sound of praying and singing of Christian songs could be heard from under the ground at Block 13. One by one the men died, as they were deprived of water and food. They were so desperate for fluid to drink that they even drank their own urine. By 14th August four prisoners were left alive. Then the moment came for a lethal injection of phenol to be administered in the left arms of the four men, including Kolbe. Kolbe prayed and gave his arm to his executioner.

News of Maximilian's death spread through the camp and was spoken of as if it had been some victory. Szczepanski wrote later, 'The lunatic programme of the Nazis was not defeated by military might. The definitive answer was given by a death in August 1941 in an underground cell in Block 13, the Block of Death, in Auschwitz concentration camp. It was given by a Polish Franciscan, Father Maximilian Kolbe, who gave an answer which no dialectic could ever provide.' On 17th October 1971 Pope Paul VI beatified Maximilian, thus making him the first Nazi victim to be proclaimed blessed by the Roman Catholic Church. John Paul II, in 1982, elevated Maximilian to the official status of martyr in the Roman Catholic Church.

Dietrich Bonhoeffer

Bonhoeffer was hanged by the Nazis at Flossenburg death camp on 9th April 1945. A memorial stone in the church at Flossenburg says: 'Dietrich Bonhoeffer, a witness of Jesus Christ among his brethren.'

Bonhoeffer was born on 4th February 1906, in Breslau, Germany. He grew up in Berlin, where his father was a Professor of Psychiatry and Neurology at Berlin University. He was the sixth of eight children in a prosperous, middle-class family.

In 1923, when he was seventeen, Bonhoeffer went to Tübingen University to study theology. He immersed himself in his studies, proving to be an independent and original thinker. His ambition was to lecture in theology at the university. As a student politics did not interest him. As a good Lutheran he believed it was his duty to support the state, but, step by step, in obedience to Christ, he was led to resist the growing evil of Nazism until he was thrown into prison and killed only three weeks before Hitler himself committed suicide.

When he was twenty-four Bonhoeffer went to America for a year, to study at Union Theological Seminary in New York. He taught Sunday School and gave Bible classes in the black ghetto of Harlem. Among these black Christians he found fellowship in Christ – a true Christian community of faith and love. And for the first time he experienced the horror of racial hatred.

Returning to Germany, he was ordained and became a student pastor and lecturer at the university of Berlin. Increasing numbers of

Christians – especially Protestants in the Lutheran churches – supported Hitler's National Socialist movement. Many regarded Hitler as their country's saviour, and defender against communism. At the university, where students and lecturers were impassioned Nazis, Bonhoeffer lectured on the evils of war.

On 30th January 1933, Hitler became Chancellor of Germany. That spring the first anti-Jewish laws were announced. To a congregation of Lutheran pastors Bonhoeffer said that the church must oppose the state when it made wrong judgments. If a car, he said, were driven by a mad driver and went out of control, then it was not enough to bind up the wounds of injured people. A spoke must be put in the wheels. Many of his congregation walked out in disgust at his words.

When the Protestant Church of Germany voted to support Hitler, Bonhoeffer became one of the leaders of the breakaway Lutheran group called 'Young Reformers'. They vowed to be true to God's word and to oppose the Aryan laws. Asked to prepare a Confession of Faith for Christians opposed to Hitler, he went to stay at Bethel – a community for the physically and mentally disabled. Here he enlisted his father's medical help to oppose the implementation of Hitler's euthanasia law. Malcolm Muggeridge writes: 'It was quite clear to him that to suppose the sick and infirm could be disposed of in this barbarous way was a worse sickness than any had to deal with at Bethel. Von Bodelschwingh [the Director of Bethel] . . . when challenged demonstrated conclusively that at Bethel there were no useless lives. The most stricken inmates could still communicate, if not in words, then in God's language of love.'

In 1933 German support for Hitler reached fever pitch. Protestants who would not support Hitler joined together to form the Confessing Church. In 1935 Bonhoeffer became head of its theological seminary at Finkenwalde. Bonhoeffer's anti-Nazi views became well-known. He lost his job at Berlin University, and in 1937 the Seminary was closed down. Bonhoeffer wrote articles for a number of periodicals. His condemnation of government policies resulted in his being condemned for meddling in politics.

In 1939, as warfare mounted, Bonhoeffer found himself in a dilemma. He was a pacifist. All war was abhorrent to him. It was impossible for him to fight for Germany. But to refuse the call-up would endanger his friends in the Confessing Church. Unable to make a decision, he sailed for America where his friends hoped he would stay till peace returned. But he could not turn his back on Germany. He wrote, 'I must live through this difficult period of our national history with the Christian people of Germany. I shall forfeit the right to share in the reconstruction of Christian life in Germany after the war, if I do not share the trials of this time with my own people.'

So after a very short time he returned – and he went back determined to do all he could to rid Germany of Hitler. In 1940 he was forbidden to preach or publish. He began to work as a German double agent. He travelled in Europe, ostensibly for the church on ecumenical missions. In reality, while pretending to find out allied military secrets, he was working with a group of conspirators seeking to destroy Hitler. He helped Jewish refugees to escape from Germany. In the winter of 1942–3 two assassination attempts failed. During this time Bonhoeffer tried to enlist the help of the British government in the plot to assassinate Hitler, and to set up an alternative government.

When Bonhoeffer was eventually arrested in 1943 it was for his involvement in smuggling fourteen Jews out of Germany. He was at first thrown into Tegel prison. This was a military prison not a Gestapo prison. Here, for the first twelve days he was allowed visits from his family, and he was also allowed to read and write letters. He hid his connection with the conspirators, whilst still communicating to them in code. Bonhoeffer spent eighteen months in Tegel prison, and here 'the theologian became a mystic, the pastor became a martyr, and the teacher produced in his *Letters and Papers from Prison*, one of the great contemporary classics of Christian literature.

One year after his arrest, when no evidence had been found implicating him in conspiracy, the charge was dropped. Whilst he was at Tegel he was given the opportunity to escape – with the help of the guards. However, he refused to run away because this would have put his uncle and brother – fellow prisoners – in danger. In July 1944 the assassination plot was discovered and the conspirators were executed. On 23rd August 1949 he wrote: 'You must never doubt that I'm travelling with gratitude and cheerfulness along the road where I'm being led. My past life is brim full of God's goodness, and my sins are covered by the forgiving love of Christ crucified.'

In October 1944 a secret file was discovered which revealed that Bonhoeffer had been working with the anti-Hitler conspirators for many years. He was moved to the Gestapo prison in Prinz-Albrecht Strasse. Here he was brutally tortured but remained unbroken, calm, cheerful, and trusting. On 7th February, 1945, he was transferred to

Buchenwald, where he was kept in the cellar of a house outside the main concentration camp. A British officer, imprisoned at Buchenwald, wrote, 'Bonhoeffer was different; just quiet calm and normal, seemingly perfectly at his ease. His soul really shone in the dark desperation of our prison. He was all humility and sweetness. He was one of the very few men I have ever met to whom his God was real and close to him.' The war was drawing to a close. The prisoners could hear American guns and expected to be released. Then, after seven weeks, Bonhoeffer was taken to the village of Schönberg. They stayed in a village school. But just after he had left, diaries were found, clearly implicating Bonhoeffer in the conspiracy. On 8th April, Low Sunday, Bonhoeffer preached a sermon on the text, 'Through his wounds we are healed'. Just as it was over, the SS arrived. 'Prisoner Bonhoeffer, get ready and come with us.' Bonhoeffer asked an Englishman, Payne Best, to give a message to Bishop Bell of Chichester, 'Tell him that for me this is the end but also the beginning.'

Not long after all the conspirators met together at Flossenburg. The prison doctor described what happened:

> Through the half-open door in one room of the huts I saw Pastor Bonhoeffer, before taking off his prison garb, kneeling on the floor praying fervently to his God. I was most deeply moved by the way this lovable man prayed, so devout and so certain that God heard his prayer. At the place of execution, he again said a short prayer and then climbed the steps to the gallows, brave and composed. His death ensued after a few seconds. In almost fifty years that I worked as a doctor, I have hardly ever seen a man die so entirely submissive to the will of God.

INDEX

MARTYRS' NAMES